"In a world marked more by incivility and talking past each other than respectful engagement, *Winsome Persuasion* is a refreshing consideration of how to pursue genuine engagement with those with whom we may have deep ideological and theological differences. . . . This is a great resource for all of us seeking to be the presence of Christ in the world."

Carol A. Taylor, president of Evangel University

"Looking for a manual on winning arguments and scoring points in the current cultural debates? Keep looking! *Winsome Persuasion* is not the culture warrior's guide to winning. If, however, you hope to learn how to listen well and be heard, how to speak truth irenically, with more light than heat, keep reading. Deeply rooted in contemporary communication theory and ancient biblical wisdom, this excellent work is a wise and effective guide to speaking truth in love."

J. Michael Thigpen, Talbot School of Theology, Biola University

"After more than twenty-five years of working with college students in campus ministry, I would argue that students living in a 'post-discourse' society need all the help they can get with learning to engage others in meaningful discussion—and not just students, but everyone who desires connections with other humans that go beneath the surface. Read this book as a prayer for change in your own life and in the lives of our communities."

Ed Uszynski, Athletes in Action, Cru

"Muehlhoff and Langer have produced a book well worth the time of any Christian who wants to be real salt and light in a difficult, pluralistic world. To be sure, not only is *Winsome Persuasion* grounded wonderfully in the Scriptures and current communication theory, but the writing is crisp, the examples and illustrations are entrancing, and the usefulness is immediate and profound. This is the perfect book for church leaders and thoughtful laypersons to read and study together."

Craig J. Hazen, Biola University, author of *Five Sacred Crossings*

"*Winsome Persuasion* could not be a more timely book! . . . This book shows us what cultural engagement can look like; wise, honest, compassionate, and helpful discourse is more important now than ever. Weaving together strands of multiple disciplines, *Winsome Persuasion* is a rare book that more than delivers on its title. Highly, highly recommended."

Mike Erre, author of *Astonished*

"In this age of shrill and often hateful public rhetoric, Muehlhoff and Langer's *Winsome Persuasion* is a breath of fresh air; wise, warm hearted, and well researched, its advice for speaking Christianly in the public square could not be more timely."

Thomas M. Crisp, professor of philosophy, Biola University

"How does a book live up to the title *Winsome Persuasion*? You're looking at it! Muehlhoff and Langer's new book models the very thing they wish to teach. Demonstrating a refreshingly relevant knowledge of culture, it's both informative and inspirational. For anyone who loves Jesus and wants the tools to effectively share him with a post-Christian world this is a must-read!"

Andy Steiger, founder and director of Apologetics Canada

"In *Winsome Persuasion*, Tim Muehlhoff and Rick Langer present both the challenge and a plan for how Christians can regain credibility and speak persuasively into a world that they no longer recognize as their own. . . . If we as Christians want to be more than political and social pawns, engaging in winsome persuasion may be the best way to present the truth of the gospel of Jesus Christ while creating space to be heard and taken seriously."

Joy E. A. Qualls, chair, department of communication studies, Biola University

"*Winsome Persuasion* is a timely and masterful book. Tim and Rick provide insightful and practical steps for Christians to communicate more effectively in our 'argument culture.' They use a delightful combination of statistics, personal examples, stories, and interactive dialogue to engage readers along the way. I hope and pray this book will receive the wide readership it deserves."

Sean McDowell, Biola University, author of *A New Kind of Apologist*

"*Winsome Persuasion* paints an intricately detailed picture of an American public square growing more and more fragmented and frustrated as her citizens entrench themselves along ideological lines. Far from leaving us in despair, though, Muehlhoff and Langer offer incisive exhortations to Christian communities to strive to heal our national divides through Christlike compassion and countercultural communication."

John W. Yates II, rector, The Falls Church Anglican

"In their excellent book *Winsome Persuasion*, Langer and Muehlhoff call us back as Christians to the art of conversation and the necessity of humble disagreement. This book both theoretically and practically lays the groundwork needed to equip Christians to engage in this fundamentally important task."

Paul Spears, director of the Torrey Honors Institute at Biola University

WINSOME PERSUASION

CHRISTIAN INFLUENCE *in a*
POST-CHRISTIAN WORLD

TIM MUEHLHOFF and RICHARD LANGER
Foreword by QUENTIN J. SCHULTZE

IVP Academic

An imprint of InterVarsity Press
Downers Grove, Illinois

InterVarsity Press
P.O. Box 1400, Downers Grove, IL 60515-1426
ivpress.com
email@ivpress.com

InterVarsity Press® is the book-publishing division of InterVarsity Christian Fellowship/USA®, a movement of students and faculty active on campus at hundreds of universities, colleges, and schools of nursing in the United States of America, and a member movement of the International Fellowship of Evangelical Students. For information about local and regional activities, visit intervarsity.org.

All Scripture quotations, unless otherwise indicated, are taken from THE HOLY BIBLE, NEW INTERNATIONAL VERSION®, NIV® Copyright © 1973, 1978, 1984, 2011 by Biblica, Inc.™ Used by permission. All rights reserved worldwide.

Cover design: David Fassett
Interior design: Jeanna Wiggins
Images: crocus: © posteriori/iStockphoto
megaphone x-ray: © Nick Veasey/Getty Images

ISBN 978-0-8308-5177-5 (print)
ISBN 978-0-8308-9113-9 (digital)

Printed in the United States of America ♾

 As a member of the Green Press Initiative, InterVarsity Press is committed to protecting the environment and to the responsible use of natural resources. To learn more, visit greenpressinitiative.org.

Library of Congress Cataloging-in-Publication Data
A catalog record for this book is available from the Library of Congress.

P 23 22 21 20 19 18 17 16 15 14 13 12 11 10 9 8 7 6 5 4 3 2 1

Y 36 35 34 33 32 31 30 29 28 27 26 25 24 23 22 21 20 19 18 17

From Tim:

To Michael, Jason, and Jeremy:

may you find wisdom in these pages that

will assist you in being God's representatives

in today's ever-changing culture.

From Richard:

To my parents, for whom I am

ever more grateful as

each year passes.

CONTENTS

FOREWORD

Quentin J. Schultze

THE FIRST AMENDMENT TO THE US CONSTITUTION is an amazing statement about the importance of democratic discourse. It says, in short, that citizens should be free to get together (freedom of assembly). As people gather, they should be free to talk (freedom of speech). And as they talk, they also should be free to write about and distribute their conversations (freedom of the press).

Then comes the zinger: no one should be excluded from such assembly, speech, and press because of their religious convictions. Religion is the only such category specifically mentioned in the First Amendment. Why? Because religion can be so divisive. In fact, nothing was more contentious in the early colonies. People were even murdered over conflicting views of faith.

Finally, says the Constitution, if anyone believes that they have been prohibited from such discourse, they have the right to take their grievance to the government. They have the right to *petition* the government. Petitioning is one of the great democratic means of persuasion. A petition gathers voices and presents them as one voice.

Democratic life is founded on open dialogue, including dialogue animated by people's deepest convictions—their faith commitments. Learning how to navigate such potentially explosive discourse is nothing short of learning how to be a productive and responsible citizen. Religion has been and will continue to be one of democracy's lightning rods.

It seems that differences of perception and opinion are built into humankind. People see reality differently. Life in a broken world—a fallen world—

is invariably complicated, confusing, and counterintuitive. When we arise each morning we might wonder what kinds of conversations we will face. How will we navigate them? How should we address conflict without folding our cards and walking away?

Faith moves forward too. Religions morph, but they rarely disappear altogether. The stunning number of Christian denominations just in the United States should convince us all that even the most faithful followers of Jesus Christ will invariably disagree on at least some of the ways to relate their common faith to cultural changes.

Moreover, as culture and society change new issues confront churches. Formerly taboo or at least private ideas emerge all around us. After a while we cannot ignore them. Slavery dogged American society leading up to the Civil War. Eventually Christians helped end slavery, but new issues arose. Today's news tracks topics that churches end up having to address whether they want to or not. Many young people are leaving churches that lack the courage to discuss faith-challenging contemporary issues. Thanks to the Internet, especially social media, we all are confronted with differences of opinion on potentially divisive topics. Even family meals become venues for learning how to practice challenging democratic discourse with kindness and respect.

This book is about navigating ever-evolving public discourse. It's about the kinds of discourse that challenge us because we are unprepared, even wary. The authors locate us in the types of social and cultural conflicts that we cannot and should not ignore. None of us can be a hermit, untouched by the social-rhetorical conflicts that energize and sometimes inflame daily discourse.

There is no turning back. The new media world engulfs us in cultural discoveries and disputes not of our making. New ideas, identities, and religious as well as secular movements appear on our radar; people we know start talking about them. Conflicts arise.

This book also is important to read because it locates Christian discourse in the age-old context of the fall—the fall from grace. We all are born into a broken world of sin. Nothing and no one is unblemished. We cannot simply look outside of ourselves for sin. We have to look inside as well.

The fault line of sin runs through every social institution and every human heart. We dwell in local, national, and global webs of injustice, exploitation, and utter self-interestedness. We all, down deep in our hearts, would like to refashion the world into our own visions of goodness—into our own images and likenesses. We are broken but ambitious control freaks. We assume that we own our tongues and keyboards. We are right and others are wrong. We know better than others. Do we?

Reinhold Niebuhr's famous prayer offers biblical wisdom as we approach a broken world: "God, grant me the serenity to accept the things I cannot change, the courage to change the things I can, and the wisdom to know the difference." That prayer should inform our discourse. It should set the scene for our daily persuasion. It should make us humble—slow to speak and quick to listen. It should also call us to engage others courageously when we honestly believe that we might be salt and light to the world.

In our counterpublics, we build Towers of Babel, rhetorical monuments to our clever thinking and efficient organizing. Evangelical Christians, for instance, have created special-interest groups that demonize opponents and create names for their own, seemingly venerated leaders. Evangelicals are too quick to hop on board the latest campaigns to fix one or another social or cultural problem. In a sense, evangelicals can be quick to sign up and speak and slow to listen to and understand others. Of course this is not merely an evangelical issue; it is a human issue. It is a root problem, evidence of the fall from grace and the worship of false gods.

During Augustine's time—about 350 years after Jesus Christ walked the Middle East—people trained as public speakers bought into the fall from grace. Rhetoricians of that era were essentially word vendors. Today we might say they were unprincipled public relations artists who knew how to use language to advance a cause without regard for truth and virtue. So when God called Augustine to follow Jesus, and Augustine decided to follow his Lord and Savior, Augustine also felt that it was time to give up his career as a rhetorician. Simply put, he believed that no one could be both a public persuader and a follower of Jesus Christ.

But after considerable biblical study, prayer, fellowship, and worship, Augustine changed his mind. He plotted a new course in the broken world. He would persuade for Jesus. He would persuade with truth. He would do it ethically as well as effectively. He would not hide his faith in the public arena. In fact, he reluctantly went on to become a priest and bishop in North Africa.

He became arguably the greatest Christian theologian from the apostle Paul to the present. He became what I would like to be: a *servant speaker*, dedicated to using the gift of language to love God, neighbor, and self.

What Augustine did is exactly what we are called to do, and what this book helps us to do: use the gift of language to be faithful agents for truth and justice in a broken but still redeemable world. Persuasion is critically important because of the gap in the world and in our own lives between the way that things are and the ways that they should be.

We are called to address this gap with our whole lives. We become witnesses to truth by how we live, not just by what we say. Our lives speak. We live with integrity when what we profess and how we live both point to the reality of Jesus Christ as the Word made flesh, killed on the cross, stored cold in a grave, and raised to be alive and communicating with the Father and Holy Spirit.

This kind of living discourse—being alive with Christ, regenerated for service of God and neighbor—is nothing short of an astonishing adventure. Every day we live in the gap between heavenly and hellish public discourse. New ideas and issues emerge all around us. New publics and counterpublics become voices in the gap. Churches split over some issues. Denominations rise and fall—like some of their leaders. Christian family members argue about public issues while sitting around the Thanksgiving table. Young people give up on "the church," sensing a lot of hypocrisy or just a derogatory spirit among Christian leaders.

This book helps facilitate the kind of conversation that we all need to be having about our own discourse. There are times when I disagree with the authors. But that's not the point of the book or of the life of faith. This book is not about the outcomes of our democratic discourse. It's about the essential process of how to address each other wisely and well in the gap between God's original creation and the promised new heaven and new earth.

Following Jesus is at least about following him faithfully into the kinds of public venues where believers and nonbelievers alike conduct their conversations about things that matter. That's what Jesus did. He was a persuader who used all of the means at his disposal. He took risks. But he did so wisely. He knew what he was talking about. He knew his audience. He knew the truth. He was the truth. As Jesus' followers, we depend on his partner, the Holy Spirit, to grant us sufficient knowledge and wise counsel.

For me, this book is a hospitable invitation to such participation in Jesus' program of public engagement. I am grateful that Tim Muehlhoff and Rick Langer were willing to put their personal thoughts and lives into the book for us to discuss.

We seem to be living in an age similar to Augustine's. It appears that we can barely trust anyone. Public rhetoric seems hollow and self-serving. Maybe, too, this is a ripe time for forming counterpublics that listen well, speak the truth, and live out what they profess. I think so. I sense that it is the right time for a book like *Winsome Persuasion*. I'm grateful for an opportunity to invite you to the democratic conversation in its pages, where no one is excluded because of their faith.

ACKNOWLEDGMENTS

TIM MUEHLHOFF

THE THOUGHTS CONTAINED IN THIS BOOK have been a long time coming, and many have helped season and spur on my ideas. One of the great joys of being part of the Biola faculty is colleagues—Doug Huffman, Jon Lunde, Gregg TenElshof, Paul Spears, Greg Ganssle, Dave Horner, Chris Grace, J. P. Moreland, Tom Crisp, Steve Porter, Craig Hazen, Joy Qualls—who are always ready to offer insight and discuss the topic *one more time!* This project benefited from a research fellowship at Biola University's Center for Christian Thought, which was made possible through the support of a grant from Templeton Religion Trust. The opinions expressed in this book are those of the author(s) and do not necessarily reflect the views of Biola's Center for Christian Thought or the Templeton Religion Trust.

A special thank you goes to my coauthor and friend Rick Langer. What a joy to write a book with such a gifted and careful thinker. Last, a deep appreciation goes to my wife, Noreen, who has tirelessly listened to these ideas—often scattered and incomplete—for the past twenty-eight years. Thank you for being such a willing sounding board and fellow counterpublic!

RICHARD LANGER

I recall an experienced pastor friend of mine who was asked by a young seminarian how long it took him to prepare a sermon. He replied, "Thirty years plus as many hours as I can find in any given week."

A book, like a sermon, is a mixture of a relatively short period of writing and a relatively long period of living. In this sense, I could never adequately acknowledge the multitude of friends and companions who contributed to the project, but I would like to identify some particular groups and individuals who have helped bring this dream to fruition.

First, my wife and family. I have been blessed with a relentlessly loving, supportive, and faithful life companion: my wife, Shari. She has often believed in me far more than I have believed in myself. She has also been my partner in raising our two children, Crystal and Mark, who have spoiled us rotten when it comes to the joys of raising children. In the past few years our family has grown to include two delightful spouses for our children (Tim for Crystal and Nicolette for Mark) and, while I was doing the final edits on this book, the further addition of two grandsons! The joy of these relationships has nourished my every endeavor.

I would also like to acknowledge the staff, elders, and congregation of Trinity Church in Redlands, California. Many of the thoughts in this book were incubated and nourished in my three decades with this wonderful congregation. More particularly, our Koinonia group—our faithful fellow pilgrims on the journey of life since 1982—has nourished us through both the best of times and the worst of times. My mind and soul were also shaped by countless cups of coffee and stimulating discussion with my reading group friends.

I would like to thank Biola University for the blessing of a faculty position that allows time for thinking and rethinking, for writing and rewriting. I'm also grateful for students in my many classes—including the Authentic Communication seminars that inspired this book. Thanks as well to countless "Coalition of the Willing" groups that have deepened my understanding of faith and learning. My coauthor, Tim Muehlhoff, and colleague Liz Hall both deserve special mention for modelling for me what might be called the Nike model of writing: "Just Do It!" Your example and encouragement is deeply appreciated.

INTRODUCTION

"WE CAN'T DO THE MEETING NEXT Thursday because of the riots."

I was puzzled to say the least. Riots on a schedule—planned in advance?

Apparently the look on my face was sufficient to prompt my friend to explain. "It's election day. There are always riots afterward. It's not a big deal—we can meet on Friday."

It was 1980, and I had been living in India for several months. I was learning to expect the unexpected. This was just one more instance of the unexpected in India. Such turmoil made me long for life back home. I mentally added democracy to my list of things that just seemed to work better in the United States.

Fast forward to 2016.

The presidential election is called early in the morning of November 9, and by evening I'm watching an AT&T van being set alight on the streets of Oakland. Shots are fired in Portland. Thousands are taking to the streets all across the country. #notmypresident is not only trending on Twitter but also spray painted on walls in urban areas in every major city. One might think that people would give Trump a chance, but not *Boston Globe* writer Michael Cohen, who bluntly states, "I don't want Trump to succeed. I want him to fail spectacularly."[1]

In days leading up to the election, I was appalled when Donald Trump was ambivalent about his willingness to accept the outcome of the election if he did not win. But as I write this, I have just clicked through a spreadsheet

---

[1]Michael A. Cohen, "I Don't Want Trump to Succeed. I Want Him to Fail Spectacularly," *The Boston Globe*, November 15, 2016, www.bostonglobe.com/opinion/2016/11/15/don-want-trump-succeed-want-him-fail-spectacularly/Xa0rVn5yjwUp1kjjRMqi6L/story.html.

listing private information, phone numbers, and email addresses of members of the electoral college. It was published by the #NotMyPresident Alliance in the hopes that members of the electoral college who had pledged to vote for Trump when appointed as electors would be pressured to vote *against* him instead.[2] It seems both sides are willing to abandon the results of the democratic process for the sake of getting their political way.

The postelection response should not have been surprising. The unraveling of public discourse had been increasingly obvious during the primaries. Donald Trump used inflammatory language with such regularity that the term *Trumpisms* entered our vocabulary—complete with a dedicated website categorizing quotations in groups with dropdown menus for easier access: Trumpisms by Region, Trumpisms on Facebook, Trumpisms on Twitter.[3] Inflammatory rhetoric bred inflammatory responses. Emmett Rensin, an editor at the politically liberal news website *Vox*, tweeted, "Advice: If Trump comes to your town, start a riot."[4] And indeed, violence occurred at many Trump rallies throughout the months leading up to the election. Rensin was suspended from his post, but he can hardly be blamed for all the violence since it began before his tweets. However, it is hard to imagine that the inflammatory rhetoric on all sides did not contribute to the inflammatory action. As of this writing a few weeks after the election, the rhetorical tone remains as strident as ever.

Perhaps it is time to remove democracy from my list of things that are working better in the United States.

It seems people are neither hearing each other nor letting each other be heard. Historically American journalism has professed to value objectivity and attempted to let both sides of an issue be heard. For example, newscasts have traditionally interviewed both Republicans and Democrats on important public issues. Presidential addresses to the nation are almost always complemented by a response from a political leader of the opposition.

---

[2]Blake Montgomery, "Anti-Trump Protesters Post Personal Information of Electoral College Members," BuzzFeed, November 17, 2016, www.buzzfeed.com/blakemontgomery/anti-trump-protesters-post-personal-information-of-electoral.

[3]Donald Trumpisms: Making America Great Again, www.donaldtrumpisms.com.

[4]Erik Wemple, "What Will a Suspension Do for a Vox Editor Who Urged Anti-Trump Riots?," *The Washington Post*, June 3, 2016, www.washingtonpost.com/blogs/erik-wemple/wp/2016/06/03/what-will-a-suspension-do-for-a-vox-editor-who-urged-anti-trump-riots/?utm_term=.9f804b3634c2.

Unfortunately, some of the most influential news sources of the Internet age shun even the pretense of being open to differing viewpoints on controversial social issues. Ben Smith, editor in chief of BuzzFeed, has helped develop the global Internet media company into one of the leading news sources in the world. Consider his response to inquiries about how BuzzFeed responded to the Supreme Court's *Obergefell* decision: "We firmly believe that for a number of issues, including civil rights, women's rights, anti-racism, and LGBT equality, *there are not two sides*."[5]

What has happened to our democracy? I was musing on this question and picked up some writings of the Czech dissident-turned-president Václav Havel. He lived in extremely volatile and dangerous political times. He was arrested and imprisoned by the communist regime in Czechoslovakia during the years before the collapse of the Eastern Bloc in 1989. He faced some equally difficult experiences when he served as the first president of Czechoslovakia in the post-communist era. These were hard times by any measure, yet it is refreshing to hear Havel talk about politics. He was firmly committed to honesty, civility, and morality as central concerns of politics, even though many thought this hopelessly naive. He mentions a particular opponent for whom "the idea that the world might actually be changed by . . . the power of a truthful word, the strength of a free spirit, conscience, and responsibility—with no guns, no lust for power, no political wheeling and dealing—was quite beyond the horizon of his understanding."[6] As Havel puts it, "There is only one way to strive for decency, reason, responsibility, sincerity, civility, and tolerance, and that is decently, reasonably, responsibly, sincerely, civilly, and tolerantly."[7] These values were so clearly manifest in the revolution of 1989 that we now refer it as the Velvet Revolution.

Havel offers us the possibility of political conquest by life, by thought, and by human dignity. A compelling vision indeed. How can we carry forward political discourse by life, thought, and dignity and avoid sinking into a morass of destructive communication, hateful rhetoric, and vindictive tribal violence?

---

[5]Dylan Byers, "Should News Outlets Declare Allegiances?," *On Media* (blog), June 26, 2015, www .politico.com/blogs/media/2015/06/should-news-outlets-declare-allegiances-209576.html (emphasis added).

[6]Václav Havel, *Politics, Morality, and Civility: An Essay* (Washington, DC: The Trinity Forum, 2006), 22.

[7]Ibid., 24-25.

This book is written to help answer this question. The question is particularly important because failed discourse is the starting point of a failed society. People who are afraid, unheard, unrepresented, and alienated from their leaders and their neighbors do not make for a healthy society. Who will stand in the breach and speak for those who have no voice? Who will choose to become peacemakers?

I hope that Christians would naturally see this as our calling. Jesus speaks a blessing for peacemakers (Mt 5:9). Proverbs encourages us to speak for those who have no voice (Prov 31:8). Peter exhorts us to engage in discourse with gentleness and respect (1 Pet 3:15). James commands us to be slow to anger and quick to listen (Jas 1:19). These statements are all biblical mandates, so surely one would think this approach comes easily to the church.

Yet in reality, or at least perception, evangelicals have not succeeded in fulfilling these mandates. It is not because we have not engaged in political action. A 2007 Barna poll indicated that 75 percent of non-Christians ages sixteen to twenty-nine believed evangelicals are too involved in politics. Clearly we have spoken up; the problem seems to be that we have spoken poorly. The same poll shows that 87 percent viewed evangelicals as being judgmental and 85 percent viewed evangelicals as hypocritical—a perception that is even shared by half of young *churchgoers*.[8]

Of course, some may wonder why we should care what others think. I have spoken with Christians who view Donald Trump's success in the recent election as a major victory in the culture wars. Indeed, they see little need for a book like ours that talks about Christian counterpublics because Trump's victory means we now hold the power—we are the public, not the counterpublic!

But I am doubtful when my fellow evangelicals shout, "We win!"

First, when it comes to winning the minds of our culture, Donald Trump's election was not much of a win. Trump won the presidency with fewer votes than Hillary Clinton received. His victory was certainly surprising, but surprise is not change. Furthermore, both Clinton and Trump achieved historically

---

[8]"A New Generation Expresses Its Skepticism and Frustration with Christianity," Barna Group, September 21, 2007, www.barna.com/research/a-new-generation-expresses-its-skepticism-and -frustration-with-christianity.

unprecedented levels of disapproval throughout the election.[9] Our culture is still committed to abortion, dismantling sexual morality, and constricting religious freedoms. I fear that those who see sweeping cultural transformation in the 2016 election are misinterpreting a receding wave as a changing tide.

Second, it is not at all clear that "we" won. Donald Trump won, but is Trump "we"? Trump has consistently stated opinions or modeled behavior that is radically at odds with the gospel. Albert Mohler, president of the Southern Baptist Seminary, strongly opposed Trump's candidacy. As he put it, "Americans have retained enough moral sense to know that personal character still matters in the choice of a babysitter. If this is true, we can hardly claim with a straight face that character is irrelevant to those who hold high positions of political leadership."[10] Mark Galli, editor in chief of *Christianity Today*, notes the depth of the division within the ranks of evangelicals when he describes Christians who look at one another and ask, "How could you, as an evangelical, possibly support your candidate?" Galli goes on to compare evangelicals to a married couple who have grown apart over the years and now look at each other and wonder whether divorce is the only option.[11] For evangelicals, there is no *we* in "We win!"

Perhaps most disconcerting is that if we tie ourselves to the Trump juggernaut, what happens when it crashes? Will our prospect for having a healthy voice and a vibrant moral witness within our culture be completely destroyed by a backlash against Donald Trump and all those who have allied themselves with his values and rhetoric?

These are perilous times for evangelicals who seek to speak in the public square. What rhetorical voice should we adopt?

Even evangelicals who do not approve of Donald Trump may nonetheless believe that we *should* be judgmental of a society as sinful and godless as ours. The time for civility is past, and the time for outrage has come. We should not worry about how the world perceives us; we know that the world

---

[9]Gary Langer, "Deep Unfavorability for Clinton, Trump Marks the Election's Sharp Divisions (Poll)," ABC News, October 31, 2016, http://abcnews.go.com/Politics/deep-unfavorability-clinton-trump-marks-elections-sharp-divisions/story?id=43177423.

[10]Albert Mohler, "Character in Leadership—Does It Still Matter?," AlbertMohler.com, June 24, 2016, www.albertmohler.com/2016/06/24/character-leadership-still-matter.

[11]Mark Galli, "After Trump, Should Evangelical Christians Part Ways?," *Christianity Today*, November 10, 2016, www.christianitytoday.com/ct/2016/november-web-only/should-evangelicals-part-ways.html.

will hate us even as they hated Jesus. It is a waste of time to make ourselves intelligible to people who have rejected the truth and are darkened in their understanding. To put it another way: Elijah never engaged in constructive dialogue with the prophets of Baal, so why not follow his example?

But there are faithful alternatives to combative public rhetoric. Let us distinguish three different postures or voices one might adopt to speak to contemporary issues: a prophetic voice, a pastoral voice, and a persuasive voice. Interestingly enough, these are analogous to different ways in which the Holy Spirit works in our lives. Table 1 sketches the differences between these voices.

Table 1. Three voices

Prophetic	Pastoral	Persuasive
appeals to revealed Word of God as final authority	appeals to shared needs and suffering	appeals to the common good and general revelation
calls for acknowledgment of sin and repentance	offers healing, nurture, and aid to those in need	seeks to change viewpoints or practices within the culture
demands of the hearer repentance and complete change in direction	meets people where they are and ministers to their needs	appeals to conscience and shared values, and seeks progressive steps toward a final goal
analogous to the convicting work of the Holy Spirit (Jn 16:8)	analogous to the comforting, helping role of the Holy Spirit (Jn 14:16, 26; 15:26; 16:7)	analogous to the Holy Spirit bearing witness (Jn 15:26-27) and restraining evil (2 Thess 2:6-7)

This book will primarily focus on speaking with a persuasive voice in a public setting. This is not meant to exclude or even diminish the need for prophetic and pastoral voices. In any given setting, public or private, it might be wise to employ any one of these three voices. However, as the Barna poll indicates, recent evangelical political action has tended to speak with the prophetic voice. If no one responds, we often feel that the only option is to turn up the prophetic volume. So we shout louder, or stage more vigorous protests, or show more horrific pictures, or warn of increasingly apocalyptic disasters. But in the face of diminishing returns, it would be good to remember that there are other options than turning up our prophetic voice. We might adopt a pastoral or persuasive voice instead; sometimes gates that are barred to angry shouting can be opened by knocking and offering to help.

But let us assume for the moment that some viewpoints are so heinous that no dialogue is necessary and seeking understanding is itself a form of compromise. What then? Do we follow Elijah's example and kill the modern equivalents of the priests of Baal with a sword? Some have adopted this rationale and engaged in shooting doctors who perform abortions or firebombing abortion clinics. But the vast majority of Christians do not advocate such extreme measures. Once violent coercion is rejected, what alternative to entering into dialogue remains? Should we talk to other people but intentionally refuse to hear and understand them? Should we simply avoid our opponents and act like they do not exist? How can these actions be reconciled with a New Testament ethic that demands that we love our neighbors and do good to those who persecute us? At the end of the day, in modern political societies there is really no alternative to conversation, constructive dialogue, and persuasion. We write this book in the hopes of helping Christians engage in helpful and constructive public conversations—even when talking to people with whom we radically disagree.

HOW THE BOOK IS ORGANIZED

In the first part we discuss key components and theories that define and describe a counterpublic. Chapter one asserts that before groups can effectively *counter* a public, they must understand both what constitutes a public and how ideas are debated within the public square. Chapter two details how Christian counterpublics are obligated to not only represent Christ's agenda but also speak in a way that honors God. As counterpublics with limited time and resources, which of God's commands or concerns should our groups prioritize and pursue? Chapter three explores the challenge of communicating a Christian agenda within today's argument culture. As representatives of Christ, how can we champion our perspective without engaging in ridicule or derision? Chapter four focuses on the crucial issue of speaker credibility. The word *credibility* comes from the Latin *credere*, which means "to believe." In communicating with others, do we make it easy or difficult for them to believe our message?

Part two takes the theories and concepts of previous chapters and applies them to engaging other people. Chapter five considers effective ways to craft our message so others will consider it on both the emotional and cognitive levels. Chapter six asks the question, When given the opportunity to deliver our message, how can we engage decision makers in a way that is compelling? Then, in championing a Christian agenda can we form partnerships or "loose connections" with non-Christian groups to meet the needs of our community (chapter seven)?

Part three considers current challenges facing Christian counterpublics. Chapters eight and nine apply the concepts of this book to a pressing cultural issue: How should we respond to the Supreme Court's decision to legalize same-sex marriage? Each author separately answers this question in these two chapters. The final chapter consists of an imaginary dialogue between the authors, which both deepens our exploration of the thorny issue of same-sex marriage and models constructive disagreement between Christians. We firmly believe that often there is not a single Christian viewpoint on a given issue, and therefore one of the places we need to model civil discourse is in conversations among ourselves as evangelicals!

UNIQUE FEATURES OF THIS BOOK

Historical sketches. American Christians commonly lament the acrimonious communication climate and adversarial relationship between the culture at large and confessing Christians. There is surely much to lament in this regard, but one thing that we should avoid is voicing our laments with apocalyptic pessimism. The end times may be near at hand, but then they may not be. It is good to remind ourselves that every generation of Christians has faced opposition, and many have faced opposition even more pronounced than what we are facing. More importantly, these Christians have left us a rich legacy of examples in the way they rose to meet and conquer the challenges of their day. This book will include a series of vignettes that highlight these examples of faithful and successful Christian counterpublics, such as William Wilberforce, Saint Patrick, and Harriet Beecher Stowe. May they remind us that the challenges we face are nothing new and that there is always reason for hope when confronting seemingly insurmountable cultural challenges.

Integration of communication theory, theology, and Scripture. Each of the issues raised in *Winsome Persuasion* will be addressed by appealing to communication and rhetoric scholars such as Aristotle, James Herrick, Lloyd Bitzer, James Carey, Jürgen Habermas, Julia T. Wood, Chaim Perelman, Lucie Olbrechts-Tyteca, and Nancy Fraser, along with noted Christian thinkers and theologians such as Augustine, G. K. Chesterton, J. P. Moreland, Quentin Schultze, Peter Berger, Tim Keller, Robert George, Richard Mouw, John Woodbridge, and C. S. Lewis. In addition, each chapter incorporates Scripture that at times both affirms and challenges communication principles and theories. We feel it is imperative that we seek truth by studying both God's Word and God's world. Our goal for this book is to take a comprehensive approach to wisdom by consulting scholars within and outside the Christian community and augmenting those insights with God's perspective via the Scriptures.[12]

Praxis. In addition to teaching, both authors have spent years communicating the Christian worldview to diverse college and community audiences. Accordingly, these chapters actively combine theory and practice. Readers consider not only relevant communication theories and principles but also how they can be applied to social issues ranging from immunization to the plight of the homeless to the Syrian refugee crisis to same-sex marriage.

"All people should be loved equally," states Saint Augustine. "But you cannot do good to all people equally, so you should take particular thought for those who, as if by lot, happen to be particularly close to you in terms of place, time, or any other circumstances."[13] The goal of this book is to spark a conversation about how to best present a perspective that is increasingly becoming the minority view. How can we set forth this distinctly Christian view to fellow community members—who providentially share a similar time and place—in a way that is compassionate, civil, and effective? If such a balance is achieved, we will serve as a vibrant contrast to our contemporary political climate.

---

[12]To be clear, we do not read secular scholars in the relevant fields merely to find negative illustrations, but to learn and see truths we might otherwise miss.

[13]Saint Augustine, *On Christian Teaching*, trans. R. P. H. Green (New York: Oxford University Press, 1997), 21.

Part I

LAYING A THEORETICAL FOUNDATION

"Desire," argues an ancient Jewish writer, "without knowledge is not good" (Prov 19:2). A common mistake in our efforts to influence others is to overlook theory and rush to application. "Just tell me how to persuade others," our students often ask. While the desire to introduce individuals to the Christian worldview is admirable, it's a mistake to overlook the usefulness of a good theory or clear definitions. In the following chapters we carefully define what it means to be a credible Christian counterpublic who can deftly and effectively communicate in today's ever-changing public square. But first, what do we mean by *counterpublic*?

1

WHAT IS A COUNTERPUBLIC?

IN SOCIAL MEDIA YOU ARE CALLED NAIVE, ignorant, and dangerous. The majority of medical experts present so-called indisputable evidence and tell you to get in step with others. Even the president of the United States publically states that the most important thing you can do for your child is the very thing you oppose. Some lawmakers suggest that your child be barred from school unless you give in to the dominant view. The issue is vaccinations, and you are utterly opposed.

You are also faced with a barrage of questions: What do you do when you find yourself in the minority? Do you compromise your convictions or stand firm? If you stand firm, how do you communicate with those in the dominant perspective in a way that doesn't quickly devolve into shouting matches—or hostile comment sections such as what followed a *Washington Post* article on vaccinations?

> ERWIN ALBER: I have long ago arrived at the conclusion that vaccination is an organized enterprise dressed up as disease prevention by means of junk science.
>
> BOB FERGY303: Are you insane?
>
> ERWIN ALBER: As Orwell said, *in a time of universal deceit telling the truth is a revolutionary act.*
>
> JIMMGT: Ewwhh boy! Nutbags are always somewhere out there.
>
> MATTHEW KAMPFF: You must have been looking in the mirror when you wrote this.[1]

---

[1]Comments on Abby Phillip, "Obama to Parents Doubting 'Indisputable' Science: 'Get Your Kids

Regardless of how you feel about vaccinations, chances are that there will come a time when on some issue you are on the outside looking in. Is your favorite political candidate somebody no one seems to take seriously? Are you on the wrong side of cultural shift so that now the majority sees your position as intolerant? Do you care about an issue that gets little attention? As your professor lectures, everyone seems to be nodding their heads in agreement, but you are not convinced and want to raise your hand and object. You are painfully aware of what public opinion is, but you aren't so sure you agree. If so, then you—like parents who refuse to vaccinate—are a counterpublic. You represent the minority perspective yet want to engage those who hold the dominant view. But how?

In order to be an effective counterpublic it is crucial to understand key concepts that lay a theoretical foundation from which you can act. In this chapter we consider what makes up a public, what the characteristics of a counterpublic are, where today's public square is, and how these concepts can be understood through a case study involving a heated debate over a depiction of Jesus on a college campus. Before we can engage others as a counterpublic, we need to first answer the question, what is a *public*?

THE PUBLIC

Just as any thoughtful discussion of postmodernism must first define modernism, so a detailed discussion of counterpublics must first focus on what is being countered—a public. Communication scholars Palczewski, Ice, and Fritch assert that a public is formed by "people coming together to discuss common concerns, including concerns about who they are and what they should do, and as a result constructing social reality together."[2] Each public must ask defining questions: What are the concerns that unify us as a group? Which concerns should be a priority? Once they are defined, how should we seek to meet these concerns? How are our values shaping how we see others and the world around us? When discussing the thorny issue of vaccinations, we quickly see two different publics emerging, each answering these questions

---

Vaccinated," *The Washington Post*, February 2, 2015, www.washingtonpost.com/news/morning-mix/wp/2015/02/02/get-your-kids-vaccinated-obama-tells-parents-doubting-indisputable-science (accessed June 1, 2015).

[2]Catherine Helen Palczewski, Richard Ice, and John Fritch, *Rhetoric in Civic Life* (State College, PA: Strata Publishing, 2012), 236.

in a different way. The pro-vaccination public argues that what unifies them is a concern for children at large. Their priority is the welfare of children entering public school systems. The concerns of the majority should trump the concerns of a fringe group who question the safety of vaccinations. The antivaccination public is equally convinced that vaccinations unnecessarily raise the risk of autism and that their children should be exempt due to personal or religious objections.

Cultural critic James Carey argues that what groups, or publics, involved in debates like these are doing is creating symbolic maps. "We first produce the world through symbolic work and then take up residence in the worlds we have produced."[3] Just as a physical map shows the landscape of a place and highlights key features—mountains, waterfalls, rivers, roads—a symbolic map lays out the conceptual features of a community through highlighting and prioritizing key concepts such as *love, honor, beauty, patriotism, sexuality, marriage, a real job,* and so on. Since words or symbols are inherently ambiguous, abstract, and arbitrary, a key part of making a symbolic map is giving definition to words. "All language," notes Jacques Ellul, "is more or less a riddle to be figured out."[4] How you figure out or define a word forms your symbolic map.

Symbolic maps are not written in isolation, but rather build on existing maps. In one of the preeminent works of twentieth-century ethical theory, *The Right and the Good,* ethicist W. D. Ross created his own symbolic map— building on Aristotle—in which he identified and defined certain qualities such as justice, non-injury, fidelity, veracity, reparation, beneficence, self-improvement, and gratitude. Ross gave each of these words or symbols a specific description. *Justice* includes both positive (preventing injustice) and negative (avoiding acts of injustice) characteristics, *non-injury* is the obligation to avoid harming others, *fidelity* is keeping promises, *veracity* is avoiding telling lies, *reparation* is making amends for wrongdoing, *beneficence* is seeking to please and serve others, *self-improvement* is bettering oneself, and *gratitude* is showing appreciation toward others for good deeds.[5]

---

[3]James Carey, *Communication as Culture: Essays on Media and Society* (New York: Routledge, 1988), 30.

[4]Jacques Ellul, "Seeing and Hearing: Prologmena," in *The Reach of Dialogue: Confirmation, Voice, and Community,* ed. Rob Anderson, Kenneth Cissna, and Ronald Arnett (Cresskill, NJ: Hampton, 1994), 123.

[5]To read more of Ross's symbolic map, see *The Right and the Good* (Indianapolis: Hackett, 1988).

What do you think of Ross's symbolic map? Is there anything missing you would add? Do you agree with a word but disagree with how it is defined? Would you throw out the entire list and start over? Even if we keep his general list, there may be strong disagreements over what constitutes justice, beneficence, or injury.

The consequences of having differing maps—or differences in how a specific map should be applied—were on vivid display during the Baltimore riots that occurred the last week of April 2015. Racial tensions erupted following the funeral of an African American man, Freddie Gray, who died a week after suffering a severe spinal injury while in police custody. Angry groups, composed mostly of teens, threw objects at police dressed in riot gear. While watching the riots unfold, Baltimore mother Toya Graham spotted her sixteen-year-old son in the crowd dressed in a black ski mask and ready to throw a brick. The video of her grabbing and slapping her son into submission went viral. While many claimed she should be awarded "Mother of the Year" and she drew public praise from the White House, others thought she should be prosecuted. "Hypocrisy of the law," tweeted one observer, identified as @cotrial; "she should be arrested for assault, battery, and abuse."[6] Professional golfer Brandon Hartzell found it ironic that NFL player Adrian Peterson was suspended and faced criminal charges for hitting his son: "We accused one person and praised another for the same action."[7] Why such different interpretations of a mother's actions? While Ross's list may help us identify broad categories such as justice or non-injury, it is up to individuals and communities to specifically place such actions within their own map. To some, the mother's actions were attempts at reparation—making amends for a wrongdoing—while others saw it as doing harm to her son. "To live within the purview of different maps," concludes Carey, "is to live within different realities."[8]

What happens when communities working off differing maps clash? Often the result is that a "dominant public tends to emerge, one that has the strength to translate its beliefs into actions affecting even people who do not

---

[6]Marisol Bello, "Mom of the Year? Baltimore Woman Isn't a Hero to All," *USA Today*, April 29, 2015, www.usatoday.com/story/news/2015/04/29/baltimore-mom-smacks-son-riots/26574143.
[7]Ibid.
[8]Carey, *Communication as Culture*, 28.

share its beliefs."[9] What allows one public to become dominant relates to a key distinction between *weak* and *strong* publics. Communication theorist Nancy Fraser defines weak publics as groups that exclusively engage in opinion formation and lack the ability to make policy decisions. In contrast, a strong public participates in identity formation but also has decision-making power.[10] Both publics can be seen in action in the vaccination debate. As we write this, a bill is racing through California's Senate Education Committee—spurred on by a measles outbreak at Disneyland Resort—that would severely limit a parent's choice not to vaccinate due to religious or personal reasons.[11] With such an important decision looming, what can parents opposed to vaccinations do? As members of a weak public they cannot pass a law or ratify a political bill, but they can seek to influence members of the strong public (the Education Committee) by holding public rallies, protesting outside the building where the committee meets, enlisting public figures to advocate for them, or making comments through social media designed to pressure decision makers.[12] When these parents seek to influence the majority they are acting as counterpublics.

CHARACTERISTICS OF A COUNTERPUBLIC

Communication scholar Daniel Brouwer identifies three characteristics of all counterpublics: opposition, withdrawal, and engagement.[13]

Opposition. What happens when you or your community feel excluded from the dominant public? You desire to take part in robust conversations that will deeply affect your community, but you have no voice. You perceive that your values are being not only ignored but attacked. Even when you do get a chance to enter the conversation, it seems that your symbolic map is easily dismissed. What unifies counterpublics is the *perception* that they are

---

[9]Palczewski, Ice, and Fritch, *Rhetoric in Civic Life*, 242.

[10]Nancy Fraser, "Rethinking the Public Square," in *Habermas and the Public Sphere*, ed. Craig Calhoun (Cambridge, MA: MIT Press, 1992), 110.

[11]Jenna Chandler, "Bill to Tighten Vaccine Rules Advances," *Orange County Register*, April 23, 2015, 4.

[12]Bill SB 277, which eliminates a parent's right to exempt their children from vaccinations, was signed by the governor of California on June 30, 2015, and became law on July 1, 2016. Counterpublics opposing the bill are now seeking signatures to force a referendum.

[13]While the concept of counterpublics is rooted in the idea of community, individuals from a specific community often find themselves acting alone in representing the group.

being excluded from communal discussions. Brouwer writes, "It's important to recognize that oppositionality is primarily perceptual; that is, counterpublics emerge when social actors perceive themselves to be excluded from or marginalized within mainstream or dominant publics."[14]

If opposition is, as Brouwer suggests, primarily perceptual, then does it allow any group to label itself a counterpublic? If perception is the main prerequisite, then "it is conceivable that anyone, including the most privileged and powerful members of society, could enact counterpublicity."[15] In addressing this concern, communication theorists suggest that any group that perceives itself as being marginalized or excluded by the dominant public must offer some form of evidence that its perception is rooted in reality. For example, among the counterpublic group Gay & Lesbian Alliance Against Defamation (GLAAD) there is a strong perception that prominent gay and lesbian characters are lacking in the movie industry. "Major studios appear reluctant to include LGBT characters in significant roles or franchises," states GLAAD's national spokesman, Wilson Cruz.[16] But can this perception be substantiated? In its first study of LGBT roles in major films, GLAAD found that of the 101 releases from Hollywood's six major studios in 2012, just fourteen films included gay, lesbian, or bisexual characters. When these characters did appear, they were often in cameos or minor roles that played no significant part in plot development. Whether the dominant public accepts, legitimates, or acts on such findings will itself take work. "The only way to make change," concludes Cruz, "is to do something about it. It takes hard work."[17] A central part of being a counterpublic is producing evidence that not only buttresses the perception of its members but also legitimates that perception with the dominant public.

Withdrawal. All counterpublics deal with the tension brought on by the dialectic of inward communication with fellow counterpublics and outward communication with dominant publics. "Those who constitute oppositional

---

[14]Daniel Brouwer, "Communication as Counterpublic," in *Communication as . . . : Perspectives on Theory*, ed. Gregory J. Shepherd, Jeffrey St. John, and Ted Striphas (Thousand Oaks, CA: Sage, 2006), 197.

[15]Christopher Duerringer, "The 'War on Christianity': Counterpublicity or Hegemonic Containment?," *Southern Communication Journal* 78, no. 4 (September-October 2013): 320.

[16]Jocelyn Noveck, "Study Finds Movies Trail Television in LGBT Roles," *Orange County Registrar*, September 6, 2013, Movies 11.

[17]Ibid.

communication need to speak among themselves in moments of retreat, regrouping, reflection, or rejuvenation."[18] During times of withdrawal, counterpublics discuss and perhaps modify the symbolic maps that fuel their vision and activism. Central to these times of regrouping are perceptual questions: How do we view ourselves, and how should we view our opposition? As a group what is our identity? With limited time and resources, which goals should we give priority? What if we can't agree? How important is it to put on a unified front?

In addition to forming an identity for themselves, counterpublics must also engage in what Robert Asen describes as "collective imagining," where individuals imagine people "different from themselves."[19] How one group imagines another will undoubtedly determine the tone of their rhetoric. Do we see those different from us as fellow citizens pursuing a common social good, or as combatants in a culture war? If members of a counterpublic regularly imagine those they are trying to persuade as uncharitable combatants in a rhetorical war, then two results may occur. First, the group may easily fall into reciprocal disdain, which can in turn lead to a type of dehumanization of the opposition. Second, during times of withdrawal counterpublics often create *hidden transcripts*, which entail a "critique of power spoken behind the back of the dominant."[20] Since they are created in private, hidden transcripts can be rhetorically harsh and contain unflattering characterizations or stereotypes of others. However, in today's savvy social media world, can hidden transcripts stay hidden?

The impact of the private being made public created a defining moment in the 2012 presidential elections. While speaking at a private fundraiser, Republican presidential candidate Mitt Romney suggested that nearly half—47 percent—of the US population would never vote for him since they did not pay taxes and were content to depend on the government. Unexpectedly, Romney witnessed his comment going viral, resulting in his being lampooned by bloggers, liberal news outlets, and *Saturday Night Live*. His name soon became linked with "47 percent." In response, Romney attempted

---

[18]Brouwer, "Communication as Counterpublic," 197.
[19]Robert Asen, "Imagining the Public Square," *Philosophy and Rhetoric* 35, no. 4 (2002): 349.
[20]James C. Scott, *Domination and the Arts of Resistance: Hidden Transcripts* (New Haven, CT: Yale University Press, 1990), xii.

to draw attention to a little-known clip of Barack Obama, then a state senator, advocating helping the poor through a redistribution of wealth.

In light of a rash of viral videos seemingly showing excessive use of force by law enforcement, Annapolis Police Chief Michael Pristoop regularly reminds his officers that one piece of technology has changed everything—the video capacity of a cell phone. He counsels officers "to be ever aware that everything they do should be considered public. . . . The fact they could be on camera should be foremost in their minds."[21] Like today's law enforcement, should counterpublics be ever aware that everything they say and do in private will become public? As they regularly retreat to discuss issues among themselves, how unguarded or unfiltered can they really be? While hidden transcripts may allow in-house venting or rallying the troops, what damage could occur if they went public?

Engagement. The most distinctive feature of counterpublics is a desire to engage the dominant view. "In this view, radical exclusions such as forced exile or chosen separatism, in which social actors cannot or do not address other publics, do not constitute counterpublicity."[22] In order for counterpublics to effectively challenge the symbolic maps of the dominant culture or strong publics who make policy, counterpublics must speak in a way that the public understands and finds credible. In short, a counterpublic must speak the vernacular of the public. Christopher Duerringer notes that the word *vernacular* is "derived from the Latin *verna*, which names a home-born slave in Rome."[23] These slaves exhibited the ability to talk among themselves in their native language, but also to enter public spaces and speak with confidence to a larger society using their vernacular. If these slaves wished to be heard in Rome, they "were required to render themselves intelligible to the broader public in terms of institutional languages."[24]

Not all counterpublics agree that they need to speak the dominant culture's vernacular. Some argue that one of the fundamental ways strong

---

[21]Marc Fisher and Peter Hermann, "Didn't the McKinney, Texas, Police Officer Know He Was Being Recorded?," *Washington Post*, June 8, 2015, www.washingtonpost.com/politics/didnt-the-mckinney-tex-police-officer-know-he-was-being-recorded/2015/06/08/504033e6-0df7-11e5-9726-49d6fa26a8c6_story.html.
[22]Brouwer, "Communication as Counterpublic," 197.
[23]Duerringer, "War on Christianity," 313.
[24]Ibid.

publics stay in power is by creating rules of discourse that put others at a distinct disadvantage. If you can't speak our language or follow our rules, assert the powerful, we will not give you an audience. In response, for example, some counterpublics who focus on race make provocative rhetorical choices. In an attempt to challenge the grammatical rules of the elite, bell hooks refuses to capitalize her name, while Michael Eric Dyson regularly uses quotes from noneducated people riddled with syntax errors to show that wisdom is not relegated to academics who can properly use the King's English. Each counterpublic will need to negotiate the tension of desiring to be heard without capitulating to the discursive rules or vernacular of the dominant public.

Once a counterpublic decides to engage those who hold the dominant perspective, they must present arguments in the public square.

THE PUBLIC SQUARE

While many today would agree that issues such as immigration, racism, cost of education, and same-sex marriage are important, where do people come together to discuss them? Many cultures have found it important to create a place—a public square—where people could come together to discuss issues facing a community. In ancient Greece, the need for a public square was evidenced by the agora in Athens. In Jewish cultures, the city gates served as a place where residents could debate each other and even call for elders to help moderate. "The public square," states Christian author Os Guinness, "was the civic center of the state, the physical place where citizens came together to deliberate and decide issues of common public life."[25] While the idea of a public square sounds inviting, it quickly raises questions. Where is today's public square? Does everyone have equal access? Are there individuals or groups who feel excluded? Who determines what topics are addressed and what vernacular is acceptable?

German sociologist Jürgen Habermas did the seminal work in understanding the strengths and weaknesses of a healthy public square. For Habermas, an ideal public square would have the following characteristics: it must be open to all who want to participate; it must address issues that

---

[25]Os Guinness, *The Global Public Square: Religious Freedom and the Making of a World Safe for Diversity* (Downers Grove, IL: InterVarsity Press, 2013), 55.

affect the majority of people; it should be free from manipulation or coercion; and, perhaps most importantly, opinions must be presented rationally.

While you may find this concept attractive, you may be hard pressed to think of how it applies to your community or campus. Can you think of a single physical place where fellow students, coworkers, or neighbors might go to talk things out? If you are struggling to think of a place, you are not alone. Habermas himself does not limit the idea of a public square to one location, but rather claims it is "constituted in every conversation in which private citizens come together to form a public."[26] He explains that for Britain and Germany between 1680 and 1730 the public square existed not in one centralized location, but in coffeehouses. London alone had over three thousand coffeehouses, where people would regularly meet to discuss current events and controversies. For Habermas a public square exists when citizens come together for one purpose: to engage in meaningful conversations about communal issues.[27]

Knowing that the public square functionally existed in British coffee-houses raises concerns about how British citizens could achieve Habermas's ideal public square. Did these coffeehouses meet the first criterion of being accessible for everyone? Did London's working poor have the means to attend? Were these mostly male-dominated venues open and inviting to women? If these groups were excluded, can we be assured that the issues being deliberated represented the masses, not merely the privileged?

Does today's public square more resemble the agora of Greece or the coffeehouses of Britain? The answer is a little bit of both. Versions of the agora can be seen in town hall meetings, school board sessions open to the public, or home owner association gatherings; at the same time, friends still discuss current events at the local Starbucks or pub. What makes our current communication climate so challenging is that issues are also being discussed in a million virtual coffeehouses across the world. While speaking at George Washington University, then secretary of state Hillary Clinton noted, "The Internet has become the public space of the 21st century—the world's town

---

[26]Jürgen Habermas, "The Public Sphere," in *Jürgen Habermas on Society and Politics: A Reader*, ed. S. Seidman (Boston: Beacon, 1989), 230.

[27]I'm indebted to Palczewski, Ice, and Fritch's excellent discussion of Habermas's conception of the public square in *Rhetoric in Civic Life*, 237-40.

square, classroom, marketplace, coffeehouse, and nightclub."[28] After citing protests in Egypt and Iran—which had been reported largely through social media—Clinton noted three characteristics that make the Internet so powerful: openness, scope, and a leveling effect. Many counterpublics have also taken note of the potential of the Internet to bypass traditional gate-keepers of the media and even to organize efforts. Protest.net is a collective of activists who have created a website to document and share protest efforts. Rather that relying on media establishments to cover protest activities, this site allows counterpublics to electronically get the word out.

While for many the ability to use Facebook, Instagram, or Twitter to comment on critical issues in real time gives voice to counterpublics, is this virtual public square also susceptible to the limitations of brick and mortar coffeehouses? Just as the coffeehouses of London created a divide between the rich and poor, does the virtual public square create a digital divide? Now that the world population has exceeded seven billion people, researchers wonder what the world would look like if reduced to a village of one hundred. In the latest version of a study started in 1990 and replicated in 2006 and 2012, researchers described the global village as containing 50 males and 50 females, with 26 being children, 74 adults, and only 8 age 65 and over. In relation to technology and social media, 78 villagers would not own or share a computer.[29] Thus, if the village's public square was mediated exclusively through the Internet, only 22 of the villagers would have a voice. This imaginative scenario seems to somewhat reflect today's situation in that "as of 2005, over 50 percent of Internet users came from developed countries, even though those countries account for only 15 percept of the world's population."[30]

How much should social media be utilized by counterpublics who *do* have access to Twitter, Facebook, or Snapchat? Surprisingly, opinions differ. In her 2014 Dartmouth commencement speech, Shonda Rhimes (creator and producer of *Grey's Anatomy* and *Scandal*) shocked her tech-savvy

---

[28]Hillary Clinton, "Internet Rights and Wrongs: Choices and Challenges in a Networked World" (speech, George Washington University, February 15, 2011); transcript at U.S. Department of State official blog, http://blogs.state.gov/stories/2011/02/15/internet-rights-and-wrongs-choices-and-challenges-networked-world.

[29]"If the World Were 100 People," *100 People: A World Portrait*, 2012, www.100people.org/statistics_100stats.php?section=statistics.

[30]Palczewski, Ice, and Fritch, *Rhetoric in Civic Life*, 257.

audience by asserting, "A hashtag is not helping." She continued: "A hashtag is not a movement. A hashtag does not make you Dr. King. A hashtag does not change anything. It's a hashtag. It's you, sitting on your butt, typing into your computer and then going back to binge-watching your favorite show."[31] Do you agree? April Reign, creator of the hashtag #OscarsSoWhite, countered Rhimes and argued that social media can spur on a movement. Her #OscarsSoWhite response was picked up by national media and became a social media phenomenon that forced the Academy of Motion Picture Arts and Sciences to consider major changes to its voting structure.[32] Who's right?

Perhaps it's helpful, argues author Sabina Khan-Ibarra, to distinguish between *social media enthusiasts* and *social media activists*. An enthusiast is "someone who spends a lot of time online clicking 'like,' posting things on Facebook and Twitter but not doing anything beyond that."[33] Terms like *slacktivism* or *clicktivism* have emerged to describe enthusiasts who gleefully add electronic signatures to surveys but invest little else. While it's valuable to get the word out, there is more to be done. Social media activists are those who are equally active offline. "They are the ones committed to a cause, become part of a movement and stick to the issue until there is change."[34] Counterpublics who choose to utilize social media will find in the following chapters both strategies for usage and cautions about social media.

Another issue counterpublics must address when participating in the public square is a matter of scope. Should we engage the public square on a national or local level? Counterpublics tend to adopt the attitude of being world changers, but is that the best perspective? We agree with sociologist James Davison Hunter that the public square should be seen as rooted in the narrative of a community rather than a nation. "The 'public' in public debate does not have to mean national debate. It can and should mean local and regional debate—among people who live and work in relative proximity to each other and who care about their common neighborhoods and communities,

---

[31]Erin Lee, "How Effective Is Social Media Activism?," *The Dartmouth*, February 12, 2016, http://thedartmouth.com/2016/02/12/how-effective-is-social-media-activism.

[32]Ibid.

[33]Sabina Khan-Ibarra, "The Case for Social Media and Hashtag Activism," *Huffington Post*, November 13, 2014, www.huffingtonpost.com/sabina-khanibarra/the-case-for-social-media_b_6149974.html.

[34]Ibid.

towns, cities, and regions."[35] Hunter isn't ignoring the reality that many decisions with implications for local communities are made at the national level among strong publics, but he recognizes that those spheres of power are "inaccessible to the average person."[36] The central claim of this book is that counterpublics should use whatever means possible to influence the national narrative—voting, letters to politicians, petition drives, organized marches on Capitol Hill—but should understand that the ability to evoke real change comes at the local level, with people who shop at the same stores, attend a common university, watch their kids play soccer together on Saturday mornings, and care about salient communal issues.

Regardless of the scope of the audience, when counterpublics engage in the public square they are also engaging in rhetoric.

RHETORIC

When you hear the word *rhetoric*, do you have a positive or negative response? Unfortunately, the idea of rhetoric has fallen on hard times. Many associate it with manipulation or showmanship (as in "empty rhetoric"). Rhetoric, in part, is the systematic study of what most of us do on a daily basis: persuade. From haggling about the price of car, to asking someone out on a date, to convincing a professor to alter a grade, to running a political campaign, persuasion is crucial to day-to-day existence. A central characteristic of rhetoric is that it is practical. Rhetoric is not merely sitting alone in a room and thinking of arguments—accompanied by strong emotions—to support your position or cause. Rather, it is thinking through how to present those emotions and arguments to a particular audience through the use of symbols. Symbols can be any "mark, sign, sound, or gesture that communicates meaning based on social agreement,"[37] such as music, paintings, films, advertisements, television shows, and Facebook or Instagram photos. In other words, the best way to persuade people in the public square may not be a formal speech, but rather a YouTube video that goes viral or a well-timed blog post. The modern counterpublic must be well versed in all forms of communication.

---

[35]James Davison Hunter, *Before the Shooting Begins: Searching for Democracy in America's Culture War* (New York: The Free Press, 1994), 231.

[36]Ibid.

[37]James A. Herrick, *The History and Theory of Rhetoric: An Introduction*, 5th ed. (New York: Routledge, 2013), 6.

Now that we have these concepts in place, how would they play out in the lives of common counterpublics?

A TEST CASE: THE SIXTY-FOOT JESUS

Several years ago an event happened on our campus—Biola University—that highlights the challenges counterpublics face. From 1989 to 1990, a nationally known muralist, Kent Twitchell, constructed on the side of our school's tallest building a massive mural of Jesus holding a Bible. As his inspiration Twitchell used a Russian Jewish male model named Jay Gam. The mural was officially titled *The Word*, but soon came to be known by students simply as the Jesus Mural.[38] To the administration and many students it was an object of pride, and it was soon used on promotional materials. According to the administration's symbolic map, the mural represented the school's dedication to Christ and served as evidence that we as a collective community were not ashamed of proclaiming Jesus. Yet what if you didn't agree? What if your community—consisting mostly of students of color on a predominantly white campus—was operating off a symbolic map that interpreted the mural as a constant reminder that this white Jesus made you feel excluded? How should these counterpublics have proceeded in voicing their opposition? What should have been the tone of their rhetoric? Their tone would be determined by how they collectively imagined the administration and students' support of the mural. Were the supporters faithful followers who merely wanted to show their fidelity to Christ, or members of a majority oblivious to issues of color and race? Or worse, a public who felt racially superior?

The first official protest against the mural came in 1993, when students returned from a diversity conference and wrote to sociologist and Christian activist Tony Campolo that they were disturbed that a "white supremacist" was painted on a building. Campolo wrote back and encouraged them to "tear it down."[39] The result of such collective imaging was angry letters to the school newspaper and frustrated informal meetings where students vented in hidden transcripts. The controversy would periodically resurface, but it was brought to a head in 2010 when a decision needed to be made on refurbishing the

---

[38]To view an image of the mural, google "Jesus Mural Biola University."

[39]Karen Myers, "The Story So Far: Jesus and the Mural," Biola University *Chimes*, April 15, 2010, http://chimes.biola.edu/story/2010/apr/15/jesus-mural-sofar.

mural, which had slowly become weather beaten, thus making the face of Jesus seem even whiter. Was it time to take down the mural, or restore it? To answer this question, the university president commissioned papers written by art faculty, panel discussions with students, and chapel services devoted to the issue. Student and faculty participation was high and passions ran even higher. People debated, argued, and protested in a public square consisting of social media, formal university-wide forums, classrooms, the school newspaper, and even an interview with the artist guided by the faculty of the art department.

While opinions varied, the campus debate could easily be broken into the categories of weak and strong publics. Those disturbed by the mural represented a weak public. They strove to frame the issue according to differing interpretations—fueled by contrasting symbolic maps—of the mural, but lacked the power to make the final decision. Their goals were twofold. First, they sought to convince other publics to adopt elements of a symbolic map that framed the mural as insensitive to students of color. Second, they sought to mobilize these publics to put pressure on the decision makers. In contrast, the strong public consisted of the president and board of directors who were also debating the fate of the mural behind closed doors, cultivating their own transcripts. However, this group understood that their final decision would affect students, faculty, and alumni. The difficulty for the student counterpublics was that they completely lacked access to the board of directors and had limited opportunity to engage the president. The question of how such students should present themselves in campus-wide forums, electronic chat rooms, blogs, and panel discussions with faculty and student leaders is the subject of this book. What tone should the counterpublic take? How can issues be framed using the vernacular of decision makers? What types of evidence will the strong public find convincing?

CONCLUSION

What complicates the activism of these students is that in addition to being counterpublics, they are also followers of Christ. As Christian counterpublics they had to not only strategize how to address the mural but also consider whether their actions brought honor to Christ. How can the two be balanced? The answer to this last question is the focus of our next chapter.

2

WHAT IS A CHRISTIAN COUNTERPUBLIC?

"**Religion that God our Father** accepts as pure and faultless is . . ."

I write this partial statement on the whiteboard and ask students to respond. They immediately recognize it, and without hesitation hands shoot up across the classroom. I call on a girl sitting in the front row and she confidently answers, "Caring for orphans and widows." Students around her nod in agreement. For a generation raised on social justice values, this verse (Jas 1:27) has become a type of rallying cry.

How would first-century believers have responded? For those in AD 45 reading James's letter for the first time, would the answer have been so obvious? No doubt some would have been inclined to say that true religion in God's sight is partaking of the Lord's Supper or devotion to prayer. In a time when Roman rule meant acknowledging Caesar as god, some may have responded that courageously being baptized and publically proclaiming "Jesus is Lord" would be the highest expression of fidelity. Yet James surprised these early followers by telling them that practicing true religion, in part, is being a counterpublic—caring for and giving voice to those who are neglected by the majority.

I find it interesting that when quoting this verse most people leave off the phrase "in their distress." Orphans and widows were the most oppressed and marginalized people in Jewish society. Their distress, which can be literally translated "pressure," came from their desperate need for food and shelter, and the constant search for an advocate. Having no voice in the culture exasperated this pressure. The Scriptures teach that the marginalized in society should have an advocate: the follower of Christ. To follow the teachings of the early church entails adopting a concern for the marginal or minority view—in other words, becoming a counterpublic.

If the three characteristics of a counterpublic are—as mentioned in the previous chapter—opposition, withdrawal, and engagement, then how do they apply to the Christian counterpublic? Each component provides a unique challenge.

OPPOSITION

In a classic counterpublic passage, the apostle Paul writes that Christians are "Christ's ambassadors," and it is through us that God makes his appeal (2 Cor 5:20). What is God's primary appeal? Paul answers, "He has committed to us the message of reconciliation" (2 Cor 5:19). What do you make of Paul's bold assertion? Are we really to serve as God's representatives? If that is God's calling, then it seems reasonable that he would select the most mature and capable among us. After all, IBM or Apple is not going to let just anyone be the face of their company. Not so with God. We easily forget that the passage we are considering is part of a letter to a young, struggling church situated in Corinth. Consider the following:

- Paul himself founded the Corinthian church.

- Corinth was an important port seen by many as a crossroads of the Mediterranean (a bustling city filled with temptation—think Las Vegas).

- The church mostly consisted of recent converts.

- Members were struggling to give up old ways of life (eating food offered to idols, factions, sexual issues, suing each other).

Apparently, God is content using common, in-process people as his counterpublics. In spite of their struggles, Jesus is so committed to these fledgling ambassadors that he shockingly states that how people respond to *them* is a direct indication of how they would respond to *him*: "Whoever listens to you listens to me; whoever rejects you rejects me" (Lk 10:16). This tight association between Jesus and his ambassadors was dramatically illustrated to Paul. While persecuting Christ-followers under the name of Saul, he encountered Christ unexpectedly on a deserted road leading to Damascus. "Why do you persecute me?" Jesus forcefully asked. Saul was stunned and confused. To him, he was only persecuting a fringe group called the Way. "Who are you?" he replied. "I am Jesus, whom you are persecuting" (Acts 9:4-5). It was a response Paul never forgot and one that, through his writings, is passed on to all Christian counterpublics.

To make matters more difficult, Jesus tells us that the message of reconciliation we've been given will be seen as an affront to those in power and will cause much hardship. "Blessed are you," Jesus tells his followers, "when people insult you, persecute you and falsely say all kinds of evil against you because of me" (Mt 5:11). The message God has given us can—and in many cases will—cause deep social and relational division, even separating families so that brothers betray brothers and parents disown children (Mt 10:35). In short, Jesus warns, expect to be hated (Jn 15:18).

However, have these dire predictions of opposition come to fruition? It's not enough to *expect* to be hated to claim counterpublic status. For Christians in the West today, can such opposition be demonstrated? When I present such questions to my religious friends, they look amazed and slightly perturbed. "Of course we are being attacked" is the general response. "Don't you watch the news?" To be fair, they have good reason to feel attacked. From Sean Hannity to Mike Huckabee to Kirk Cameron, we are fed steady stories of seemingly systematic, anti-Christian opposition designed to frighten and mobilize. For example, In Todd Starnes's book *God Less America* readers encounter a dire warning on the inside cover: "We are in a war for our country." The description continues:

> Our government is waging an all-out assault on our freedom, and religious liberty is fast becoming the civil rights issue of our generation. Could it be that one day the pastor of the local church will be arrested for preaching hate? Is it possible that Christian business owners could be forced to close down for refusing to violate the tenets of their faith? Will evangelical organizations be labeled domestic hate groups for defending the traditional definition of marriage? This day may, in fact, already be upon us.[1]

To prove his case, Starnes provides pages of examples meant to shock us into action. While examples taken from social media and news headlines seem to buttress his claims, do they meet an academic standard?

---

[1]Todd Starnes, *God Less America: Real Stories from the Front Lines of the Attack on Traditional Values* (Lake Mary, FL: FrontLine, 2014), front flap.

Though not as sensationalistic as Starnes, researcher George Yancey also suspects there is an anti-Christian bias prevalent among pockets of society. He identifies a type of *Christianophobia*, which he defines as "an unreasonable hatred or anger toward Christians."[2] But can he prove it? Yancey's methodology includes both a quantitative and a qualitative component. The quantitative element is rooted in the 2012 American National Election Survey (ANES) and consists of a sample size of 5,105 individuals. Respondents were asked to rank their affection or disaffection for a number of groups, ranging from zero to hundred. "Based on calculations done with this variable we were able to determine that among religious groups only atheists faced more disaffinity than Christian fundamentalists."[3] While this disaffinity exists, it seems to be mostly localized to individuals who are "highly educated, wealthy, politically progressive and white."[4] The qualitative aspect focused on narratives from culturally progressive activists with a sample size of 3,577 respondents. They were asked a series of open-ended questions about their attitude toward the Christian Right. "The only difference I see between [a] Christian fundamentalist and [an] Islamic fundamentalist is terrorism," responds a male in his late forties. "We cannot allow them [Christian Right] to get a solid foothold in our government," asserts a female in her mid-sixties.[5] While such comments are disconcerting, Yancey again notes that the respondents are, like in the quantitative sample, mostly highly educated, white, wealthy, and progressive.

While Yancey is convinced that Christianophobia exists, he cautions readers to avoid two common mistakes. First, some Christians exaggerate claims of persecution, and soon "almost everything these Christians do not like in our society prompts a claim to persecution."[6] Second, in an attempt to avoid claiming victimhood, others minimize or outright ignore Christianophobia. The answer, concludes Yancey, is somewhere in the middle.

In the end, what separates the works of Yancey and Starnes? After all, each contains both narrative and statistics. Perhaps what most separates the

---

[2]George Yancey, *Hostile Environment: Understanding and Responding to Anti-Christian Bias* (Downers Grove, IL: InterVarsity Press, 2015), 11.
[3]Ibid., 156.
[4]Ibid.
[5]Ibid., 19-20.
[6]Ibid., 24

two is restraint. For example, in addressing the issue of homosexuality and same-sex marriage, the two take radically different approaches. Yancey, in an attempt to avoid needlessly inflaming the issue, restrains himself from directly addressing the topic. "Such a subject may take a book-length treatment and I do not possess the expertise in this subject to write such a book. There are simply too many twists and turns in this subject for it to be easily dealt with in the few pages of a chapter." He concludes, "This book will be controversial enough without me walking into that minefield."[7] In contrast, Starnes satirically addresses the issue in a chapter titled "So Absurd It Could Be True: The Great Interspecies Marriage Act of 2023," where he envisions a fictive futuristic news release from the Associated Press:

> (AP) THE FUTURE—A divided Supreme Court finally legalized interspecies marriage, striking down a key section of a federal law that denied veterinary benefits to humans and pets, marking what activists are calling the greatest civil rights ruling of the twenty-first century.[8]

The chapter concludes with a sarcastic announcement that PetSmart is launching an interspecies bridal registry.

What impact might it have on counterpublics to regularly ingest the hyperbolic writings of authors such as Starnes? Church historian John Woodbridge suggests that inflammatory, culture war language affects the Christian community in two ways. First, culture war rhetoric conditions us to interpret mere disagreement as personal attack. When you read Starnes, the rhetorical heat that confronts you page after page is unavoidable. Instead of citizens disagreeing about their vision of a community, you encounter opposition portrayed as individuals who hate you and your community. Second, culture war rhetoric can easily become a type of "self-fulfilling prophecy exacerbating the very conflicts it seeks merely to describe."[9] In short, each time we describe reality, we perpetuate it. If all we see are enemies on the other side bent on our destruction, then we will adopt a warlike response. Woodbridge offers a different metaphor, in which neighborhoods and schools are seen not as battlefields but as mission fields,

---

[7]Ibid., 23
[8]Starnes, *God Less America*, 102.
[9]John Woodbridge, "Culture War Casualties: How Warfare Rhetoric Is Hurting the Work of the Church," *Christianity Today*, March 6, 1995, 22.

where grace-filled communicators operate. "Our home and church do not become military bunkers, but havens of hospitality with the sign 'Welcome' displayed over the front doors."[10]

A natural inclination for Christian counterpublics will be to utilize social media to engage others. In later chapters we discuss specific strategies for communicating through social media; for now, *Christianity Today* writer John Dyer offers a somber warning: "What few of us realize is that when we press those 'Publish,' 'Post,' 'Comment,' and 'Send' buttons, we are making the shift away from merely 'believing' truth and stepping into the arena of publishing that belief."[11] According to Dyer, when we post our convictions we place ourselves under James's warning, "Not many of you should become teachers, my fellow believers, because you know that we who teach will be judged more strictly" (Jas 3:1). While we strongly advocate the use of social media to be effective counterpublics, we encourage an honest evaluation of what topics individuals are qualified to address, careful fact checking, and cultivating a civil tone. Unfortunately, we seldom take time to do any of these. Dyer concludes, "Social media relentlessly asks us to publish our personal opinions on anything and everything that happens. There is no time for reflection in prayer, no place for discussion with other flesh-image bearers, and no incentive to remain silent."[12]

WITHDRAWAL

All counterpublics must take time to step away from the cause and meet as a public to regroup. The same is true of Christian counterpublics, who need to occasionally pull back and address their agenda, how to stay motivated, and how they should envision other publics.

Agenda. Unique to Christian counterpublics is that our agenda is given to us via the Scriptures. As we've already considered, the apostle Paul states that our central God-given message is bearing witness to God's reconciling all things to himself (2 Cor 5:19). A key result of this reconciliation will be the restoration of God's shalom, which is evidenced by "universal flourishing,

---

[10]Ibid., 25.
[11]John Dyer, "Not Many of You Should Presume to Be Bloggers," *Christianity Today*, March 11, 2011, www.christianitytoday.com/ct/2011/marchweb-only/bloggers.html.
[12]Ibid.

wholeness, and delight."[13] The difficulty comes when Christian counterpublics want to be more specific about an agenda. Of all that the Scriptures teach, what should my group focus on? Is there one agenda that fits all? What happens when counterpublics disagree on what aspects of the agenda should receive priority?

On September 28, 2009, representatives of the Orthodox, Catholic, and evangelical traditions met in New York to sign a statement that came to be known as the Manhattan Declaration, drafted by Robert George (Princeton University), Timothy George (Beeson Divinity School), and the late Chuck Colson (founder of the Chuck Colson Center for Christian Worldview). The declaration acknowledged that while the Christian moral tradition contains many aspects, pressing cultural concerns mandated that Christians marshal their attention and resources specifically on three issues. Each issue was described and argued for in powerful narrative supported by Scripture: the plight of the unborn (Gen 1:27; Jn 10:10), traditional marriage (Gen 2:23-24; Eph 5:32-33), and religious liberty (Is 61:1; Mt 22:21). The declaration was signed by leading pastors, clergy, politicians, activists, and authors.[14] With biblical support and a who's who of religious leaders, the matter seemed settled.

Not so, argues Jonathan Merritt. Often referred to as the voice of young evangelicals, Merritt states that evangelical counterpublics under thirty are not comfortable with such a narrow agenda. It's not that they don't acknowledge the plight of the unborn or the attack on traditional marriage; they just are uncomfortable with limiting their focus to the usual concerns of the culture wars. "Previous generations may be somewhat excused for a narrower agenda, but this generation will not be," explains Merritt. Through the Internet and short-term mission trips focusing on social justice needs, young evangelicals have been "assaulted by the world's ills—stories of poverty, hunger, genocide, disease, and unnecessary suffering around the globe—we can't ignore them."[15] In one sense, what Merritt acknowledges is indisputable: to focus on one issue is to ignore another. Consequently, with

---

[13]Cornelius Plantinga Jr., *Not the Way It's Supposed to Be: A Breviary of Sin* (Grand Rapids: Eerdmans, 1995), 10.

[14]"Manhattan Declaration: A Call of Christian Conscience," November 20, 2009, http://manhattandeclaration.org.

[15]Jonathan Merritt, *A Faith of Our Own: Following Jesus Beyond the Culture Wars* (New York: FaithWords, 2012), 124.

limited time, resources, and volunteers, each counterpublic will have to decide which aspects of the biblical agenda should be prioritized and which set aside. While freedom to decide most certainly can be given to Christian counterpublics, what if differing agendas conflict?

A clash of agendas surfaced when humanitarian organization World Vision announced that its US branch would no longer discriminate against employees in same-sex marriages. The backlash from pockets of the Christian community was swift. One day after the announcement, World Vision estimated it lost financial support for more than two thousand child sponsorships. Twitter and Facebook campaigns, along with Christian leaders and entire denominations, urged individuals to consider pulling support. In order to stem financial losses estimated in the millions, World Vision president Richard Stearns reversed their policy and asked supporters for forgiveness for a temporary lapse of judgment. Yet not all were ready to forgive. In a scathing article, "How Evangelicals Won a War and Lost a Generation," religion writer Rachel Held Evans mirrored the anger of many that children had been used as bargaining chips in a Christian war against gays. "When Christians declare that they would rather withhold aid from people who need it than serve alongside gays and lesbians helping to provide aid, something is wrong." Evans concluded that what the issue revealed is "just how misaligned evangelical priorities have become."[16] When and how Christian counterpublics address disagreements over biblical agendas and priorities will require careful mediation, understanding, and charity.

How difficult it is to arrange Christian priorities was in full display in three essays written by evangelical theologian Wayne Grudem leading up to the 2016 presidential election. In his first essay Grudem acknowledges that Donald Trump the candidate is brash, egotistical, married three times, and by his own admission unfaithful in those marriages. Yet, evoking Jeremiah 29:7, he argues that this "flawed" candidate is still best for the welfare of the nation.[17] However, after the infamous *Access Hollywood* tape surfaced of a

---

[16]Rachel Held Evans, "How Evangelicals Won a War and Lost a Generation," *CNN Belief Blog*, March 31, 2014, http://religion.blogs.cnn.com/2014/03/31/how-evangelicals-won-a-culture-war-and-lost-a-generation.

[17]Wayne Grudem, "Why Voting for Donald Trump Is a Morally Good Choice," *Townhall*, July 28, 2016, http://townhall.com/columnists/waynegrudem/2016/07/28/why-voting-for-donald-trump-is-a-morally-good-choice-n2199564.

2005 interview in which Trump spoke of grabbing women by their private parts and attempting to seduce married women, Grudem responded by writing a second essay revoking his support. Reminding readers of the prohibition against adultery (Ex 20:14), he concludes, "I cannot commend Trump's moral character, and I strongly urge him to withdraw from the election."[18] Ten days later Grudem surprisingly reversed course, stating he was again voting for Trump. "Since I find both candidates morally objectionable, I am back to the old-fashioned basis on which I have usually decided how to vote for my entire life: *Whose policies are better?*"[19] All Christian counterpublics will no doubt feel the angst experienced by Grudem in how to prioritize Christian values. In our attempt to secure political power—for the good of the city—can we still maintain our moral voice? How can both be prioritized or balanced?

The biblical agenda given to Christian counterpublics does not merely provide utilitarian goals, such as electing candidates or establishing laws, but also relational goals, such as restoring civility, promoting shalom, and loving those who oppose us. James Davison Hunter argues that such relational goals are worthy aims for all counterpublics; success should not be measured merely in "political terms but in social terms; in the de-escalation of tensions, in the development of a small measure of mutual understanding, and in the outcomes of real people's lives."[20] The ancient writers of the book of Proverbs would agree with Hunter's assessment: "When the LORD takes pleasure in anyone's way, he causes their enemies to make peace with them" (Prov 16:7). The realism of the verse is striking and hopeful. Not all disagreements can be resolved, it acknowledges; yet is it possible to live at social peace in the midst of disagreement? It is pleasing to God when Christian counterpublics add to their rhetorical goals promoting shalom with those who oppose them.

Times of withdrawal can also allow counterpublics to address seasons of discouragement. Due to their strong desire to see God's shalom permeate

---

[18]Wayne Grudem, "Trump's Moral Character and the Election," *Townhall*, October 9, 2016, http://townhall.com/columnists/waynegrudem/2016/10/09/trumps-moral-character-and-the-election-n2229846.

[19]Wayne Grudem, "If You Don't Like Either Candidate, Then Vote for Trump's Policies," *Townhall*, October 19, 2016, http://townhall.com/columnists/waynegrudem/2016/10/19/if-you-dont-like-either-candidate-then-vote-for-trumps-policies-n2234187.

[20]James Davison Hunter, *Before the Shooting Begins: Searching for Democracy in America's Culture War* (New York: The Free Press, 1994), 234.

his creation, Christian counterpublics are acutely aware of the lack of it in our troubled world. In a personal letter, apologist Francis Schaeffer voices this concern: "Surely if there was ever a dark age in history, and one which needs a calling forth unto a deeper spiritual walk and close waiting upon our dear God, this is our generation. The longer I am back in the United States, the more I tremble for my beloved land. I wonder if we are not coming close to the end of civilization."[21] Surprisingly, Schaeffer penned this in 1954—pre-dating the sexual revolution, the AIDS crisis, *Roe v. Wade*, the bloody struggle of the Civil Rights movement, divorce culture, the Rwandan genocide, the explosion of sex trafficking, and the proliferation of pornography, to name a few. Christian counterpublics, like Schaeffer and those forming the L'Abri communities, are prone to focus on the encroaching darkness. In light of this, Christian counterpublics need to regularly renew a vision for shalom. Where can such motivation come from? In part, by looking to the past and future.

Motivation for modern Christian activists can be taken from early counterpublics who founded our country. Many of us forget that the signers of the Declaration of Independence did so facing great duress and threat of punishment. England viewed this seminal document as a symbol not of independence but of treason and threatened to hang all who sup-ported it. John Witherspoon, representative of New Jersey, signed the Dec-laration. As a husband and the father of ten children, why would he put himself at such risk? "It is only the fear of God, can deliver us from the fear of man," Witherspoon preached from the pulpit.[22] Seeking God's favor above that of the dominant public reflects Jesus' exhortation that we should "rejoice and be glad" when opposition comes, knowing that our reward—God's affirmation—will be great (Mt 5:12).

Acknowledging that the darkness will one day recede also renews counter-publics. Nobel Peace Prize winner and Holocaust survivor Elie Wiesel stays motivated in fighting for human rights by leaning on two words: "My favorite expression is 'and yet.' It's true there's much injustice in the world,

---

[21] Francis Schaeffer, *Letters of Francis A. Schaeffer: Spiritual Reality in the Personal Christian Life*, ed. Lane T. Dennis (Westchester, IL: Crossway, 1985), 45.

[22] John Witherspoon, "Ministerial Character and Duty," in *The Works of the Rev. John Witherspoon* (Philadelphia: William W. Woodward, 1802), 2:562.

and yet we try to prevail."[23] Christian counterpublics also seek to prevail in current struggles, spurred on by Wiesel's conception of the *and yet*. While the lack of shalom in today's world is deeply discouraging, we know that in the New Jerusalem God's rule and subsequent peace will be fully restored (Rev 21:1-7).

ENGAGEMENT

After times of renewal, counterpublics seek to engage dominant publics. Before engagement can occur, decisions need to be made about scope and target audience. Do we seek to enter into the national narrative or pursue change at the local level? For many, the issue is moot since it seems Jesus sets the scope in commanding us to take his message to all nations. In what has come to be known as the Great Commission, Jesus instructs his disciples to "make disciples of all nations, baptizing them in the name of the Father and of the Son and of the Holy Spirit" (Mt 28:19). While it sounds daunting, many Christian counterpublics have adopted a goal of being world changers and influencing entire cultural narratives. But doesn't the Great Commission conflict with our assertion in the previous chapter that the focus of counterpublics should be rooted in the local, not national debate?

Christian leaders and authors have sought to put Christ's commission in perspective for current activists. Pastor and Christian statesman John Stott argues that, unintentionally, we may have given the Great Commission too prominent a place. "Please do not misunderstand me. I firmly believe that the whole church is under obligation to obey its Lord's commission to take the gospel to all nations. But I am also concerned that we should not regard this as the only instruction which Jesus left us."[24] Stott reminds us that Christ also issued the second great commandment (Mt 22:39, quoting Lev 19:18), calling us to love our neighbors as we do ourselves. If our scope is too large, can we really love and attend to our neighbor? Christian author Eugene Peterson argues that the gospel has always been rooted in a particular locale—a limited and bounded area. If not put in the right perspective, the

---

[23]David Ferrell, "A Voice That Stays Strong: Despite Age and Heart Surgery, Elie Wiesel Fights on for Human Rights," *Orange County Registrar*, April 17, 2014, News 3.

[24]John Stott, *Authentic Christianity: From the Writings of John Stott*, ed. Timothy Dudley-Smith (Downers Grove, IL: InterVarsity Press, 1995), 321.

Great Commission can cause us to overlook local work as we seek bigger and better projects. "We are particularly vulnerable to devaluating place because we are used to trafficking in large ideas, proclaiming the gospel to all the world and telling the stories of courageous missionaries across the seas."[25]

While the Great Commission is conceptually our goal, it seems to practically be played out locally. In one of his first postresurrection appearances, Jesus addresses his disciples and adds insight into how the Great Commission will be accomplished: "You will be my witnesses in Jerusalem, and in all Judea and Samaria, and to the ends of the earth" (Acts 1:8). In others words, the gospel will spread to the world by moving from locale—Jerusalem—to locale—Judea—to locale—Samaria. This advancement requires time and committed labor. Stott notes that one of recurring mistakes of the modern church is to deviate from Paul's methodology by being "too superficial (making brief encounters and expecting quick results), whereas Paul stayed in Corinth and Ephesus for five years, faithfully sowing gospel seed and in due time reaping a harvest."[26]

Last, and most important, the larger the scope, the less effective your message becomes. Why? As stated in the previous chapter, one of the key goals of a counterpublic is to gain access to and influence strong publics, or those who have the power to make decisions. At a national level few of us have access or credibility to influence strong publics. Yet at the local level not only do we have access to strong publics such as civic leaders, parent-teacher association representatives, and school board members, but we can actually become part of those strong publics. As citizens we can seek the welfare of our community by seeking out leadership positions. Training for how to obtain such positions may be becoming more available. Conservative activist David Lane is seeking to recruit and equip one thousand pastors to run for local political office. "Believers have been comfortable taking a back seat. We need a bigger place at the table," states trainee Mitch Brooks, who is a pastor in Belton, South Carolina. "We believe that, in a lot of areas, we have some insight."[27] Conservative writers Cal Thomas and Ed

---

[25]Eugene Peterson, *Subversive Spirituality* (Grand Rapids: Eerdmans, 1997), 191.

[26]Ibid., 329.

[27]Aisha Bhoori, "Evangelical Group Training Pastors to Run for Elected Office," *Time*, June 12, 2015, http://time.com/3919862/american-renewal-project-pastors.

Dobson agree with Christians seeking community leadership positions and explain that the Religious Right's failure in evoking national change is not due to a lack of effort, mobilization, or conviction. "We failed because we were unable to redirect a nation from the top down. Real change must come from the bottom up, or better yet, from the inside out."[28]

Even if counterpublics adopt a local perspective, they must still make ideas known in their community's public square. While we'll have more to say about this in upcoming chapters, the first goal for Christian counterpublics is Habermas's first criterion of a healthy public square—openness to all. Today, it may seem that all perspectives are welcome *but* the Christian view. After witnessing an alarming trend toward secularization, former Lutheran minister and political theorist Richard John Neuhaus coined the phrase "naked public square" to describe political debate stripped of religious voices. Christians are not the only ones alarmed by a public square that selectively excludes certain voices. Philosopher Robert Ansen notes, "Practicing democratic discourse fairly and justly depends indispensably on enabling inclusion."[29]

With a diverse public square comes a commitment to not merely tolerate different perspectives but engage them. Princeton University is home to diverse and even polarizing views. Robert George is a deeply religious educator who coauthored the Manhattan Declaration and is an outspoken defender of rights of the unborn. Also at Princeton is Peter Singer, a moral philosopher who specializes in applied ethics, who argues that newborns lack the essential characteristics of personhood such as rationality, autonomy, and self-consciousness. Thus taking the life of a newborn is not the same as killing a self-conscious, rational person exhibiting autonomy.[30] Knowing George's religious convictions, one would expect him to want to silence Singer or exclude him from the public square. Nothing could be further from the truth. Rather, George argues that Singer not only has the right to make arguments for his position but also deserves that others seek to understand and consider his views. For George, a commitment to truth and a healthy public forum demands this type of posture—a posture he

---

[28]Cal Thomas and Ed Dobson, *Blinded by the Might: Why the Religious Right Can't Save America* (Grand Rapids: Zondervan, 1999), 100.

[29]Robert Ansen, "Imagining the Public Square," *Philosophy and Rhetoric* 35, no. 4 (2002): 345.

[30]For an introduction to Singer's ethical symbolic map, see Peter Singer, *Rethinking Life and Death: The Collapse of Our Traditional Ethics* (New York: St. Martin's Griffin, 1996).

equally expects from Singer and those who find George's own views radical and offensive.[31] To exclude radical secular views from the public square would result in it becoming naked to the nonreligious. In today's combative communication climate, securing a public square open to all—even if it means allowing radical views—is the first priority of engagement.

CHRISTIAN COUNTERPUBLICS AND THE CHURCH

One may read this description of Christian counterpublics and wonder where the church fits in. Or, more directly, is not the church supposed to be God's counterpublic? Why should Christians organize counterpublics at all—why not just be the church?

Ultimately, the church is intended to be God's counterpublic. It is (or is meant to be) the place where the corporate life of humanity is lived in shalom and where Jesus is worshiped as Savior and King. Furthermore, the church is where the corporate witness to Christ toward the surrounding society is to be centered. When we find ourselves living in a society where God is not honored and the prevailing culture is opposing his vision for the cosmos, the church is his primary agent for effecting change. So, yes, the church is God's counterpublic, and as much as possible we advocate carrying out the activities of a counterpublic through the local church. However, this does not mean there is no place for organizations outside of the church that contribute to the task of being a counterpublic. Indeed, there are several possible benefits that such organizations might offer.

Specialization. These organizations could be analogous to parachurch mission agencies, which develop training and support mechanisms for sending and sustaining missionaries on the field. They allow individual local churches to send missionaries to many places that would be difficult to reach if they had to develop an international infrastructure on their own. In the case of counterpublics, this infrastructure might include relationships with political leaders, school boards, social service agencies, foundations, universities, media outlets, lobbyists, and many other groups or individuals who are active in public issues.

---

[31]To hear George discuss Singer and his vision for a healthy, inclusive public square, listen to his discussion with Cornell West and Rick Warren at Biola University, "The Cost of Freedom: How Disagreements Makes Us Civil," April 2015, www.youtube.com/watch?v=XNDQj8QK8Zc.

Cooperation between churches. Again, similar to parachurch agencies that allow several different churches to support a single missionary, churches can join together under the umbrella of a third-party organization to become a counterpublic. Individually, small churches may not have a voice that would be heard in a crowded public square, but by banding together they can make themselves heard.

Avoiding legal entanglements. In the United States, there are fairly strict laws that separate church and state and therefore limit the lobbying and political activities of a church. Organizing a separate nonprofit organization or foundation has often proven to be the best way to avoid the legal entanglements that come when a counterpublic addresses political concerns.

Diversity of opinion within a congregation. If a church adopts a single stance on a controversial issue, members who see that issue differently may feel exclude or rejected. Working through a third-party organization may avoid this problem because it allows different members to align with different groups that are in keeping with their various convictions.

Benefits such as these make organized Christian counterpublics a helpful contribution to the mission of the church.

CONCLUSION

While James offers a powerful description of religious acts that God considers pure and faultless, he also identifies what is deemed worthless. "Those who consider themselves religious and yet do not keep a tight rein on their tongues deceive themselves, and their religion is worthless" (Jas 1:26). In today's vitriolic communication climate, few seem able or willing to rein in verbal attacks. In such a climate, how should a Christian communicator present his or her message in a way that is civil and uncompromising? In chapter three we will explore how Christians can serve as gracious communicators in an argument culture.

SAINT PATRICK AND IRISH CIVILIZATION

ONE MORNING IN AD 401, a young man named Patricius was walking along a beach in western Britain with his family when a fleet of Irish long-boats rushed ashore. The warriors crashed onto the beach with braying war horns, terrorizing Patricius and his family as they fled toward town. The warriors demolished the village, discovered Patricius in the ruins, and dragged him aboard a boat bound for the east coast of Ireland.[1] He was sold to an Irish warlord named Miliucc and began living like an animal, spending his days in the wild as a shepherd-slave, terrorized by his master. In his desperation, he found his nominal Christianity slowly taking on a more substantial form. He began to pray many times a day, and he discovered a rising love and faith in God within his heart. He would stay out in the forests and awaken before daylight to pray in the snow and rain, warmed only by the Spirit of God burning in his heart.[2]

After six years of servitude, Patricius heard a mysterious voice assuring him he would soon return to his homeland. Not long thereafter he heard the same voice say, "Come and see, your ship is waiting for you." Answering what he deemed to be the call of God, he fled two hundred miles across Ireland to a harbor far in the south, where he boarded a ship to Gaul. Upon arrival he found his way to a monastery, where he studied to become a priest, and ultimately he returned home to Britain. But after many years of faithful service, he heard another voice crying, "We beg you, holy youth . . . come and walk again among us."[3] Hearing this as a call from God, he rose to answer and served the remainder of his life among the Irish, with whom he had lived as a slave so many years before.

---

[1] Mary Cagney, "Patrick the Saint," *Christian History* 60 (1998), www.christianitytoday.com/ch/1998/issue60/60h010.html.

[2] *Confession of St. Patrick*, Christian Classics Ethereal Library, www.ccel.org/ccel/patrick/confession.iv.html.

[3] Ibid.

Patricius, of course, is better known today as Saint Patrick. The story of his return to Ireland chronicles one of the most remarkable counterpublics in all of church history, and it exemplifies each of the three marks of a counterpublic: opposition, withdrawal, and engagement.

PATRICK'S MISSION AS A COUNTERPUBLIC

Opposition. It is hard to imagine a time or place that was more opposed to the gospel than fifth-century Ireland. Their economy was built almost entirely on raiding, slavery, and warfare. For several centuries before and after the birth of Christ, the Irish marauded the English coast with relentless zeal. Those who survived their raids were taken captive and sold as slaves. Imagine the horror of serving an Irish war chieftain whose home was protected by a palisade of sharpened trees capped with the heads of slaves captured while trying to escape. Indeed, the skulls of victims found many uses, including being sculpted into ceremonial drinking bowls or used as footballs in victory celebrations. The religious life of Ireland offered no respite from bloodshed. Irish druid paganism was as terrifying as the Irish pirates themselves. Theirs was a bloody religion of human sacrifices, strangled or beheaded to please the druid gods. Several remarkably well-preserved victims have been found in peat bogs. Vessels with them are adorned with images of gods deriving erotic pleasure from eating human beings whole. In short, the realities Patrick confronted in fifth-century Irish life make the challenges facing most other counterpublics pale in comparison. Even more remarkable is that despite the opposition, Patrick's efforts were overwhelmingly successful. Within thirty years his small band had converted between 30 and 40 percent of Ireland to Christ. Human sacrifice was eliminated, and Irish slavery and slave trade were almost entirely abolished.

How did Patrick accomplish such a remarkable transformation in such a short time?

Withdrawal and engagement. Patrick sought to fulfill his calling to Ireland by building monastic communities. Ian Bradley, a scholar of Celtic Christianity at St. Andrews University, compares Celtic monastic life to Egyptian monasticism of the fourth and fifth centuries. Though there are many similarities, a striking difference is that the Egyptian monks generally practiced radical separation from the world, whereas the Celtic monasteries provided places of sanctuary but were also intensely involved in the affairs of the world and the lives of the people they served.[4] George Hunter, professor of church growth and evangelism at Asbury Seminary, makes a similar comparison as he notes that Egyptian monasteries were organized to protest and escape the materialism of Rome and the corruption of the church. The monks built them to cultivate and save their own souls. The Celtic monasteries, in contrast, were organized to save other people's souls.[5] So Patrick's monasteries shared with all monasteries the function of being a place of *withdrawal*, but they were unique in their simultaneous commitment to *engagement*.

How did Celtic monastic communities accomplish these seemingly paradoxical purposes? Similar to other monasteries, a Celtic monastery was enclosed by a ditch or wall, but the function of the enclosure was entirely different. Rather than blocking out the world, it served more like the lines on a playing field. As one passed through the gate, one entered into a playing field with entirely different rules. Within the Celtic monastic enclosure the rules of the kingdom of God applied. The community was an outpost of the kingdom—a foretaste of heaven. What would one day be true in the new heavens and new earth was anticipated and modeled within the walls of the Celtic monastic community. This included all the multitudinous activities of ordinary life. Celtic monasteries were populated with craftsmen, artists, farmers, families, and children. Cows were herded, sheep were sheared, cloth was made, and crops were cultivated. The earth yielded its fruit for the good of human beings and in cooperation with God's design. As Philip Sheldrake aptly phrases it, "monastic settlements [were] anticipations of paradise in which the forces of division, violence and evil were excluded. Wild beasts were tamed and nature was regulated. The privileges of Adam and Eve in Eden, received from God but lost in the Fall, were reclaimed." The enclosures integrated all the elements of human life, as well as all classes of human society.[6]

Patrick's vision of integrating both sacred and secular also found expression in distinctive forms of prayer associated with the daily tasks of

---

[4]Ian C. Bradley, *Colonies of Heaven: Celtic Models for Today's Church* (London: Darton, Longman & Todd, 2000), 11.

[5]George Hunter, *The Celtic Way of Evangelism* (Nashville: Abingdon, 2000), 28.

[6]Philip Sheldrake, *Living Between Worlds: Place and Journey in Celtic Spirituality* (London: Darton, Longman & Todd, 1995), 39.

living. There were prayers for planting, meals, journeys, and welcoming guests. The echoes of these prayers and practices are found in the old Gaelic prayers repeated in some of the most remote sections of the British Isles up into the twentieth century. Consider this prayer for lighting a morning fire:

> I will kindle my fire this morning
> In presence of the holy angles of heaven,
> God, kindle Thou in my heart within
> A flame of love to my neighbor,
> To my foe, to my friend, to my kindred all,
> To the brave, to the knave, to the thrall.[7]

The beauty of this prayer comes in no small part from the intimate proximity of daily tasks of ordinary human life and the spiritual mission to love both God and neighbor.

Emphasizing the role of cultural engagement in the Celtic monastery should not make one doubt the importance of spiritual retreat and contemplation. Life within the monasteries was intentionally structured so there was a rhythm of engagement in and withdrawal from the world.[8] Contemplation was not just for the "professional" ascetics. Patrick and his followers believed that "all people were called from birth to the experience of contemplation," so places were constructed within the enclosure for solitude and contemplation.[9] And certainly the most influential leaders of Patrick's movement often found withdrawal to be essential. Columba alternated periods of intense activity running the monastic community on Iona with months of solitude on the island of Hinba. Cuthbert would withdraw from running the community at Lindisfarne to his hermit cell on the uninhabited Farne islands. Dyfrig regularly retreated from the busy monastery at Llantwit Major to Caldy Island.[10] These leaders of cultural engagement found their lives unsustainable without seasons of retreat and solitude.

But what is most unique about Patrick's mission was its successful transformation of Irish culture. How did he foster such effective engagement? In

---

[7]James Carmichael Watson and Angus Matheson, *Carmina Gadelica: Hymns and Incantations with Illustrative Notes on Words, Rites, and Customs, Dying and Obsolete* (Edinburgh: T. and A. Constable, 1900), 233.

[8]Bradley, *Colonies of Heaven*, 17.

[9]Ibid., 20.

[10]Ibid., 18.

short, he did it by faithful action at a *local level.* He was absolutely committed to the conversion of the entirety of Ireland, but his strategy was always expressed by working in very localized communities. Patrick returned to Ireland at age forty-eight, which was about the normal life expectancy at that time. He had no idea how long his ministry would last, but from the first moment he returned to Irish soil he was building a work that would continue long after he was gone. He arrived with twelve companions and a simple plan. He would approach a tribal chieftain to seek his conversion, or at least permission to form a community of faith adjacent to the tribal settlement. The team would then become involved in the life of the community, engaging them in conversation and acts of service such as mediating disputes and tending the sick. Those who were responsive would join the apostolic band and worship with them. If God blessed the efforts, they would build a church. When the group moved on, Patrick would leave a protégé behind to serve the fledgling church while taking one or two young people to join in planting a new church near another tribal settlement.[11]

This simple plan was repeated again and again until an Irish civilization arose, like a phoenix, from the ashes of war, slavery, and human sacrifice.

LESSONS FROM PATRICK

Arrows and spears. Some Christians worry that cultural engagement will deflect the church from its primary mission of proclaiming the gospel. In other words, Christians are called not to engage culture but rather to convert sinners, and we do this by proclaiming the gospel and calling our hearers to repent. This sort of thinking involves two mistakes, and Patrick offers a helpful corrective to both.

The first mistake is reducing the gospel to a command to convert. The teachings of the gospel certainly begin with conversion to Christ, but they are not completed until Christ is honored as king in every aspect of creation and every sphere of human endeavor. His proper claim is to preeminence over all creation. Therefore, we cannot neglect the stewardship of creation, activities of human governments, the physical suffering of the poor and disabled, the stultifying and oppressive nature of slave labor, and a host of

---

[11]Hunter, *Celtic Way of Evangelism*, 21-22.

other reminders that human life on earth is radically disordered and often in direct rebellion against the lordship of Christ. Our mission as his disciples is as comprehensive as his lordship. There is not a single square inch of planet earth that is not our concern. Patrick's mission among the Irish is a wonderful example of this sort of holistic gospel vision.

The second mistake is to assume that verbal preaching and cultural engagement are mutually incompatible. This is surely not the case. Our good works among people are a central focus of New Testament teaching, and they are often associated directly with our witness before others. Good works are good in their own right, but they are also good for establishing the credibility of both individuals and the church as a witness to the works and person of Christ. Doubtless there are times when Christians have abandoned their verbal witness for the sake of social activism. Many consider the social gospel movement of the early twentieth century to be such a time. However, there are many times and places in church history when these two concerns have gone hand in hand, and Patrick's mission to the Irish is certainly one of the foremost among them.

The importance of having faithful verbal witness and faithful social action operating together is illustrated by one of the earliest lessons humanity learned about making effective weapons. Arrows and spears are two of the most ancient and universal of human weapons. They rely on a similar construction that attaches a sharpened head to a long stick or pole. Both of these elements are necessary to make the weapon effective. Detached from its shaft, the spear tip or arrowhead is no more than a pointed rock that will tumble through the air and bounce off its target. On the other hand, throwing a shaft without a hard, sharp object at the head is equally ineffective. Effective arrows and spears must have both operating together. In similar fashion, the gospel preached is the arrowhead, and the gospel lived is the shaft. Though the contemporary church often does both, and at times does both very well, it seems rare that it does both well together. Bifurcating cultural practice from gospel preaching is as futile as having one warrior throw an arrowhead while another throws a stick. The power of Patrick's model is that he did both together.

Opposition is opportunity. The harsher the oppression, the deeper the wounds and the more desperate the need for the gospel. Patrick landed in an Ireland awash with blood. A peace-filled monastic community was a colony of heaven in a continent of hell. Creating enclaves of human flourishing and divine peace and reconciliation made the most compelling of arguments in favor of the gospel he preached.

What similar opportunities confront contemporary American Christians? Though slavery is no longer permitted and our wars are in distant lands, we still have our share of oppression and suffering. In particular, consider the destructive and disordered sexuality of contemporary America. Christians have seen this problem and responded in a prophetic key. We have expressed the outrage that God must feel at the sexual devastation wrought by our culture. The result, however, has largely been resentment and ever greater expressions of sexual excess by our culture. Perhaps it is time to learn a lesson from Patrick and focus more on building communities that play by the rules of the kingdom of heaven rather than dismantling communities that violate those rules. This does not mean refusing to speak against sexual sin, but it might mean adopting more of a pastoral than a prophetic tone.

A good example of this appears in the words of a Christian counselor who found herself dealing regularly with adolescents:

> Counseling these young people, for whom the doors to sexuality have been swung wide open since puberty, is like being an emergency-room physician with the survivors of a school-bus wreck. . . . At times it feels unspeakably sad. Those who ushered in the 1960s flung open the door of sexual restraint, but those who followed walked through it more blindly—and with devastating consequences. In just one generation, we have lost so much of our moorings . . . something beautiful [has been] lost between the sexes, something that surely God must grieve.[12]

This counselor adopts tones of empathy and grief rather than anger and condemnation, and she prompts us to consider the largely unfulfilled opportunity the Christian community has to speak into this unspeakable sadness. What if we built communities in which teenage sexuality did not look like a school-bus wreck? What if, inspired by Patrick's example, we built communities whose sexual practices were both wholesome and winsome,

---

[12]Paula Rinehart, "Losing Our Promiscuity," *Christianity Today* 44, no. 8 (July 10, 2000): 35.

and then invited others to join our communities? What a welcome sanctuary we could offer those who stagger with the wounds of empty and disordered sexuality! Rather than focusing our rhetoric on the sins of secular society, we could offer communities that protect sexuality from exploitation and violence; give and receive sexuality as a gift, not a commodity bought and sold on the open market; provide guidance, boundaries, and traditions for the young, including rites of passage and public celebrations that might help children develop a healthy sexual identity; value both marriage and singleness as viable paths of human life; and nurture the young and care for the elderly as expressions of abiding love, not as part of a service industry. The church is a large, transgenerational community that is in it for the long haul. It is perfectly placed to draw a boundary line and live as a colony of heaven embodying God's vision and values for human sexuality.

Love the beautiful wherever it may be found. One of the observations commonly made by Patrick's biographers is the depth of love he felt for the Irish people and their culture. For all of Irish culture's appalling problems, Patrick was keenly aware of its beauty. He found himself in the midst of loyal, courageous, and generous people—qualities that he could not help but extol when he described the Irish to others. He found people who were deeply in awe of the beauty of nature, and whose posture toward creation served as a ready foundation for Christian worship. Having been a slave himself, he deeply empathized with the plight of the slaves who surrounded him—all too many of which were Irishmen enslaved by their brethren. In short, Patrick could admire and praise the image of God in all he encountered, no matter how badly it was tarnished. We could all learn from Patrick's ability to appreciate goodness even when surrounded by people, times, and places that seem to shout of badness.

3

COUNTERPUBLICS IN
THE ARGUMENT CULTURE

"I WISH I CAN TAKE THEM BACK!"

Perhaps the most controversial words uttered by conservative shock jock Glenn Beck came during his acceptance speech for an award for defending the First Amendment. Beck surprised many by accepting responsibility for how his on-air tirades put Americans at "each other's necks" and contributed to a deeply fractured nation. "For any role that I have played in dividing, I wish I can take them back."[1]

Beck is not alone in noticing how uncivil we've become. A nationwide study found that each generation in America believes we are becoming increasingly uncivil. "More than nine in 10 of each adult generation—Millennials, Gen Xers, Boomers and the Silent Generation—believe that civility is a problem. . . . The generations are also in agreement that incivility has reached crisis proportions in America."[2] Sadly, incivility is becoming the new normal as we discuss differences. Within this vitriolic communication climate, counterpublics must learn to address those with whom we disagree. To counteract this negative climate, we must understand the characteristics of the argument culture, how it influences us, and how as Christian communicators we can offer an alternative.

---

[1]"Glenn Beck Says He Regrets Dividing People," Associated Press, June 6, 2013, www.cbsnews.com/news/glenn-beck-says-he-regrets-dividing-people.

[2]*Civility in America 2014*, Weber Shandwick, Powell Tate, and KRC Research, 3; www.webershandwick.com/uploads/news/files/civility-in-america-2014.pdf.

COMMUNICATION SCRIPTS AND
THE ARGUMENT CULTURE

Scripts govern our lives. Scripts are memorized routines related to particular people and situations. They are our personal understanding of how certain situations are *supposed* to proceed—what should happen first, second, and so on. We have scripts for almost all of our daily interactions. When we step into a crowded elevator, we know that we are supposed to face forward and watch the numbers. When a salesperson asks if she can be of assistance, we know that we are supposed to respond, "Just looking, thank you." We know how much we are to share with a new acquaintance, and to not discuss politics, religion, or finances with family members. Children learn specific scripts that walk them through anticipated interactions step by step. We have a "stranger at the door" script, a "phone rings when Mommy is in the shower" script, and a "stranger who asks if you want a ride" script. Scripts are good and helpful in many situations. They help us deal with the complexity of the world around us. No one approached by a salesperson wants to stop and ask himself, *Now, what would be the most appropriate response to this individual in this setting?* The script tells us quickly how to respond, and we move on.

These scripts are not created in isolation, but rather are deeply influenced by our cultural surroundings. In addition to a salesperson or child-stranger script, we are seeing evidence of a cultural script that dictates how we approach and discuss differences. Georgetown linguist Deborah Tannen labels this script the *argument culture*, and claims it "urges us to approach the world—and the people in it—in an adversarial frame of mind."[3] Tannen notes that the argument script is learned early on. The Western tradition of education is modeled after that of the ancient Greeks, who, in all-male schools, taught students to stake out a position and defend it at all cost. The result was intense rhetorical battles with clear victors and losers. In fact, the "Latin term for school, *ludus*, also referred to play or games, but it derived from the military sense of the word—training exercises for war."[4]

The argument script can be broken down into key elements that guide our communication when we encounter those with whom we disagree.

---

[3]Deborah Tannen, *The Argument Culture: Moving from Debate to Dialogue* (New York: Random House, 1998), 3.
[4]Ibid., 258.

Consideration equals condoning. When communities are entrenched in ideological positions, any serious consideration of an alternative perspective is seen as compromise. To suspend judgment long enough to understand a person's point of view from an opposite, and often demonized, position is seen as being traitorous to your community's convictions. Alarmingly, this view is often strongly held by persons of faith—including my students. In my introduction to communication theory course, students are surprised to see a particular book on the syllabus: the Qur'an. If students are surprised, parents are shocked, and some angered. "I didn't send my daughter to Biola—Bible Institute of Los Angeles—to read the Qur'an!" stated a concerned mother over the phone. As the semester goes on, those in my class report odd reactions from fellow students who see them walking around campus with a Qur'an: "Why are you reading that?!" "Thinking of switching religions?" "Should I be concerned?" "Your time would be better spent reading the Bible."

It seems that students and parents are fine with considering an opposing view so long as the purpose is to attack it. While my students do eventually critique the Qur'an from a Christian perspective, they don't start there. Rather, the first step is to understand the text. However, for those immersed in the argument culture, to suspend judgment long enough to understand a view is seen as an unnecessary risk. "Asking your students to read the Qur'an is dangerous," stated one parent in an email. Many of the negative reactions to my assignment seem to be fear based. If I consider other's perspectives, where could it lead?

Valuing monologue over dialogue. The argument script eschews authentic dialogue in favor of assertive monologue. For many, dialogue with the opposition is a dangerous proposition that may lead to a questioning of long-held values and ideological commitments. The danger of learning something new is avoided by adopting what Reuel Howe identifies as "calculated monologue," in which a person draws conclusions in advance of the actual conversation.[5] The goal is not to have a give-and-take exchange of ideas but to dismantle ideas ascribed to the other prior to the discussion. In fact, monologue communicators often develop a form of "agenda anxiety"

---

[5]Reuel Howe, *The Miracle of Dialogue* (New York: Seabury Press, 1963), 81.

as the conversation progresses, growing increasingly fearful that they'll not have time to cover all the points of attack developed prior to the meeting.[6]

Not merely disagreeing, but demonizing. Tannen asserts that the argument culture "encourages those on one side to demonize those who take the other view, which leads in turn to misrepresenting the work of those who are assigned to the other camp."[7] Demonization begins when one group identifies the beliefs and convictions it holds sacred. Then that group uses inflammatory language to describe how the other group maligns these core beliefs. They further stir up emotions by presenting the views of the other so simplistically as to foster disbelief and ridicule.

For example, in their book conservative writers Suzanne Venker and Phyllis Schlafly first identify key values of conservative women, such as marital fidelity, welcoming and valuing children, supporting husbands, helping men lead, and prioritizing family over careers by esteeming women as homemakers. They veer into demonization when they imaginatively construct "The Ten Feminist Commandments" that directly counter conservative values:

- Thou shalt pursue demanding careers and pay other women to raise thy children [prioritizing family].
- Thou shalt be allowed to have an abortion at any time for any reason [valuing children].
- Thou shalt be allowed to divorce at any time and keep custody of the children [fidelity in marriage].
- Thou shalt belittle men until their manhood is gone [male leadership].
- Thou shalt not take thine husband's name [supporting husbands].
- Thou shalt demean all full-time homemakers and conservative women [women as homemakers].[8]

Venker and Schlafly inflame passions when they portray their stated core beliefs as targets, using overly simplistic descriptions of complex values held

---

[6]Ibid., 75.

[7]Tannen, *Argument Culture*, 30.

[8]Suzanne Venker and Phyllis Schlafly, *The Flipside of Feminism: What Conservative Women Know— and Men Can't Say* (Washington, DC: WND Books, 2011), 185.

by an opposing community. But how would feminists respond to these commandments meant to represent them?

Communication and gender scholar Julia Wood argues that in its broadest sense feminism is an opposition to oppression in any form. Thus, if the struggle of feminism were realized, then women would have the freedom to *either* choose a career or assume the role of a traditional stay-home parent, depending on different seasons of life. Conversely, a feminist agenda would afford these same options to men.[9] Feminists are demonized when none of the nuances described by Wood are acknowledged or explored but are merely caricatured.

Online disinhibition. If you've spent any time traversing social media, you know that humility and civility are rare, while demonization of others is prevalent. Why? Mass communication scholars have identified a trait they label "online disinhibition," where individuals feel unrestrained by normal social conventions, resulting in unfiltered communication. One key trait of disinhibition is the feeling that we are invisible as we communicate. Thus, I can express exactly what I think of your post, tweet, or blog without fear of repercussion. This feeling of invisibility has several dramatic effects on my communication.

Shielded from the impact of communication. When speaking face-to-face, I immediately experience the result of my choice of words or tone. If I call you a name, belittle your perspective, or shout, I face the impact of my communication choices. If I'm in a restaurant and yell, people will turn to look, or I can see the hurt on your face and will adjust my tone. However, if I'm online, I can take off the rhetorical gloves and not experience the immediate results. In fact, when online I often have no idea how my communication is affecting others.

Real-time responses. I read an uncivil post or blog about a topic I care about and decide to respond. With powerful emotions surfacing, I wing it as I craft a rebuttal. The more I write the angrier I get. *Flaming* is a term used to describe emails or text messages sent while in a rage. Flaming often includes profanity, all capital letters, and excessive exclamation points or question marks: "Do YOU know what I'm TALKING ABOUT?!?!" Long before the rise of online disinhibition, Jewish wisdom writers observed that "like a city whose walls are broken through is a person who lacks self-control" (Prov 25:28).

---

[9]Julia T. Wood, personal correspondence, June 10, 2014.

IMPACT OF THE ARGUMENT SCRIPT

What are the cumulative results of the argument culture and its communication script? First, we are—consciously and subconsciously—tempted to mimic the incivility we see regularly occurring in social media and from spokespeople like Glenn Beck and his self-professed diatribes. Neuroscientists have identified and labeled certain neurons as "monkey see, monkey do" or mirror neurons, which contribute to the way we learn by observing others. "Whenever we see a behavior, there is a silent echo; a neurological mirror of ourselves doing that behavior resides in the brain. This is a wonderful thing as we can learn by watching others, but it can also have negative effects."[10] As we consume media through a plethora of devices, what do we learn by watching? Sixty percent of Americans say that they regularly witness incivility in government, pop culture, media, schools, and professional sports. Such statistics led researcher Jack Leslie to conclude that civility continues to erode on a national level.[11] As we watch crisis proportions of incivility, how often does a silent echo in our brain occur, prompting us to mirror what we see?

Second, the argument script invariably leads to gridlock. Before defining dialogic gridlock, communication scholars William Wilmot and Joyce Hocker ask readers to envision themselves gridlocked in traffic. "You may feel full of road rage, derisive of the stupid other drivers, furious at the system, defeated and hopeless, or numb and tuned out."[12] What makes this type of gridlock so frustrating is that you have to share the road with others; opting out of sharing the road is unfeasible. The same frustration occurs for counterpublics who share a community with other counterpublics and members of the dominant culture. Thus Wilmot and Hocker define relational gridlock as "unproductive interdependence."[13] Those caught in gridlock exhibit the following:

- Communication is happening, but leads nowhere.

- You gradually become more entrenched and unwilling to compromise.

---

[10]William Struthers, "The Effects of Porn on the Male Brain," *Christian Research Journal* 34, no. 5 (2011): 17.

[11]*Civility in America 2014*, 2.

[12]William Wilmot and Joyce Hocker, *Interpersonal Conflict*, 8th ed. (New York: McGraw-Hill, 2011), 15.

[13]Ibid.

- Communication is void of humor or affection.

- Vilifying each other leads to more extreme and polarizing views.

- Ultimately, you simply disengage.[14]

Mark Osler, professor of law at the University of St. Thomas in Minneapolis, argues that gridlock—particularly in the political arena—is rooted in religious beliefs. Osler states that for many religious conservatives "the root of knowledge is a bedrock certainty of a literal reading of the Bible" that encourages people of faith to view our world as being locked "in a battle between good and evil." Within such a perspective, "bending to the other side becomes unthinkable. A loss or even a compromise is something terrible—it is a victory for evil."[15] The result is gridlock fueled by religious zeal.

Finally, the gridlock and animosity generated by the argument script have created an unexpected opportunity. "Has the nation's harsh political rhetoric become more than just talk—to the point of being dangerous?" asked the editors of *USA Today*.[16] "Guns. Speech. Madness. Where we go from Arizona" reads the cover of *Time* magazine.[17] Each was responding to the tragic shooting of US Representative Gabrielle Giffords and eighteen others during a public meeting in Casas Adobes, Arizona, on January 8, 2011. Court records revealed that the shooter, Jared Loughner, had shown a deteriorating mental state months before his attack, evidenced by Internet rants about government. How much did his exposure to the rants of social media and news outlets add to his deterioration?

While impossible to answer, the question was unsettling enough that individuals from the Right and Left responded. Liberal-minded talk show host Keith Olbermann suspended his "Worst Person in the World" segment—where nominees were almost exclusively taken from voices on the Right—and conservative Sarah Palin removed from her website a map with crosshairs on twenty Democratic-held congressional districts—including

---

[14]Ibid.

[15]Mark Osler, "My Take: The Religious Roots of Our Political Gridlock," *CNN Belief Blog*, December 5, 2012, http://religion.blogs.cnn.com/2012/12/05/my-take-the-religious-roots-of-our-political-gridlock/?hpt=hp_t1.

[16]Susan Page and Fredreka Schouten, "Gabrielle Giffords Shooting Fuels Debate over Rhetoric," *USA Today*, January 10, 2011, http://usatoday30.usatoday.com/news/washington/2011-01-09-ariz-shooting-political-rhetoric_N.htm.

[17]*Time*, January 24, 2011, cover.

Giffords's. President Obama's response to the shooting was to deliver an impassioned speech where he urged our nation to pause and "make sure that we are talking with each other in a way that heals, not a way that wounds."[18] Sadly, it seems his plea has gone unheeded.

After a sixteen-year run on *The Daily Show*, Jon Stewart announced he was stepping down because he found covering politicians had become "increasingly depressing."[19] Stewart isn't the only person to find the incivility of our political process depressing. The negative effects of the argument culture as evidenced by vitriolic politicians is deeply influencing how young people view public service. During the 2012 presidential election the *Washington Post* conducted an interview of high school and college students asking them to rank potential career options. If each job paid equally, would the respondent rather be a business owner, teacher, salesperson, or mayor of a city? Nine out of ten selected something other than mayor as their first choice, while 40 percent put mayor as their least-desired option.[20]

What contributed to Glenn Beck's apology and Jon Stewart's disgust with our political discourse is an argument script in which we don't merely disagree with each other but despise and wish harm toward others. During the early years of Barack Obama's presidency, a campaign appeared consisting of bumper stickers and T-shirts that read "Pray for Obama: Psalm 109:8." Religion professor Elizabeth McAlister points out that many observers would miss the ironic message, as Psalm 109:8 reads, "May his days be few; may another take his office." The next verse in context, McAlister states, is chilling: "May his children be fatherless and his wife a widow" (Ps 109:9 ESV). Kansas House Speaker Mike O'Neal, learning of the bumper sticker campaign, wryly commented that he could finally offer "a Biblical prayer for our president!"[21]

---

[18]Helene Cooper and Jeff Zeleny, "Obama Calls for a New Era of Civility in U.S. Politics," *New York Times*, January 12, 2011, www.nytimes.com/2011/01/13/us/13obama.html?_r=0.

[19]Anita Bennett, "Jon Stewart Says 'Dissatisfaction,' Presidential Politics Caused Him to Quit 'Daily Show,'" *The Wrap*, April 19, 2015, https://celebrity.yahoo.com/news/jon-stewart-says-dissatisfaction-presidential-politics-caused-him-155834611.html.

[20]Richard Fox and Jennifer Lawless, "Turned Off by Politics," *Washington Post*, November 24, 2013, A23.

[21]Elizabeth McAlister, "They're Praying for the Worst. Is That Wrong?," *Los Angeles Times*, June 25, 2014, www.latimes.com/opinion/op-ed/la-oe-mcalister-negative-prayer-20140625-story.html.

Can Christian counterpublics take advantage of our nation's tiredness of gridlock and the dangerous implications of the argument script? If so, what can we do differently?

A CHRISTIAN RESPONSE TO THE ARGUMENT SCRIPT

If Christian counterpublics want to enter into today's argument culture, what will it take to deviate from the argument script with those outside the Christian community? While later chapters will address how to develop ethos, craft sound arguments, and present them in a civil way, we assert that the starting place for a Christian counterpublic entering the argument culture is compassion.

Compassion should be a central trait of Christian counterpublics due to God's compassionate relationship with us. The psalmist states that God not only crowns us with compassion (Ps 103:4) but also, like an earthly father, is relationally compassionate toward us (Ps 103:13). Old Testament scholar John Goldingay argues that God's compassion toward an oft-rebellious Israel entailed much patience. "Even when confronted by his children's rebellions, a father shows compassion. Indeed, it is their rebellions that test the reality of his compassion."[22] Our job as counterpublics will often entail bestowing compassion—like our heavenly Father's—toward the very people who rebel against God's plan for the world—shalom. Our compassion will consist, in part, in the following principles.

Compassion is rooted in caring for others. As already noted, a central part of gridlock is the absence of affection. Regardless of our disagreements with others, affection should be present in all our exchanges. As Christian communicators we are called not to merely tolerate others, but to love them. In turn, our love fuels compassion, resulting in a deep concern for the other. Through his many encounters with Jewish leaders, Paul developed a reputation as a troublemaker (Acts 24:5) opposed to their laws and the authority of the temple (Acts 21:28). These leaders could easily have concluded that Paul was motivated by an agenda spurred on by hatred toward fellow Jews. In a stirring passage, Paul feels compelled to communicate his deep care for his opposition. "I have great sorrow and unceasing anguish in my heart," he

---

[22]John Goldingay, *Psalms*, vol. 3, *Psalms 90–150*, Baker Commentary on the Old Testament Wisdom and Psalms, ed. Tremper Longman III (Grand Rapids: Baker Academic, 2008), 172.

writes concerning the Jewish people (Rom 9:2). The word *sorrow* can be translated as pain, torment, or grief and is often used of persons in mourning.[23] Paul is deeply concerned for the eternal destiny of "my people, those of my own race" (Rom 9:3). Shockingly, he is even willing to become "cursed" and subsequently "cut off from Christ" for their sake (Rom 9:3).

As counterpublics, do we show the same concern for those we wish to persuade? Do we, like Paul, feel tormented by the plight of those outside the Christian community? Do we love those who oppose us? Christian author Daniel Taylor suggests we often fall short. "If you are loved, you generally know it. And you know it in great part by how someone acts toward you. The simple fact is that the people whose behavior we believe is sinful do not report that they feel loved—or anything close to it."[24] Our concern for others cannot merely be a tactic to improve our rhetoric, but must be heartfelt.

Compassion is not limited to sympathy, but includes empathy. The word *empathy* is derived from two Greek words meaning "feeling inside." Thus, empathy means attempting to experience a person's perception—and accompanying emotions—by temporarily taking on that person's point of view as if your own. In contrast, *sympathy* comes from the Greek for "feeling with." Sympathy entails coming alongside a person and acknowledging his or her emotions. "When you sympathize, the confusion, joy or pain belongs to another. When you empathize, the experience becomes your own, at least for the moment."[25] The call to empathy is seen in the writer of Hebrew's admonishment not only to remember and acknowledge the sufferings of believers who are being mistreated in prison (sympathy), but to do so "as if *you yourselves* were suffering" (empathy) (Heb 13:3).

Unfortunately, those representing the Christian perspective often fail to be sympathetic or empathetic. Whatever one thinks about Bruce Jenner's decision to go public as Caitlyn Jenner by gracing the cover of *Vanity Fair* magazine, Jenner has garnered the admiration of millions, even receiving ESPN's 2015 Arthur Ashe Courage Award. Her decision to no longer remain silent about a lifelong struggle—encompassing Jenner's record-setting

---

[23]Kenneth S. Wuest, *Wuest's Word Studies from the Greek New Testament* (Grand Rapids: Eerdmans, 1984), 1:152.

[24]Daniel Taylor, "Deconstructing the Gospel of Tolerance," *Christianity Today*, January 11, 1999, 50.

[25]Ronald Adler, Lawrence Rosenfeld, and Russell Proctor II, *Interplay: The Process of Interpersonal Communication*, 11th ed. (New York: Oxford University Press, 2007), 106.

decathlon gold medal performance in the 1976 Olympics—gives voice to a transgender community composed of people who identify with a gender that torturously doesn't fit their sex. Our response to Jenner—and the thousands she represents—must be both biblical and compassionate. Many struggle to find the balance.

Months before Jenner appeared in *Vanity Fair*, former Baptist pastor and Republican presidential candidate Mike Huckabee addressed the plight of the transgender community while speaking at the 2015 National Religious Broadcaster's Convention in Nashville, Tennessee. "Now I wish that someone told me that when I was in high school that I could have felt like a woman when it came time to take showers in PE," said Huckabee, garnering laughs from the audience. "I'm pretty sure that I would have found my feminine side and said, 'Coach, I think I'd rather shower with the girls today.'" As laughter continued to grow, he concluded, "You're laughing because it sounds so ridiculous doesn't it?"[26] Comparing the lifelong struggles of transgender people like Jenner to a high school boy feigning femininity to get a free peep show lacks both sympathy (acknowledging the pain of self-identified transgender people) and empathy (imagining what their struggle would feel like), resulting in a response void of compassion.

I recently shared the thoughts you've just read during a radio interview. The producer informed me that the station received a fair amount of negative responses. "We must have a biblical stance on this issue! God made us either male or female, we do not have the right to surgically alter his work!" emailed an angry listener. Their protests seem to be rooted in confusion between the content and relational aspects of communication. The content level is the literal meanings of the words we are using that convey our message. The relational level expresses the amount of affection, respect, and compassion between people. Both levels can be seen in Paul's command to speak "the truth [content level] in love [relational level]" (Eph 4:15). Our critique of spokespeople like Huckabee is not against his content or biblical convictions, but how he addressed transgender people on the relational level (mocking instead of compassionate). Bruce Jenner's former pastor, Josh Cobia, made a disheartening observation after Jenner came out in

---

[26]Eric Bradner, "Huckabee: I Wish I Could've Identified as Female in High School Gym," *CNN Politics*, June 3, 2015, www.cnn.com/2015/06/02/politics/mike-huckabee-transgender-caitlyn-jenner.

Vanity Fair. The only compassion Caitlyn seemed to receive was from non-believers, noted Cobia, with Christians either remaining silent or being negative.[27] Could our silence or mocking comments be indicative of our lack of compassion? "For the mouth speaks," asserts Jesus, "what the heart is full of" (Lk 6:45).

Compassion entails confronting the uncompassionate. The biblical call to compassion is often abandoned when debate with those outside the Christian community becomes heated and passions run high. How can we remain compassionate during such exchanges? In short, we practice with each other. To Christians scattered throughout the culture, Peter writes, "Finally, all of you, be like-minded, be sympathetic, love one another, be compassionate and humble" (1 Pet 3:8). By practicing sympathy and compassion with each other, we prepare to be compassionate to outsiders. Yet how should we react when fellow Christians adopt the argument script and fail to be sympathetic or compassionate—not only to each other, but to those outside our community? What should you do when a fellow believer speaks harshly or derogatively toward the very people we are called to care for? We suggest that, at that moment, we assume a *traitorous identity*.

A traitorous identity is assumed when a "group member criticizes attitudes or actions that are common and accepted among members of that group."[28] The concept, borrowed from gender theorists, could apply to a pro-feminism man who sits in a meeting where male friends are telling sexist jokes. Should he remain silent or speak out? If he confronts the others, will he been seen as a traitor to the group? "People who perform traitorous identity are not really 'traitors' to their group," notes Julia Wood. "Rather, by questioning certain behaviors, they are challenging the group to become better."[29]

Should we not do the same as Christian counterpublics? For example, John argues that if anyone claims to love God but hates another person, how can God's love be manifest in him (1 Jn 4:20)? How then should we respond if, behind closed doors, believers are saying hateful things about others? Do

---

[27]Billy Hallowell, "Pastor Reveals Details About Caitlyn Jenner's Reported Church Attendance," *TheBlaze*, June 5, 2015, www.theblaze.com/stories/2015/06/05/pastor-who-worked-at-church-attended-by-jenner-family-caitlyn-has-taught-me-more-about-jesus.

[28]Julia T. Wood, *Gendered Lives: Communication, Gender, and Culture*, 11th ed. (Stamford, CT: Cengage Learning, 2015), 83.

[29]Ibid.

we remain silent, or do we risk speaking up? If we do speak, are we going to come across as holier-than-thou or harsh toward fellow believers? Paul is instructive when he writes, "Do not let any unwholesome talk come out of your mouths" (Eph 4:29). In other words, our response to the uncompassionate cannot itself be harsh or uncompassionate. Rather, speak "only what is helpful for building others up according to their needs" (Eph 4:29). Our goal in addressing uncompassionate statements by fellow believers is to help us as a community attain biblical standards that reflect God's heart.

Compassion is unconditional. The argument script dictates that we should respond compassionately only to those who are compassionate to us. Daniel Taylor observes that many followers of Christ seem to have bought into this relational principle. "The sad truth is that, in our battle with a hostile culture, we have adopted the culture's tactics. We fight ugliness with ugliness, distortion with distortion, sarcasm with sarcasm."[30] In stark contrast, Paul tells us that our compassion must extend to all—including our enemies. Before Paul tells us to feed and give drink to the very people that would cause us harm, he writes, "On the contrary" (Rom 12:20). What is Paul's command contrary to? In part, an argument script that repays evil with evil (Rom 12:17).

CONCLUSION

The argument script—full of ill will and potential harm—will only be countered by offering prayers for those we oppose and adopting a new communication script filled with love, truth, and compassion. Christian love and compassion were on vivid display after the worst mass shooting in US history, on June 12, 2016. Early Sunday morning, forty-nine people were murdered at an Orlando gay nightclub called Pulse. The shooter, Omar Mateen, had pledged allegiance to ISIS and voiced disgust toward homosexual people. Breaking a long-held policy of not opening on Sundays, Chick-fil-A opened Orlando branches to serve the more than six hundred law enforcement officers and people waiting in line to donate blood. Chick-fil-A had faced criticism and boycotts from the LGBTQ community because of comments made by the company's CEO supporting

---

[30]Taylor, "Deconstructing the Gospel of Tolerance," 50.

traditional marriage based on the Bible. Acts of compassion and kindness can powerfully propel people past the argument culture toward unity. "Following a crisis like the one in Florida," notes psychologist Art Markman, "people across the country were thinking of themselves as Americans—a group that is inclusive—rather than maintaining this social distance."[31]

---

[31]Jenna Birch, "Acts of Kindness Emerge from Orlando Nightclub Tragedy," Yahoo, June 13, 2016, www.yahoo.com/beauty/acts-of-kindness-emerge-from-orlando-nightclub-194633459.html.

4

CREDIBILITY OF A COUNTERPUBLIC

AS A THIRTY-YEAR VETERAN OF REPORTING, Brian Williams had seen it all. While he was covering the Iraq war in 2003, his helicopter came under fire from a rocket-propelled grenade launcher. As the flood waters of Hurricane Katrina submerged New Orleans in 2005, Williams faithfully reported from the French Quarter in a hotel overrun with gangs. Watching a dead body float by his window unnerved him, yet despite being emotionally frayed and sick from dysentery, he stayed at his post. Such reporting earned the trust of the American public; in 2015 Williams was ranked as the twenty-third most trusted person in the country, on par with actor Denzel Washington and economist Warren Buffett. Fast forward four months, and Williams's ranking had fallen to 3,352, putting him in the company of rapper Eminem and *Playboy* founder Hugh Hefner. What happened?

Reports surfaced that Williams had exaggerated or lied about his stories. While some helicopters had come under enemy fire, Williams was in a separate helicopter that arrived an hour after the attack. Hotel mangers and rescue workers countered that the French Quarter where Williams reported remained mostly dry, making the claim of a floating body highly unlikely. Executives at NBC suspended Williams for six months, resulting in his apologizing for embellishing stories and being demoted to a struggling cable news outlet.[1]

Communication comes to us "embodied," notes rhetorical scholar Roderick Hart. "Most people cannot separate the substance of a message from

---

[1] "Williams Delivers Apology but Stops Short of Admitting He Lied," *Orange County Register*, June 20, 2015, News 6.

its author."[2] As counterpublics, our message does not exist independently from *who* we are. From Aristotle to modern philosophers studying intellectual virtues, the credibility of a person is foundational to effective communication. What constitutes credibility and how it can be cultivated are key questions for us as we serve as counterpublics.

CREDIBILITY

The word *credibility* comes from the Latin for "to believe." The goal of a counterpublic is to create messages that make it easy for others to believe. In his classic *On Rhetoric*, Aristotle suggests that a message's power to persuade is rooted in three factors: the logic of the argument (*logos*), the speaker's ability to project a trustworthy persona (*ethos*), and the speaker's ability to awaken the emotions of the audience (*pathos*). Aristotle is clear that an argument can be compromised by the speaker's lack of character. In fact, he argues that character (*ethos*) is the controlling factor in persuasion.[3] Brian Williams, after doubts about the truthfulness of his reporting surfaced, did not become less intelligent or passionate; his lack of character in how he described events canceled out his audience's ability to believe him. Aristotle is particularly helpful in that he breaks *ethos* down into three aspects: wisdom (*phronēsis*), virtue (*arēte*), and good will (*eunoia*). Using these three categories as a launching point, we explore the need for each.

Wisdom. Effective communicators know the facts of their arguments and are able to present them in a persuasive manner free of contradiction. While later chapters will explore how to arrange and present facts, our focus here is on the need to know *all* the facts not just those pertaining to our particular perspective. For Aristotle, one of the most useful aspects of rhetoric is that it teaches us to understand the pros and cons of any issue. Understanding both sides of an issue is especially important when the issue is complex and people are sharply divided. If individuals feel overwhelmed with the amount of information or diverse opinions surrounding an issue, they rely on those who profess expertise. For example, your friend tells you that she wants to buy a new smart phone but doesn't have time to check out all the myriad of options. If you position yourself as someone who has done extensive

[2] Roderick Hart, *Modern Rhetorical Criticism*, 2nd ed. (Boston: Allyn & Bacon, 1997), 84.
[3] Aristotle, *On Rhetoric*, trans. George A. Kennedy (New York: Oxford University Press, 1991), 39.

research before purchasing a phone, your credibility will undoubtedly increase. However, if during the conversation it becomes obvious that you have only researched and settled on a Samsung—neglecting other options such as iPhones—your credibility will be compromised.

As Christian counterpublics our tendency is to limit our inquiry to merely knowing our side of an issue. Syracuse University professor Rosaria Champagne Butterfield, before her conversion to Christianity, observed that Christian students she encountered often "refused to read material in university classrooms on the grounds that 'knowing Jesus' meant never needing to know anything else."[4] In short, many Christians are well educated, but not well rounded. This tendency toward intellectual isolation is especially true when we feel attacked and emotions run high.

"Professor Makes Students 'Stomp on Jesus,'" screamed the headline of an article describing an in-class assignment that seemed to target Christians. Under the direction of Florida Atlantic University professor Deandre Poole, students were instructed to stomp on a piece of paper with the word *Jesus* written on it. One student protested. "I'm not going to be sitting in a class having my religious rights desecrated," he told a television reporter.[5] What followed were national protests from religious groups, objections from the governor of Florida, a lawsuit aimed at the university, and death threats toward the professor, resulting in his being put on leave for his own protection. In such volatile situations, is it even necessary to argue both sides of an issue? What possible explanation could be offered? Echoing Aristotle, the university administration responded: "We find it outrageous that critics of Dr. Poole immediately condemn his exercise without fully knowing the facts."[6]

Poole, a self-professed Christian who has taught Sunday school at his local church for twenty years, explains that the exercise isn't original to him but is taken from the instructor's guide to a leading textbook, *Intercultural Communication: A Contextual Approach*, which has been used nationwide for thirty years. The point of the exercise isn't that students will actually step

[4]Rosaria Champagne Butterfield, *The Secret Thoughts of an Unlikely Convert: An English Professor's Journey into Christian Faith* (Pittsburgh, PA: Crown & Covenant, 2012), 4.

[5]Todd Starnes, "Professor Makes Students 'Stomp on Jesus,'" Todd Starnes on Radio, 2013, http://radio.foxnews.com/toddstarnes/top-stories/professor-makes-students-stomp-on-jesus.html.

[6]Scott Jaschik, "'I Was Doing My Job,'" *Inside Higher Ed*, April 1, 2013, www.insidehighered.com/news/2013/04/01/interview-professor-center-jesus-debate-florida-atlantic.

(not stomp) on Jesus when they're asked to, but that most will refuse because of the importance of symbols. "When students hesitate to step on the word 'Jesus,'" explains the author of the textbook and originator of the exercise, Jim Neuliep, "they understand that a piece of paper has meaning to them because of the word, which helps them understand the force of symbols."[7] Many critics have asked, why aren't students required to write *Muhammad* on a piece of paper? Neuliep concedes that if he were teaching in a different country, he might make the point with a different name. For the exercise to work, the word needs to have significant meaning for students. "If I asked them to write my name on the paper, they would step on it," states Neuliep.[8] Is an exercise designed to show the power of symbols worth the potential for offending religious students? Regardless of our answer, our perspective will take on credibility only if we understand the complex arguments—pro and con—surrounding an issue.

While some may grant the importance of understanding the perspective behind a professor's provocative classroom activity, isn't it too risky to ask Christians to be able to argue both sides of issues such as same-sex marriage, gender, evolution, abortion, or atheistic challenges to faith? Researcher David Kinnaman, in exploring why young Christians are leaving faith communities, argues that our sheltering of young minds from the perspectives of others is ultimately detrimental. "In short, many young Christians feel overprotected. Millions of young believers perceive that the church has kept them fearful of and detached from the world—a world, mind you, that they are called by their faith in Christ to redeem."[9] Such overprotection leads to self-doubt: if you feel the need to shelter me from arguments, they must be persuasive and potentially dangerous to my faith.

Kinnaman's concern finds support with those who hold to inoculation theory. According to this theory, individuals gradually exposed to counter-arguments are better prepared to respond to these arguments when actually challenged. Hearing counterarguments allows individuals the opportunity to process challenges and develop responses. Much like vaccination, when

---

[7]Scott Jaschik, "He Didn't Say 'Stomp on Jesus,'" *Inside Higher Ed*, March 28, 2013, www.inside highered.com/news/2013/03/28/professor-whose-exercise-caused-stomp-jesus-controversy.
[8]Ibid.
[9]David Kinnaman, *You Lost Me: Why Young Christians Are Leaving Church and Rethinking Faith* (Grand Rapids: Baker Books, 2011), 98.

an individual is exposed to mild versions of a differing perspective, he or she can develop levels of resistance. Furthermore, a person who has not been vaccinated may be more likely to be persuaded to change belief or to avoid the discussion at all costs, stopping all dialogue in the process.

In his classic study, William J. McGuire separated students into four groups and presented each with the wildly counterintuitive idea that brushing your teeth promotes tooth decay. The article they were to read included pseudoscientific statements such as "Brushing your teeth wipes away saliva, which is a natural deterrent to tooth decay." The first group received no preparation other than being told they were going to read an article promoting a particular idea. The second group merely received reinforcement of a prior belief (brushing your teeth is good) before reading the article. The third group received a warning that they were about to read something that would challenge prior beliefs. The fourth group, prior to reading the article, was provided with a mild version of the argument and given a refutation of it. McGuire was interested in which group would experience the most change. Predictably, the group with the *least* change was those who had received a preview of the argument and a refutation. What was surprising was which group experienced the *most* change: group two. Armed only with an affirmation of what they already believed, this group felt deceived when they encountered seemingly strong counterarguments. Not only was this group susceptible to the arguments, they also attached negative emotions to those who only provided an affirmation of prior beliefs.[10]

The outcome of this study has clear ramifications for Christian counterpublics. If we only arm individuals with affirmation that the biblical position is true without presenting them with clear counterarguments, we not only set them up for failure when they encounter articulate opposition, but we run the risk of losing their trust. "Were you not aware that there are powerful arguments against our position?" "If you knew these arguments existed, why didn't you tell us?" "What else are you shielding us from?"

In his letter, Jude warns us that sometimes the ungodly will purposely infiltrate our community to wreak havoc. One of the telltale signs that

---

[10]For more on inoculation theory, see John A. Bana and Stephen A. Rains, "A Meta-Analysis on Research on Inoculation Theory," *Communication Monographs* 77, no. 3 (2010): 281-311.

people are not true Christ followers is that they "slander whatever they do not understand" (Jude 10). To gain credibility and protect our youth from crippling self-doubt, we must understand not only facts associated with our perspective but facts used by others. The first responsibility of a counter-public is not to refute or slander a particular view but to understand it.

Virtue. For Aristotle, virtue is rooted in objective features of humanity. When he identified virtues, he understood himself to be identifying features of human nature, not merely cultural preferences. Though most communication theorists today view virtues as a social construct, they are still extremely important for effective communication. Rhetoricians Kinneavy and Warshauer explain that understanding what an audience deems virtuous is crucial since *ethos* is "exhibiting that quality of character that culture, and not the individual, defines as virtue."[11] In some cases speakers may feel a tension between the virtues of society and their own personal ethics. However, whether virtues are objective or a social construct, many of Aristotle's virtues are still broadly acknowledged today. Especially important for counterpublics are virtues such as justice, courage, self-control, magnanimity, gentleness, prudence, and wisdom. Such virtues entail certain actions, while other actions—such as insulting people for pleasure—are precluded. "The cause of pleasure to those who give insult is that they think they themselves become more superior by ill-treating others."[12]

It should also be noted that just as some virtues are associated with actions, other virtues are associated with thinking. Modern philosophers have recognized various intellectual virtues—such as open-mindedness, courage, tenacity, fair-mindedness, curiosity, and humility—that flow from a person's intellectual character, which can be defined as "the force of accumulated thinking habits that shape and color every decision we make."[13] Perhaps the most important and misunderstood of the intellectual virtues is *humility*. How much would the argument culture script described in the previous chapter be altered if people assumed a humble rather than arrogant position toward others?

---

[11]James Kinneavy and Susan Warshauer, "From Aristotle to Madison Avenue: Ethos and the Ethics of Argument," in *Ethos: New Essays in Rhetorical and Critical Theory*, ed. James S. Baumlin and Tita French Baumlin (Dallas: Southern Methodist University Press, 1994), 175.

[12]Aristotle, *On Rhetoric*, 126.

[13]Philip E. Dow, *Virtuous Minds: Intellectual Character Development* (Downers Grove, IL: IVP Academic, 2013), 22.

Philosopher and educator Philip Dow notes that because "intellectually humble people value truth over their egos' need to be right, they are freed up to admit the limits of their own knowledge."[14] Embracing intellectual humility does not mean that individuals lack confidence or will change their position at the slightest challenge. "It only means that they are submissive to the truth and are, therefore, capable of expanding their understanding of the world in a way arrogant people are incapable of doing."[15]

The ancient writers of the book of Proverbs advocate the virtue of humility and give warning against its counterpart, pride. While the result of pride is destruction and disgrace, the humble person will experience honor, riches, and fullness of life (Prov 11:2; 18:12; 22:4; 29:23). The defining trait of a humble person is listening to advice (Prov 12:15). Notice the writer did not say the advice would always be followed, but it would be humbly considered. In commenting on this verse, Old Testament scholar Derek Kidner asserts that a prime way a wise communicator checks for prejudice—which is often not readily apparent to us—is to be open to the views of others.[16]

In addition to being open to others, we need to ask ourselves probing questions. Philosopher Elizabeth Krumrei-Mancuso suggests the following questions to help discern one's personal humility:

> Even when you feel strongly about something, are you still aware you could be wrong?
>
> Do you trust that truth has nothing to fear from investigation?
>
> Do you reserve the right change your mind? Or do you feel weak or ashamed to change a strongly held opinion?
>
> Do you feel like you need to hide past errors in your thinking?
>
> Do you approach others with the idea that you might have something to learn from them?[17]

While most Christians are open to exploring how these questions may be answered in relation to political or philosophical issues, we often struggle

---

[14]Ibid., 72.

[15]Ibid.

[16]Derek Kidner, *Proverbs: An Introduction and Commentary*, Tyndale Old Testament Commentaries (Downers Grove, IL: InterVarsity Press, 1964), 97.

[17]Elizabeth Krumrei-Mancuso, "Are You Intellectually Humble? 13 Tough Questions," *The Table*, September 17, 2014, http://cct.biola.edu/blog/2014/sep/17/cultivating-humility-follow-we-know-part.

to answer them in relation to our faith. After all, in a Christian community where steadfastness and unwavering resolve are rewarded, is it possible to assume a humble stance toward religious convictions? Psychology professor Joshua Hook, a self-professed Christian who studies matters of faith, suggests we struggle to hold our Christian beliefs and convictions with humility for several reasons. First, we have a lot invested in being right about our worldview. It is our faith commitments that give us a sense of purpose, peace, and the comfort of surviving death. Yet if we humbly accept the possibility that we might be wrong about parts of our worldview, our levels of peace diminish and existential anxiety increases. In addition, Hook explains that many of us have a "brick wall" approach to faith. "We have to be absolutely certain about each conviction and how they fit together, or else the whole wall falls apart."[18] For example, if a Christian comes to believe that macroevolution is true after all, then suddenly God no longer exists and the Bible is full of nonscientific myths. One brick (rejecting a literal reading of Genesis) causes the entire wall (God and the veracity of Scripture) to collapse.

Accepting a humble approach to our Christian convictions means that that we embrace the reality that all of us have blind spots, lack of information, and biases that keep us from seeing and knowing things clearly. As Paul states, "For now we see only a reflection as in a mirror; then we shall see face to face. Now I know in part; then I shall know fully, even as I am fully known" (1 Cor 13:12). Assuming such a humble position allows us to connect with individuals and groups who differ from us. Embracing our limitations allows us to enter these exchanges with the attitude that we can gain new information and learn from others.

Goodwill. A speaker exhibits goodwill by not only being motivated by the needs of the audience but putting those needs above his or her own. The greater good may outweigh the individual desires of the speaker. Only when the audience recognizes and acknowledges that the goodwill gestures being made by the speaker are directed *to them* will the message be persuasive. Central to a posture of goodwill is acknowledging the worthiness

---

[18]Joshua Hook, "Humility and Religious Convictions," *The Table*, August 11, 2014, http://cct.biola .edu/blog/2014/aug/11/humility-and-religious-convictions.

of another.[19] What happens when we do not respect the worthiness of another? "People have contempt for those things that they think of no account, and they belittle things of no account," asserts Aristotle.[20] Belittling manifests itself in a communication style marked by contempt, spite, and insult. How might counterpublics hold firm to their positions and yet still acknowledge the worthiness and needs of their opponents?

Gilbert Keith Chesterton—better known as G. K. Chesterton—was a prolific writer, philosopher, lay theologian, literary critic, and fierce debater. During his lifetime he squared off against some of the sharpest intellects of his day, including George Bernard Shaw, Rudyard Kipling, and H. G. Wells. While the debates were often loud and spirited, Chesterton seemed to be able to maintain a spirit of goodwill toward his adversaries. "He is something of a pagan," stated Chesterton referring to Shaw, "and like many other pagans, he is a very fine man."[21] Despite his disagreement with Shaw's socialist and antireligious views, Chesterton's respect for Shaw is apparent in a section of his autobiography completed just before his death: "I have argued with him [Shaw] on almost every subject in the world. . . . It is necessary to disagree with him as much as I do, in order to admire him as I do; and I am proud of him as a foe even more than as a friend."[22] Though H. G. Wells, with his humanistic worldview, often felt the heat of Chesterton's logic and oratory skills, he also experienced his goodwill. Far more than merely a debate opponent, Wells knew he was the object of Chesterton's unwavering concern. He once commented that if he made it into God's good graces "it would be by the intervention of Gilbert Chesterton."[23]

SPIRITUAL *ETHOS*

While Christian counterpublics no doubt should heed Aristotle's insight into the components of *ethos*, we have additional considerations. As Christ followers we should, as the apostle Paul states, "grow to become in every

---

[19]Ronald Polansky, *The Cambridge Companion to Aristotle's Nicomachean Ethics* (Cambridge: Cambridge University Press, 2014), 321.

[20]Aristotle, *On Rhetoric*, 125.

[21]Zachry O. Kincaid and Darren Sumner, "G. K. Chesterton: A Gallery of Beloved Enemies," *Christian History* 75 (2002): 41.

[22]Ibid., 42.

[23]Ibid., 43.

respect the mature body of him who is the head, that is, Christ" (Eph 4:15). As we seek to challenge the perspectives of others, do we reflect not only Aristotle but Christ? In his commentary on the book of Daniel, John Lennox notes, "Surely it is but elementary spiritual logic that if we wish to persuade others that God is real and that it is possible to have a vibrantly meaningful relationship with him, we shall have to be personally loyal to God and his Son and adjust our lives to be consistent with our fundamental Christian confession, 'Jesus Christ is Lord.'"[24] Are we consistent with what we profess? Peter provides a list of characteristics he argues should be true of people of faith: "Finally, all of you, be like-minded, be sympathetic, love one another, be compassionate and humble" (1 Pet 3:8-9).

These characteristics can serve as type of checklist to gauge our credibility as Christian counterpublics. For instance, as we seek to advance our position with others are we *sympathetic* and *compassionate* communicators? Both of these words carry the idea of the "fellow-feeling we should have towards those who suffer."[25] The first-century world was a cold and uncaring place— void of any organized welfare system—that afforded early disciples the opportunity to establish a reputation for doing good. Have we as modern followers continued in that tradition, increasing our credibility? Many would answer in the negative. In 2010 eighteen thousand respondents in twenty-three countries were asked, "Is religion a force for good?" The results were sobering. More than half (52%) answered no. Tragically, European countries with rich Christian roots had the most negative views, with only small percentages seeing religion as a positive influence (Belgium 21%, France 24%, Great Britain 29%, Sweden 19%). In the United States, 35% of those surveyed voted no to the claim that religion is a force for good.[26]

Reclaiming* ethos *one tweet at a time. If half of respondents no longer believe religion is a force for good, how can we show a watching world that we are serious about becoming followers of Christ who think deeply about issues of faith, service, and neighbor love? How can we introduce others to

---

[24]John C. Lennox, *Against the Flow: The Inspiration of Daniel in an Age of Relativism* (Grand Rapids: Monarch Books, 2015), 59.

[25]Kenneth Wuest, "1 Peter in the Greek New Testament," in *Word Studies from the Greek New Testament* (Grand Rapids: Eerdmans, 1984), 2:86.

[26]"Ipsos Global @dvisory: Is Religion a Force for Good in the World?," Ipsos News & Polls, November 26, 2010, www.ipsos-na.com/news-polls/pressrelease.aspx?id=5058.

a thoughtful, credible view of Christian counterpublics? In our estimation, Twitter can provide snapshots of the important issues contemporary followers of Christ are discussing. While there are many today who effectively utilize Twitter—Jonathan Merritt, Alan Noble, Richard Clark, Alissa Wilkinson, Katelyn Beaty—Christena Cleveland and Wesley Hill particularly encourage us.[27]

Christena Cleveland is a social psychologist at Duke University who focuses on issues of reconciliation and race. She does not shy away from asking hard questions that are at the center of our credibility as peacemakers. She asks: "Why is the Church divided into over 40,000 denominations? Why do Churches in the same town often have very little to do with each other?"[28] Cleveland invites Twitter followers to listen to a podcast where she provocatively answers these questions. In a retweet she encourages us to diversify our theological reading by checking out a list of the ten most important nonwhite theologians.[29]

Wes Hill, assistant professor of New Testament at Trinity School for Ministry, quotes Rowan Williams in reminding us, "Christianity is a tradition constantly in search of its own center."[30] With so many pressing social issues, what should be at the center for Christian counterpublics? In another tweet he encourages us to ask a question relevant to all Christian activists: "Imagine if evangelicals were interested in planting churches where the suicide rate is the highest?"[31] Inviting others into such rich conversations—140 characters at a time—helps counteract the stereotype that Christians are shallow and anti-intellectual. In contrast, it builds *ethos* by exhibiting a desire to foster wisdom and goodwill as salient issues are discussed.[32]

However, Christian communicators should be aware that our tweets could erode our *ethos*. President Donald Trump is a salient example of the complexity of Twitter. Trump values this medium in that it allows him to

---

[27]While we do not always agree with their views or answers, we are encouraged by the questions they are asking and their constant desire to push our thinking.

[28]Christena Cleveland, @CSCleve, May 23, 2016, https://twitter.com/cscleve; retweet of Nomad Podcast, @nomadpodcast.

[29]Cleveland, May 17, 2016; retweet of Englewood Review of Books, @ERBKS.

[30]Wesley Hill, @wesleyhill, May 31, 2016, https://twitter.com/wesleyhill.

[31]Hill, May 12, 2016.

[32]This is not to suggest that Cleveland and Hill only discuss deep issues on Twitter. Each includes fun facts about themselves—favorite foods, how to spend a lazy day off, informal photos, guilty pleasures—but they regularly include weighty questions, quotes, and resources.

directly communicate with his followers—22 million by his estimation—without having to go through a traditional media gatekeeper like the *New York Times*. However, how he tweets about potentially volatile issues has come under critique. When protests rejecting his election broke out in major cities, Trump dismissed the hurt of disenfranchised voters by saying how "very unfair" it was that "professional protestors" were making waves. After charges of insensitivity he changed course and tweeted: "Love the fact that the small groups of protesters last night have passion for our great country. We will all come together and be proud!"[33] However, had irreversible damage already been done? In other words, could the dismissive tone of the first tweet be counteracted by the second? Understanding the power of Twitter to establish or detract from a speaker's *ethos* is crucial in today's media-savvy climate.

The complexity of ethos. Several factors make our understanding of *ethos* even more complex. First, Aristotle distinguishes between two types of credibility. *Initial credibility* is based on a person's prior reputation, status, and professional or educational credentials, while *derived credibility* emerges during a talk as the audience judges the speaker's argument, evidence, style, virtue, and expertise. The difficulty with being a counterpublic is that derived credibility is not merely personal but also communal. The community or organization to which you belong can compromise your personal credibility. In one-on-one encounters you can control your tone, message, and level of civility. However, as a counterpublic you may not be able to control who speaks for your community or in what manner. Each counterpublic group will have to answer key questions: Will there be one spokesperson for our group? If so, will other members ever be allowed to publicly present a different message? Who ultimately has the power to craft and deliver public messages?

Also, when an audience listens to a speaker address controversial issues, their judgment of the speaker's credibility is heavily based on perception of bias. Communication theorists Inch, Warnick, and Endres note that it is "vital that recipients perceive a source as being free of bias and vested interest

---

[33]Meghan Keneally, "Donald Trump's Latest Tweet Flips on 'Professional Protesters,'" *ABC News*, November 11, 2016, http://abcnews.go.com/Politics/donald-trumps-latest-tweet-flips-profes sional-protesters/story?id=43466841.

and concerned primarily with their welfare."[34] In other words, as Christian counterpublics, are we sincerely committed to the welfare of the overall public or merely interested in advancing our agenda? When outsiders interact with our community, do they witness open-mindedness to opposing ideas or an unyielding rhetorical stance that never acknowledges other viewpoints or needs? "Research has also shown that when arguers are expected to have a personal interest in one side of an issue and actually favor the other side, they have high credibility."[35] For example, former US surgeon general C. Everett Koop—an outspoken Christian—made the surprising decision to support offering clean needles to drug addicts in an effort to stem the AIDS crisis.[36] While many conservatives and religious leaders opposed the move, Koop's credibility increased with many liberals for being willing to balance Christian convictions about drug use with the safety of addicts as broader solutions were sought.

The Scriptures seem to support the complex view of *ethos* considered in this chapter by alluding to key concepts advanced by Aristotle. Consider Paul's counsel to Timothy, his young protégé: "Command and teach these things [intelligence]. Don't let anyone look down on you because you are young, but set an example for the believers in speech [derived credibility], in conduct [initial credibility], in love [goodwill], in faith and in purity [virtue]" (1 Tim 4:11-12).[37]

In light of a complex view of *ethos*, every counterpublic must answer salient questions. First, *what is the level of credibility that precedes you?* What does the audience or strong public know of you and your group before you utter your first word? Just as there is individual *ethos*, institutions also have a certain collective *ethos*. In 1999, Amway made the costly

---

[34]Edward Inch, Barbara Warnick, and Danielle Endres, *Critical Thinking and Communication: The Use of Reason in Argument*, 5th ed. (Boston: Allyn and Bacon, 2006), 332.

[35]Ibid.

[36]Tim Franklin, "Koop Backs Clean-Needle Program," *Chicago Tribune*, March 2, 1988, http://articles.chicagotribune.com/1988-03-02/news/8804030857_1_clean-needle-programs-aids-epidemic-disease-through-sexual-contact.

[37]Augustine, who understood both the abuses and usefulness of rhetoric, states that "more important than any amount of grandeur of style" is the "life of the speaker." Interestingly, Augustine concedes that a discerning learner can glean valuable information from a speaker who "lives a wicked life." However, while such a speaker may offer insight to others, the speaker's own soul does not benefit because he refuses to apply the very insights he offers. Saint Augustine, *On Christian Teaching*, trans. R. P. H. Green (New York: Oxford University Press, 1997), 147.

decision to attempt to shed its negative reputation—and the nickname
Scamway, used by those frustrated with high-powered sales tactics—by
changing its name in North America to Quixtar.[38] Christian organizations
have followed suit, with Campus Crusade for Christ—a counterpublic dedicated to global evangelism—shedding the divisive word *crusade* and
adopting the abstract moniker Cru. When counterpublics operate within
communities or organizations, the collective *ethos* follows and marks them.
Second, *what is the level of* ethos *cultivated during your speech or interaction
with the public?* Does the audience perceive that you have a grasp on the
facts? Do you come across as a virtuous speaker who mirrors the values of
the broader community? Do you exhibit goodwill, or do you seem belittling?
Last, *what is your perceived level of credibility after the exchange?* We should
evaluate our exchanges with others not only on the content level—coherent
arguments supported by compelling evidence—but also on the relational
level—the amount of goodwill and civility cultivated during the interaction.

Private ethos **and Snapchat.** In a time when people have grown cynical
due to private scandals of leaders being made public, we begin to wonder
whether we can trust our spokespeople. Do they live out in private what
they so articulately present to us in public? Perhaps an app like Snapchat
can increase perceived credibility. Snapchat allows users to send images or
short videos that disappear after a brief time. Far from being polished, this
app lets viewers see—often in real time—what is dominating a person's
thoughts. "Snapchat isn't the place where you go to be pretty," argues *New
York Times* technology writer Jenna Wortham. "It's the place where you go
to be yourself."[39]

While frivolous photos and light content often dominate Snapchat,
could it not be used to express weightier issues? For instance, while I may
publicly speak about the needs of the poor, do I think of them when I go
about daily life? Showing a grainy video of my interacting with the needy
gives viewers a snapshot of how my convictions follow me as I traverse my
day. The ephemeral nature of Snapchat also allows me to share thoughts
that are still in process, thoughts I'm not ready to make permanent in a

[38]In 2007 the name Quixtar was abandoned and the corporation settled on the name Amway Global.
[39]Jenna Wortham, "How I Learned to Love Snapchat," On Technology, *New York Times Magazine*,
  May 22, 2016, 21.

speech, Facebook post, or blog. Snapchat expands my rhetorical vocabulary by allowing me to communicate through images what I struggle to express through text. One image of a person living on the street in filth perhaps will do more than paragraphs of narrative. Wortham concludes, "Words alone can be imperfect. Text barely captures even a fraction of that emotional depth and texture, even when we can type as much as we want."[40] Rhetoricians understand that an image can, and often does, surpass a thousand words.

CONCLUSION

In 2015, the Associated Press requested the release of a deposition in a 2005 civil case against Bill Cosby by a woman who accused him of drugging her in order to obtain sex. The AP had learned that the one-thousand-page deposition included Cosby admitting he had obtained prescription drugs with the intent of giving them to women. Obviously, Cosby's lawyers stringently fought against the release of such damning testimony. In ruling that the deposition would be made public, the judge, Eduardo Robreno, gave the following reasoning: "The stark contrast between Bill Cosby, the public moralist, and Bill Cosby, the subject of serious allegations concerning improper (and perhaps criminal) conduct, is a matter to which the AP—and by extension the public—has a significant interest."[41] The high moral bar established by Cosby was his undoing. He arrogantly set a public standard that he privately undermined. The same could easily be true of Christian communicators who call others to a high standard of virtue and goodwill. Are we just loud public moralists, or do we advocate a standard—rooted in the Scriptures—that governs our public and private lives? Our credibility, or *ethos*, will be determined by our answer.

---

[40]Ibid., 18.

[41]Leonard Pitts Jr., "Bill Cosby, Public Moralist, Silenced," *Seattle Times*, July 12, 2015, www
.seattletimes.com/opinion/bill-cosby-public-moralist-silenced.

JEAN VANIER AND L'ARCHE

ON THE EVENING OF AUGUST 4, 1964, Jean Vanier walked into his home in a small village about sixty miles north of Paris with three unusual companions. Dany, Raphael, and Philippe were residents of a mental asylum who had just been released into Jean's care to begin an experiment in residential living. Moved by the words and example of a Dominican priest and spiritual mentor, Jean wanted to see whether there was something he could do for mentally handicapped persons. The idea of a residential home presented itself, and Dany, Raphael, and Philippe were to be the first residents. The first evening proved memorable. Dany had lived all his life in a highly structured institution. He constantly wore a collar and spat at anyone who approached him. The sudden change in his environment made him extremely insecure, and he began to hallucinate. He ran out into the quiet streets of the village and began accosting passers-by with menacing gestures. When finally returned to the house, he roamed back and forth in a state of anxiety. Sleep was impossible for Dany and the other occupants. The next morning, Jean sadly called the asylum and asked them to come and collect Dany.[1]

It was hardly an auspicious start, but Raphael and Philippe remained and joined Vanier, a former naval officer, in forming a small community they called L'Arche. In the intervening years the organization has grown into a vast network of 147 communities in thirty-five countries across five continents. It is a tale of a remarkably effective Christian counterpublic. It is also particularly illustrative of certain qualities of counterpublics addressed in the previous two chapters. Chapter three examined the sort of compassion that characterizes a Christian alternative to the argument culture, suggesting that such compassion is born of true *affection* for people, is willing to enter into the world of others and *empathize* with them, and is willing to *confront*

---

[1]Kathryn Spink, *Jean Vanier and L'Arche: A Communion of Love* (New York: Crossroad, 1991), 39-40.

the uncompassionate and *advocate* for those who cannot effectively advocate for themselves. Chapter four discussed credibility and the importance of virtue, particularly the virtue of *humility*. Jean Vanier and the L'Arche communities are beautiful examples of all of these traits.

COMPASSION WITH AFFECTION

The L'Arche communities began with the simple affection of hospitality—Vanier chose to share his home with Raphael and Philippe. He saw disabled persons not as projects but as friends and companions. The fundamental relationship was "living with" rather than "doing for," and this has remained the ethos of L'Arche communities throughout their history. As their website notes, "people with intellectual disabilities are at the heart of L'Arche—not as clients, patients, or recipients of services but as friends, teachers and companions."[2] John Swinton describes the L'Arche communities as places where people with intellectual disabilities live with people who do not share that life experience, not as caregiver and cared for but as fellow human beings. As Swinton puts it, "L'Arche is truly odd—it refuses to do what society thinks it should."[3]

A famous example of this oddness appears in the life of Henri Nouwen, an Ivy League professor and writer who spent the last ten years of his life living in a L'Arche community in Toronto. Among his responsibilities during this time was caring for a disabled person named Adam. What could be more odd than an Ivy League professor befriending a person with profound mental disabilities? Author Philip Yancey was struck by this oddness while writing a piece on Nouwen late in Nouwen's life. Nouwen claimed he had gained more from his relationship with Adam than Adam had gained from him. Yancey was puzzled and probed this claim more deeply. Nouwen acknowledged it had been difficult for him at first; physical touch and the messiness of caring for an uncoordinated person did not come easily. But he developed a deep affection for Adam, and in the course of events he came to see himself reflected in Adam's profound disabilities. Nouwen began to learn "what it must be like for God to love us—spiritually uncoordinated,

---

[2]"Discover," L'Arche International, 2015, http://wp.larche.org/discover.
[3]Stanley Hauerwas and Jean Vanier, *Living Gently in a Violent World: The Prophetic Witness of Weakness*, ed. John Swinton (Downers Grove, IL: InterVarsity Press, 2008), 17.

retarded, able to respond with what must seem to God like inarticulate grunts and groans." Nouwen had always struggled with two competing voices: one calling him to "succeed and achieve," the other inviting him "simply to rest in the comfort that he was 'the beloved' of God." It was only in his final decade, through Adam and the L'Arche community, that Nouwen could truly listen to the second voice.[4]

COMPASSION WITH EMPATHY

Nouwen's story is not only an example of compassionate affection but also a model of genuine empathy. Nouwen learned to not just "feel for" Adam but to "feel with" him. He felt movements within his own soul arising in response to his activity with Adam. He found unexpected joy and release in this deep but unlikely relationship. There is a hospitality of soul that visitors to L'Arche communities often feel, which is nicely expressed in their original vision of forming loving communities that say, "I'm glad you exist."[5] L'Arche's commitment to the glad embrace of others has enabled them to cross a remarkable range of cultural, religious, and social boundaries. Their communities are found in some of the most impoverished and violent places in our war-torn world. Vanier himself continues to live within the communities he has founded, currently in the original L'Arche in Trosly-Breuil, France, when he is not traveling and speaking.

Another aspect of Vanier's empathy is his sensitivity to religious challenges posed by living in close community. Because of his devout Catholic convictions Vanier had taken it for granted that he and Raphael and Philippe would go to Mass each morning, until one day when Philippe asked why he had to go. Instead of reacting defensively, Vanier entered into the feelings Philippe expressed. Philippe had settled very well into his new life and would have made almost any concession to avoid being returned to the institution. Indeed, Vanier had little doubt Philippe would be willing to go to Mass if he had to, but should he have to? Vanier decided that the more fragile a person's liberty, the more it must be respected and protected.[6] Especially

---

[4]Philip Yancey, "Yancey: The Holy Inefficiency of Henri Nouwen," *Christianity Today*, December 9, 1996, www.christianitytoday.com/ct/1996/december9/6te080.html.
[5]Hauerwas and Vanier, *Living Gently in a Violent World*, 69.
[6]Spink, *Jean Vanier and L'Arche*, 42.

for a community of disabled persons, it was essential that worship be freely offered. He made a seminal decision at that point that no one would be required to worship. As he puts it, "We welcome people because they are people and not because they are baptised."[7]

COMPASSION WITH ADVOCACY

It is hard to adequately appreciate the L'Arche communities without first contemplating the radical disenfranchisement of disabled persons in contemporary society. L'Arche serves as a counterpublic for disabled persons by accepting them as they are, loving them as friends, treating them as equals, and living with them in community. Much of this can be taken for granted in ordinary human relationships, but it is extraordinary for people living with disabilities. In fact, almost nothing can be taken for granted about the way people with disabilities are treated in broader human society. Prevailing attitudes toward them bring to mind the words of Aristotle quoted in chapter four: "People have contempt for those things they think of no account."

Vanier tells of an assistant in a L'Arche community who heard a mother say to her child, "I would have aborted you if I could." He has gone into schools and heard kids say, "If I have a monster within me, I will get rid of it."[8] This is not just adolescent insensitivity—we live in a world where disability is often "solved" by abortion. Recent estimates are that 92 percent of all women in the United States who receive a prenatal diagnosis of Down syndrome choose to terminate their pregnancies.[9] Vanier notes similar trends in France, suggesting that within a few years there will be no more children with Down syndrome because they will all have been aborted.[10] John Swinton, a mental health nurse turned theologian and ethicist, wryly relates the comments of his friend John, who has Down syndrome, responding to these statistics: "That doesn't make us feel very welcome, does it?"[11]

---

[7]Ibid., 45.
[8]Hauerwas and Vanier, *Living Gently in a Violent World*, 69.
[9]Susan Donaldson James, "Down Syndrome Births Are Down in U.S.," *ABC News*, November 2, 2009, http://abcnews.go.com/Health/w_ParentingResource/down-syndrome-births-drop-us-women-abort/story?id=8960803.
[10]Hauerwas and Vanier, *Living Gently in a Violent World*, 69.
[11]Ibid., 11.

But such is our world. It would have been easy for Vanier to pick up the tools of the argument culture and advocate with outrage. But he chose to lay these tools aside and offer something radically different: compassionate community instead of hostile rhetoric. He did not argue for treating mentally disabled persons as equals; rather, he formed communities where their equality was a fact. Vanier and the L'Arche communities do not just say to those with disabilities, "I am glad you exist"; they prove it by living with them.[12] They often confront those who shut doors in the faces of disabled persons by joyfully opening a door to welcome them in. It is a beautiful testimony in any time and place, but it stands out all the more against the landscape of the argument culture.

HUMILITY THAT BUILDS CREDIBILITY

There is a deep humility at the core of L'Arche. It is built on the premise that there should be a level playing field for disabled and nondisabled people alike. Differences in abilities do not create two classes of people or a hierarchy of worth. Stories from the L'Arche communities challenge common perceptions about who is "abled" and who is "disabled." Vanier noticed early on that Raphael and Philippe had a striking capacity for communion and tenderness. They possessed fruit of the Spirit that Vanier lacked and abilities in which he was greatly deficient. They would never teach him about leadership or intelligence, but they would be his teachers by awakening qualities of the heart rather than the mind.[13] L'Arche is a place where biblical teaching about the humble being exalted and the last becoming first comes to life.

L'Arche embodies the conviction that disabled persons make necessary and positive contributions to humanity in general and the church in particular. Far from being ballast or burdens, disabled persons are essential to the flourishing and proper function of communities. Paul's words should make this obvious to Christian communities:

> The eye cannot say to the hand, "I have no need of you," nor again the head to the feet, "I have no need of you." On the contrary, the parts of the body that seem to be weaker are indispensable, and on those parts of the body that we think less honorable we bestow the greater honor. . . . God has so composed

---

[12]Ibid., 69.
[13]Spink, *Jean Vanier and L'Arche*, 42.

the body, giving greater honor to the part that lacked it, that there may be no division in the body, but that the members may have the same care for one another. (1 Cor 12:21-25 ESV)

As clear as this passage is, Vanier argues that its message is almost completely disregarded in our ecclesiology. "Who really believes it?" he asks.[14]

It is a fair question. A friend of mine is a special education professor at a Christian university. He asked a member of the Bible department why he did not talk more about disabilities in his classes. The Bible professor commented that he would teach more about it if the Bible spoke more about it. My friend was stunned and began to describe the intimate connection between disability, poverty, and the gospel. The treatment of the disenfranchised—whether lame, blind, deaf, mute, poor, fatherless, or ill—is a major concern of both the law and the prophets. Individuals with disabilities are central characters in many stories in the Gospels, and as a group they are frequently mentioned as prime beneficiaries of the ministry of Jesus and the new covenant. And because those with disabilities are almost always among the poorest of the poor, every passage of Scripture that describes the suffering of the poor covers those who are disabled under its umbrella. How could this be missed as a central teaching of Scripture? It is as if our ability to see blinds us to those who are blind and our ability to hear deafens us to the deaf. We do not relate to their stories, so we act like their stories were not told. If we want to read Scripture well, we need to learn from our brothers and sisters with disabilities.

Vanier also notes that disabled persons are essential because they often embrace the values of the gospel more than the values of the culture at large: "The mystery of people with disabilities is that they long for authentic and loving relationships more than for power. They are not obsessed with being well-situated in a group that offers acclaim and promotion. They are crying for what matters most: love."[15] Furthermore, interacting with people with disabilities often transforms those who are not disabled. Vanier relates a story of a very successful and chronically busy Parisian businessman whose wife was stricken with Alzheimer's disease. He did not want her institutionalized,

---

[14]Hauerwas and Vanier, *Living Gently in a Violent World*, 74.
[15]Ibid., 30.

so he was pressed to feed and bathe and clothe her. As a result, he later said, "I have changed. I have become more human." He also recounted a time in the middle of the night when his wife came out of her fog for a moment and said, "Darling, I just want to say thank you for all you're doing for me." The businessman found himself weeping and weeping.[16] In a materialistic culture that reduces people to their function and aspires to consumption and power, those with disabilities are not only helpful—one wonders whether we can be truly human without them.

Finally, it should be noted that the humility and compassion of Vanier and the L'Arche communities have certainly been effective in building credibility. In July 2015, L'Arche International was granted special consultative status at ECOSOC, the branch of the United Nations that promotes social and economic development. The result is that L'Arche will be consulted on all issues related to disability as the UN seeks to implement the Convention on the Rights of People with Disabilities, which was ratified in 2006. Vanier has also received a wide variety of recognitions, including the Companion of the Order of Canada, the Legion of Honour (France), the Pope Paul VI International Prize, the International Peace Award (Community of Christ), and the Rabbi Gunther Plaut Humanitarian Award. Most recently, he joined luminaries such as Mother Teresa, Aleksandr Solzhenitsyn, Desmond Tutu, and the Dalai Lama as a recipient of the Templeton Prize.

---

[16]Ibid., 66.

Part II

ENGAGING

OTHERS

How do we take the concepts we've been considering and use them to engage communities whose beliefs are radically different from our own? It's impractical to devise specific scripts for every possible scenario you may encounter. Communication situations and audiences are simply too diverse. What we need are broad principles that can aid counterpublics in constructing messages that may be disseminated through blogs, speeches, podcasts, emails, letters to the editor, articles, or YouTube videos that may go viral. The very first step is to identify the problem you want to address through your message.

5

CRAFTING YOUR MESSAGE

IN HIS CLASSIC *ON CHRISTIAN DOCTRINE,* Saint Augustine reminds us that it's not enough to merely understand or become passionate about a particular perspective, doctrine, or worldview. Being an effective communicator also entails being able to persuade others of these truths and evoke the same emotions you feel. He writes, "So is he persuaded if he loves what you promise, fears what you threaten, hates what you condemn, embraces what you commend, sorrows at what you maintain to be sorrowful; rejoices when you announce something delightful, takes pity on those whom you place before him."[1] Notice that Augustine is talking about not merely presenting intellectual arguments but crafting a message that surfaces powerful emotions such as love, fear, hate, and sorrow, culminating in a person acting on what the speaker presents.

When was the last time you heard a sermon or lecture that moved you? The speaker so presented the facts that you felt *compelled* to act even if it was inconvenient to do so. How did he or she do it? What makes one talk engaging and persuasive and another flat or inconsequential? A crucial part of being a counterpublic is motivating people to hate the things you hate, love what you cherish, and feel sorrow over issues you find disheartening. In short, effective communicators prompt the audience to consider the world as they do. In this chapter we discuss how to craft messages that invite the audience to consider issues through your perspective.

---

[1]Saint Augustine, *On Christian Doctrine,* trans. Laurence J. Lafleur (Indianapolis: Bobbs-Merrill, 1960), 136-37.

IDENTIFYING THE PROBLEM

Rhetorical arguments come into existence, note rhetorical scholars Kuypers and King, in the same sense "that an answer comes into existence in response to a question or a solution in response to a problem."[2] What is the problem you feel needs to be addressed by your community? What potential solutions are those in power not considering? *Exigence* is a word crafted by Lloyd Bitzer to describe a "thing which is other than it should be."[3] Simply put, what is currently happening in your community that should not be? Consider the following scenario.

As a Christian counterpublic your group takes seriously the Scripture's command to not close our hearts toward those in need (1 Jn 3:17). It deeply concerns you that homeless people often endure cold nights shivering in blankets or worn sleeping bags. The harsh reality is that on any given night over half of the homeless in your city cannot find a place to sleep in a county shelter. Tragically, they are forced to sleep under bushes, on park benches, or on the sidewalk. While the overall issue of homelessness is beyond the resources of your group, is there a way you can restore some dignity and keep them safe?[4] What if the homeless who have cars could legally sleep in them at night? While not a solution to the bigger issue, it is a step in the right direction. The more your group discusses this option, the more committed and passionate you become. However, you understand that there are many who oppose your solution and that similar ideas have previously been defeated. In fact, three out of four cities statewide—including your city—have laws prohibiting the very solution you are advocating.[5] How can you convince the strong publics in your community to enact your solution?

SELECTING AN AUDIENCE

While you may be passionate about your cause, the goal isn't merely to present your case to anyone who will listen. Rather, you want to address

---

[2]Jim Kuypers and Andrew King, *Twentieth-Century Roots of Rhetorical Studies* (Westport, CT: Greenwood Press, 2001), 282.

[3]Lloyd Bitzer, "The Rhetorical Situation," *Philosophy and Rhetoric* 1 (December 1968): 6.

[4]This is not merely a hypothetical situation. In Orange County, California—where both authors live—the option of allowing the homeless to sleep in cars has become a divisive and hotly contested issue.

[5]Madison Jaros and Rebecca Turley, "Should the Homeless Be Allowed to Sleep in Their Cars?," *Orange County Register*, July 4, 2015, News 16.

what scholars call the rhetorical audience. The rhetorical audience is made up of strong publics who have the power to enact—or deny—the solutions you and your group are advocating. What is it that *they* would find compelling or persuasive? "It is indeed the audience which has the major role in determining the quality of argument and the behavior of orators."[6] How can a speaker know beforehand that what he or she is presenting will be persuasive? The answer lies in addressing a series of audiences that help you craft a persuasive message.

Starting with you. The first step in crafting a message is to treat yourself as a type of audience. What arguments concerning a particular issue do *you* find persuasive? Do the facts really support your position? What counter-arguments can you think of? Are these arguments strong enough that you might need to revise your position? Do you find yourself exaggerating facts in order to make your case stronger? While we may be tempted to lie or exaggerate when speaking with others, are we willing to lie to ourselves? The benefit of treating yourself as an audience, assert rhetorical scholars Perelman and Olbrechts-Tyteca, is that you "cannot avoid being sincere" and you are "in a better position than anyone else to test the value" of your own arguments.[7] While self-deception is always a possibility, we can hope that most of us want to be sure that what we are advocating really is the best position supported by facts. "Just as one attaches more importance to arguments presented in closed session than those presented at a public meeting, the secrecy of self-deliberation seems to guarantee its value and sincerity."[8]

Using yourself as an audience finds support not merely among communication scholars but with other noted intellectuals. Blaise Pascal asserts that the best test of truth is "your own assent to yourself, and the constant voice of your own reason."[9] In fact, Pascal argues that many of the problems facing society could be solved if individuals would take time to sit alone in a room and work through pressing issues, paying attention to how their intellect and heart guide them. In his preface to the *Meditations*, René Descartes describes

---

[6]C. H. Perelman and L. Olbrechts-Tyteca, *The New Rhetoric: A Treatise on Argumentation*, trans. John Wilkinson and Purcell Weaver (Notre Dame, IN: University of Notre Dame Press, 1969), 24.

[7]Ibid.

[8]Ibid., 41.

[9]Blaise Pascal, *Pensées*, trans. A. J. Krailsheimer (London: Penguin Classics, 1995), 220.

how the truths he arrived at were first discovered by arguing with himself, and that his writings are, in part, an attempt to see whether he can "persuade others by means of the same reasons that have persuaded me."[10]

Returning to the plight of the homeless, why do *you* think it is important to fight for their right to sleep in cars? As a Christian counterpublic you believe that each person—being made in the image of God—has inherent dignity. Allowing individuals to sleep in the privacy of a car restores a semblance of that dignity. What prompts you to act is knowing that Christians should serve as advocates for those who have no voice or status (Jas 1:27). Being an advocate entails seeking to ensure the relative safety afforded by the option of sleeping in a car. What harm could there be in allowing the few homeless people who have cars to sleep in them?

Before we consider the next step in crafting your message, we need to address two common mistakes counterpublics make. First, in our self-deliberations we tend to focus only on our own arguments. As you formulate your opinion and look at evidence that supports your view, it is easy to become cemented in the persuasiveness of your own argument. How can people ignore what deeply concerns us? How closed minded do you have to be to reject our arguments? How could anyone be so uncaring as to ban the unfortunate from sleeping in their cars? As we mentioned earlier, how you imagine those who disagree with you greatly establishes the relational aspect of communication and the amount of respect you afford others. We often forget that people on the other side are individuals who also have thought deeply about this issue and are guided by what they consider to be compelling reasons accompanied by equally strong passions. In our self-deliberations we must remember the humanity and complexity of those who oppose us.

The second mistake in self-deliberation is failing to consider other perspectives. When you think through an issue it is imperative to avoid merely seeking out arguments that support your position; you must also expose yourself to points of view that challenge your conclusions. Mirroring Aristotle's commitment to *ethos*, we cultivate wisdom by being able to articulate diverse perspectives. In my senior seminar for communication majors, students are

---

[10]René Descartes, *Meditations on First Philosophy*, trans. Laurence J. Lafleur (Indianapolis: Bobbs-Merrill, 1960), 11.

required to read authors on both sides of an issue. Not only do they read Kevin DeYoung's book *What Does the Bible Really Teach About Homosexuality?*, which presents a traditional interpretation of key biblical texts, but they also consider Christian ethicist David Gushee's argument for full acceptance of same-sex marriage in the church presented in *Changing Our Mind*. Initially the goal is not to evaluate each position, but to understand and articulate each side.

Once your arguments are formed, it's time to test them to see whether they are persuasive. How would members of the rhetorical audience respond to your suggestions? The next audience to help you refine your message is someone who represents the very people you are trying to persuade.

Testing your ideas. While our arguments seem persuasive to us and find support with fellow counterpublics, how can we know they'll be equally persuasive with those of a different point of view? Perelman and Olbrechts-Tyteca suggest we find a single critic who holds the same perspective as the group we are trying to persuade. They call this person the "audience of one."[11]

Armed with your arguments you meet at Starbucks with a neighbor who has participated in city politics for years. You explain how your faith motivates you to be concerned about the plight of the homeless. "Allowing them to sleep in their cars not only affords them dignity, but helps them be safe." After a brief pause, your neighbor responds, "While your faith is admirable, as a nonreligious person it's a nonfactor for me. I agree that we should be concerned about people's safety, but whose safety are we talking about?" You ask for clarification. Looking down at his coffee he replies, "One of the main reasons the option you are suggesting has been shot down in the past is that it causes massive safety and logistical problems for other residents, especially shop owners." He explains that national statistics show that the homeless are often perpetrators of property crimes against both residences and businesses. "Also, what do you do if a homeless person pulls up in a car in front of someone's house or business and stays there for weeks or months? Will we have to pass a law that prohibits anyone—including homeowners or

---

[11]Interestingly, these scholars do not necessarily mean you should talk to an actual person. As part of a mental exercise you could create a symbolic audience of one from articles, books, or blogs articulating the other side. We advocate that when possible you engage an actual person who disagrees with you.

shopkeepers—from parking there? I'd be careful of the legal can of worms you are about to open." When you are ready to leave, your neighbor offers a surprising piece of advice. "I hope you won't be offended, but I think I might keep it quiet that you are religious or belong to a specific church. When I was a civic employee some of the most hostile and demanding people who came to meetings or wrote letters were people who thought they were doing God's work. Sorry if that seems harsh."

After the conversation you realize there are several issues that you need to address. First, while your faith provides you with a moral imperative to act on behalf of the homeless, everyone does not share it. In fact, being religious may be an unexpected hindrance. Second, your neighbor helped you realize that in your zeal to protect the homeless you may have caused others to feel unsafe. Third, perhaps more attention needs to be given to the legal ramifications of the suggestion you are offering. What laws will need to be created to make your group's suggestions enforceable? It would be folly to simply ignore the objections uncovered during the conversation. It becomes increasingly obvious that you are not ready to present your suggestions to the strong public. What alterations do you need to make to your message?

Crafting universal arguments. What often short-circuits a good argument is being too limited in scope. What one specific audience finds convincing, another may find lacking. For example, for your community the Bible's admonishment to help the homeless or outcast is persuasive. In fact, it's all the motivation your group needs. Yet communicators need to consider not merely what they find persuasive, but what other groups of rational people would equally find persuasive.

Building on the discussion of virtue in the previous chapter, the key is to craft arguments that reflect not merely your community's values but also universal cultural values. What values have people—regardless of historical or cultural context—tended to adhere to in daily living? When we look at civilizations as a whole, notes C. S. Lewis, we observe that almost all cultures, past and present, surprisingly have roughly the same moral intuition. Each of these cultures "had an idea that they ought to behave in a certain way."[12] Lewis is arguing against the popular idea that different civilizations and

---

[12]C. S. Lewis, *Mere Christianity* (New York: Macmillan, 1960), 21.

different ages had radically different moralities. "If anyone will take the trouble to compare the moral teaching of, say, the ancient Egyptians, Babylonians, Hindus, Chinese, Greeks and Romans, what will really strike him will be how very alike they are to each other and to our own."[13] It's crucial to note these diverse cultures developed mostly independently of one another. They were not having international conference calls comparing moral codes and reworking their lists to cultivate consensus. Yet consensus is exactly what emerges when we compare them. It's as if a billion musicians, in thousands of different geographical locations, were playing off the same music sheet.[14]

Thus, the goal is to craft a message that reflects values you share with the people you wish to engage. What need or value would the strong public embrace in relation to the issue of the homeless? In the 1940s psychologist Abraham Maslow sought to identify certain needs that motivate individuals to act. He placed the needs in a hierarchy starting with basic or deficiency needs (physiological, safety, love, and esteem) and moving toward self-actualization. Maslow argued that basic needs must be attended to before one can seek higher needs. The longer a basic need goes unmet, the more motivated people become to address it. Notice that *safety* is one of the basic needs of all humans. If Maslow is right, then we can be assured that everyone—including members of the strong public—value the need for safety. In your message you must offer a plan that meets the safety needs of everyone, not merely the homeless. This ubiquitous need can serve as a starting point in the conversation.

THE POWER OF IMAGES

When crafting your message make sure to consider how images might play a role in communicating with those inside and outside your group. "Imagine if the civil rights activists photographers had Twitter and Instagram, their powerful photos would have been able to spread courage, pride, and righteousness around the globe at the speed of light," suggests Sadie Yankello.[15]

---

[13]Ibid., 19.

[14]If you are interested in digging deeper into this argument, see J. P. Moreland and Tim Muehlhoff, *The God Conversation: Using Stories and Illustrations to Explain Your Faith*, rev. ed. (Downers Grove, IL: InterVarsity Press, 2017).

[15]Sadie Yankello, "Activist Photographers of Today," Brooks Museum blog, February 11, 2015, www.brooksmuseum.org/blog/posts/activist-photographers-of-today.

Instagram is a social networking app made for sharing photos and videos from a smartphone and is slowly replacing other social media options. According to a 2014 Pew study, Instagram had more users than Twitter. "While 23 percent of Americans now use Twitter, 26 percent use Instagram—up from 17 percent in 2013 and 13 percent in 2012."[16]

The power of Instagram is that photos can create image events. Image events are attempts to use visual rhetoric to challenge the way groups conceptualize a certain issue. After the fatal shooting of Michael Brown on August 9, 2014, in Ferguson, Missouri, by a white police officer, social media exploded with videos and pictures of an unusual form of protest that came to be known as "die-ins." These consist of large groups of black protesters lying on the ground playing dead. The provocative visual rhetoric used in Ferguson soon spread as die-ins were enacted throughout the country, educating viewers on perceived injustices.

While visual rhetoric is powerful, it is difficult to predict how viewers will react. Often images are shared without an easily available explanation or desired interpretation. Visual communication scholar Rick Williams explains that what makes the effects of visual rhetoric so unpredictable is that our "initial, primary response to visual cognition is preconscious."[17] Before you make images public it is wise to test them on members of the audience you wish to persuade to gauge their initial reaction. Does the image excessively inflame passions, making communication difficult, or does it evoke an emotional response that causes others to conceptualize the issue in helpful ways? The goal of our messages—regardless of the form—is to create starting points.

STARTING POINTS

Starting points are values or areas of agreement shared by the speaker and the audience that allow the conversation to develop.[18] Far too often

---

[16]Aaron Blake, "The Political Potential of Instagram," *Washington Post*, February 4, 2015, www .washingtonpost.com/news/the-fix/wp/2015/02/04/why-the-two-parties-need-to-figure-out-instagram-now.

[17]Rick Williams, "Theorizing Visual Intelligence: Practices, Development, and Methodologies for Visual Communication," in *Visual Communication: Perception, Rhetoric, and Technology*, ed. Dian S. Hope (Cresskill, NJ: Hampton, 2006), 35.

[18]Perelman and Olbrechts-Tyteca, *New Rhetoric*, 20-21.

counterpublics are impatient to present the full scope of their argument and win the other side in one engagement. As a result, we rush past our commonalities to focus on our differences, inadvertently stopping the momentum of the conversation.

Christian counterpublics must face the question of whether religion is a conversation starter or stopper. Before her conversion to Christianity, professor Rosaria Champagne Butterfield would have agreed with the latter. She states that many students of faith would "bring the Bible into a conversation to stop the conversation, not deepen it." She says the phrase *the Bible says* "was the Big Pause before the conversation stopped."[19] Atheist philosopher Richard Rorty resonates with Butterfield's experience and suggests that in order for robust conversations to happen in the public square, we all—religious and nonreligious alike—must be careful not to offer justifications for our beliefs that are sure to sidetrack the discussion. He imagines a person of faith, motivated by her understanding of God's will, attempting to convince an atheist of the immorality of abortion. Rorty suggests the atheist should respond, "OK, but since I don't think there is such a thing as the will of God, and since I doubt that we'll get anywhere arguing theism vs. atheism, let's see if we have some shared premises on the basis of which to continue our argument about abortion."[20]

Popular Christian author Rob Bell views not only religion as a conversation stopper but the word *God* itself. "When a word becomes too toxic and too abused and too associated with ideas and understandings that aren't true to the mystery behind the mystery, it's important to set it aside and search for new and better ways to talk about it."[21] Bell's solution is to replace *God* with the descriptor "soul of the universe" when talking about complex spiritual realities. Not everyone agrees with Bell's attempt to open dialogue by eliminating the word *God*. Religion writer Jonathan Merritt ponders, "To me, creating a God-less religion is a little like baking biscuits without butter—it can be done, but in some way, it ends up lacking an intractable ingredient

---

[19]Rosaria Champagne Butterfield, *The Secret Thoughts of an Unlikely Convert: An English Professor's Journey into Christian Faith* (Pittsburgh, PA: Crown & Covenant, 2012), 4.

[20]Richard Rorty, "Religion as Conversation-Stopper," in *Philosophy and Social Hope* (New York: Penguin, 1999), 171.

[21]Jonathan Merritt, "Is 'God' a Trigger Word?," BuzzFeed, October 22, 2015, www.buzzfeed.com/jonathanmerritt/god-a-trigger-word#.aj8Xpqzv5J.

that made it what it was."[22] Whether you side with Bell or Merritt, Christian counterpublics must acknowledge that linguistic choices have lasting ramifications in *how* or *if* a conversation develops.

The impact of our language was illustrated by Ronnie Floyd, president of the Southern Baptist Convention, when he passionately denounced the Supreme Court decision on same-sex marriage by unequivocally stating, "The Supreme Court of the United States is not the final authority, nor is the culture itself, but the Bible is God's final authority about marriage and on this book we stand."[23] While his rhetoric may help mobilize Southern Baptists, is it the best starting point in conversing with those who oppose him?[24] What would Floyd say to those who don't accept the Bible as God's final authority on marriage or don't share Floyd's conception of God? Are there, as Rorty suggests, premises that could help start a conversation about differences? If so, what could they be?

Concerning the thorny issue of abortion, could we could agree that a woman—especially in light of historical abuses—generally has the right to govern what happens to her body? When seeking to resolve this issue, can we affirm that the plight of *both* the mother and the fetus should be taken into consideration? Can we also agree that if an abortion is to happen, it should be made as safe as possible? While each of these premises no doubt will eventually bring up strong objections from both sides, they are meant to be starting points allowing deeper discussion to develop. These points are not "niceness, or pseudounanimity, but a core package of values and rights we can affirm together while we continue to disagree on some fundamental understandings of the ultimate nature of things," states Christian author Daniel Taylor.[25] As you craft your message, the goal of a starting point is to allow you to eventually address the ultimate nature of things, where your

---

[22]Ibid.

[23]Jonathan Merritt, "Three Things You Need to Know About Southern Baptists' Anti-gay Marriage Resolution," Religion News Service, June 18, 2015, http://jonathanmerritt.religionnews.com/2015/06/18/3-things-you-need-to-know-about-southern-baptists-anti-gay-marriage-resolution.

[24]While Floyd's speech was given to Southern Baptists, the difficulty is that his statement went public, putting Southern Baptists in an intractable position—if you don't accept the Bible as authoritative, then we have nothing to discuss.

[25]Daniel Taylor, "Deconstructing the Gospel of Tolerance," *Christianity Today*, January 11, 1999, 52.

explicit faith commitments will no doubt come into the conversation—at the right time. A word spoken at the right time, argue ancient Jewish writers, is like finely crafted jewelry (Prov 25:11).

How would starting points work in real life? Imagine you are part of a group that knows what you are planning will be flatly rejected by city officials (strong publics). The convictions of your community are not only in the minority but are offensive to others. How could you start the conversation? These were the very questions a counterpublic group in Detroit, Michigan, was facing. The group, the Satanic Temple, wanted to erect a one-ton, nine-foot-tall bronze statue of an occult figure with two young children at its feet, lovingly looking up at its goat-like face. The statue would be placed on the waterfront in the heart of Detroit. Religious organizations and civic leaders passionately objected and put great pressure on the members of the strong public who would render a decision. From a communication standpoint, the Satanic Temple seemingly had no chance. How could you possibly persuade a community—with a significant Catholic population—to accept such an outlandish statue? Surely these counterpublics were doomed to fail. Right?

On July 27, 2015, over seven hundred people attended a gathering to celebrate the unveiling of the occult statue. How did they do it? Strategically, members of the Satanic Temple did not *start* with their radical belief that Satan is to be admired as an example of those who resist authority.[26] Rather, as a starting point they shared with the press their mission statement, which is, according to Detroit chapter spokesperson Jex Blackmore, to "encourage benevolence and empathy among all people, reject tyrannical authority, advocate practical common sense and justice, and be directed by the human conscience to undertake noble pursuits guided by the individual will."[27] Affirming values—benevolence, empathy, common sense, justice—that resonated with members of the strong public helped rhetorically pave the way to their most important starting point—religious liberty. Temple members argued that they fully supported the right to voice religious views in the

[26]See the mission statement of the Satanic Temple at http://thesatanictemple.com.

[27]Tom Greenwood, "Satanic Statue to Be Revealed in Detroit on Saturday," *Detroit News*, July 22, 2015, www.detroitnews.com/story/news/local/detroit-city/2015/07/22/satanic-statue-revealed-detroit-saturday/30508189.

public square without fear of retribution. While these religious opinions may be offensive to some, our country was built on the right to express them. Though city council members recoiled at the idea of drawing attention to Satan, the starting points offered by temple members began a conversation that resulted in the group being allowed to express their convictions in the form of a provocative statue.

Oddly, Christian counterpublics should be encouraged by the success of these unique counterpublics. The reaction you had to learning of the Satanic Temple and its goal to erect a statue is the same reaction many have to our conservative religious beliefs. The effectiveness of this counterpublic also illustrates two key points applicable to all who hold a minority perspective.

PLAUSIBILITY STRUCTURES

The first objective of the temple members was not to win people over to their unique and disturbing view of Satan. Rather, they sought to affirm an idea already within another community's *plausibility structure*. Peter Berger, a sociologist who coined the term, explains that beliefs become plausible if those around us support them. "We are all social beings, we were created as social beings and much of what we think about the world depends on support by important people with whom we live." Thus, it would "be very difficult to be a Catholic in a Tibetan village. It would be difficult to be a Buddhist in a Catholic village in the south of Italy."[28] Berger expands the common scholarly definition of a plausibility structure as merely a set of beliefs a person is willing to consider as being true. What people are willing to consider as true, asserts Berger, is inextricably linked to social forces around them.

In the classroom I find it interesting to ascertain what fits within my students' plausibility structures. "How many think it's plausible that Big Foot exists?" After the laughter dies down, there are only a few who raise their

---

[28]"Rethinking Secularization: A Conversation with Peter Berger," interview by Albert Mohler, *Thinking in Public*, October 11, 2010, www.albertmohler.com/2010/10/11/rethinking-seculariza tion-a-conversation-with-peter-berger. For more of Berger's thoughts on plausibility structures, see *The Sacred Canopy: Elements of a Sociological Theory of Religion* (New York: Anchor Books, 1967). Berger offers a sobering thought for Christian counterpublics: "Probably for the first time in history, the religious legitimations of the world have lost their plausibility not only for a few intellectuals and other marginal individuals but for broad masses of entire societies" (p. 124).

hands. "How many think it's possible that hell doesn't exist?" No hands go up. Why? Berger would suggest that while believing Big Foot exists might evoke odd looks or laughter, it still could find some support among fellow students at a conservative religious university (if Yeti or Abominable Snowmen do exist, God created them). More importantly, it doesn't violate any core beliefs in the plausibility structure of the community. However, the belief that hell isn't real will not only lack public support by students and faculty, it also violates a salient conviction of the overall structure. A student can still entertain the implausibility of hell, but the plausibility structure of the community will make harboring such a belief difficult and isolating.[29]

Consider the role plausibility structures played in the success of the message offered by the Satanic Temple. Members understood that their belief that Satan was a virtuous entity had little chance of being supported by council members whose plausibility structure was rooted in traditional Christian beliefs. How could council members go back to their community if they affirmed a positive view of Satan? These members would find virtually no support from their community, thus rendering the idea implausible. Instead, the Satanic Temple wisely offered a belief—religious freedom—that easily fit into the council members' plausibility structures. While the council no doubt would face criticism for their decision to allow the statue, they could argue that it was a necessary byproduct of upholding a higher belief—freedom to voice religious views.

The key to crafting a successful message is to find starting points consisting of beliefs that the strong public already finds plausible. Persuasion entails offering a person not only facts and evidence but also an alternative community and corresponding plausibility structure. A friend once commented to me that he could never become a Christian because of his firm belief in evolution. He couldn't imagine going to his secular colleagues and informing them that he now believes God supernaturally created humankind. I informed him that becoming a Christian does not necessarily mean abandoning evolution and that some within my community find it entirely plausible that God used the complexity of evolution as part of creation.

---

[29]What could make a belief that hell doesn't exist feasible is finding a subculture on campus— filled with people an individual deems important—that allows or supports that idea. Thus the subculture's plausibility structure, not the dominant culture, determines what is permissible.

Admittedly, Christians who affirm what is commonly called theistic evolution are a minority compared to those who believe God created a literal first couple, but that option does exist within the plausibility structure of a Christian worldview. Christian author Timothy Keller makes a similar point when he states, "Since Christian believers occupy different positions on both the meanings of Genesis 1 and on the nature of evolution, those who are considering Christianity as a whole should not allow themselves to be distracted by this intramural debate."[30] As Christian counterpublics we must present those we seek to persuade with an inclusive plausibility structure that represents the breadth of opinions and possibilities within our community, not merely our personal convictions.

SACRED CORES

In crafting a message we need to carefully consider what makes up the sacred core of the community we are addressing. This core is the set of values or beliefs cherished by members of a particular community. The sacred, notes sociologist James Davison Hunter, "expresses that which is non-negotiable and defines the limits of what they will tolerate."[31] Violating a sacred core typically evokes a harsh response. It's a lesson Joe Gordon learned the hard way.

With ankles shackled, American citizen Joe Gordon stood in an orange prison uniform awaiting his punishment. He was sentenced to two and a half years in a Thai prison. His crime? While in America he translated and posted online excerpts of a banned biography that insulted Thailand's king, thus violating the country's laws—referred to as *lese majeste*—that prohibit defamation of the royal family.[32] While visiting Thailand for medical treatment, Gordon was promptly arrested and thrown in jail. Some observers argue that Gordon's sentence was light compared to a twenty-year sentence handed down to a sixty-one-year-old Thai native convicted of sending four text messages judged offensive to the queen. Gordon and other

---

[30]Timothy Keller, *The Reason for God: Belief in an Age of Skepticism* (New York: Dutton, 2008), 94.

[31]James Davison Hunter, *Culture Wars: The Struggle to Define America* (New York: Basic Books, 1993), 322.

[32]Associated Press, "American Sentenced to Two Years for Thai Royal Insult," *USA Today*, December 8, 2011, http://usatoday30.usatoday.com/news/world/story/2011-12-07/Thailand -american-prison/51722776/1.

critics of the Thai government paid dearly for violating a country's sacred core. A strong reaction surely would have also occurred if members of the Satanic Temple had publically violated core beliefs of Detroit's predominantly Catholic community. While advocating for an occult statue no doubt put a strain on the communication climate with Detroit's leaders and community members, outright disrespecting of God or the Virgin Mary would have ended the conversation.

The imprisonment of Gordon and the provocative goals of the Satanic Temple dramatically illustrate the importance of sacred cores, but the same principles apply to working to allow the homeless in your community to sleep in cars. What values are paramount to city planners (strong publics)? Does their sacred core include an unwavering commitment to local shop owners—who are the heart and soul of your town—to keep the homeless from setting up camp in broken-down cars, resulting in leery customers? As we seek to craft persuasive messages, we must be aware of and respect the core beliefs of other communities. To neglect gathering this information risks entering a rhetorical minefield without knowing what topics could derail your message and render your content useless.

There comes a time when it's necessary to directly critique the non-negotiable beliefs of another community. How should we package our critique? Peter gives us a clue when he admonishes believers that we should present our worldview "with gentleness and respect" (1 Pet 3:15). Let's consider what gentleness does *not* look like. If you want to provoke anger from someone, respond to his or her convictions with emotionless nonchalance. In other words, I treat your conviction as merely a point being made in a debate. Rather than acknowledging the deep emotions that accompany your view, I dispassionately offer my counterargument. After all, there is a debate to be won! Regardless of how persuasive my argument is, I will undoubtedly come across as detached and harsh. We would do well to remember the ancient writer's admonishment that a harsh word "stirs up anger" (Prov 15:1).

What might gentleness in addressing a group's sacred core look like? Our answer in part comes from an unlikely source. David Roman is a unique theater critic who focuses on what has been labeled "AIDS theatre." This comprises not only formal staged productions but short one-act plays, improvisational sketches, and even impromptu performances done outside a theater. The purpose of these performances is to draw attention to the AIDS crisis, challenge misconceptions about those with AIDS, and call people to action. Often the cast is composed of people afflicted with AIDS who are in various stages of treatment. Some are investing their last days, months, or years in the production. Now, how would you like to be a theater critic critiquing these heroic performances? Welcome to David Roman's world. How do you critique sick or dying cast members who are often too fatigued to produce what is traditionally identified as good theater? Roman's response is to enact *critical generosity*, which he defines as "a new mode of criticism appropriate to the demands of the historical conditions."[33] While he does critique the actual performance, he never looses sight of the deep passion and sacrifices of the performers.

As Christian counterpublics, when we address the sacred core of a group we must adopt a form of critical generosity. This begins with communicating to others that we are fully aware we are treading on their deepest convictions and do not do so lightly. We must express to the group that it hurts us to know we are hurting them. It brings us no joy to critique what is so dear to them. Next, if possible acknowledge what is admirable about their core or the dedication they have to it. Finally, be honest in your critique. In an odd piece of advice, the writer of the book of Proverbs states that "an honest answer is like a kiss on the lips" (Prov 24:26), suggesting that honesty—in contrast to speaking of a person disparagingly in private—is as much a sign of respect and intimacy as a kiss. To honestly, compassionately, and gently address the core of another group could surprisingly cultivate begrudging respect.

CONCLUSION

It is understandable to associate Augustine, author of seminal works such as *City of God* and *Confessions*, with complex content. However, he believed that a message could be deeply—and even mystically—transmitted through a creative presentation. Specifically, he felt the use of imagery could help others not only learn but find pleasure as the message comes alive.[34] In the next chapter we consider how our carefully crafted content can be presented in a way that moves the intellect and emotions of the audience.

---

[33]David Roman, *Acts of Intervention: Performance, Gay Culture, and AIDS* (Bloomington: Indiana University Press, 1998), xxiv.
[34]Augustine, *On Christian Teaching*, 31.

6

DELIVERING YOUR MESSAGE

IT'S THE MOMENT WE LOVE. The theater goes quiet and we lean forward. The judge asks the defense to give a final summation. The facts seem overwhelming against the accused as the lawyer approaches the jury. A group of worn soldiers faces an entrenched enemy who has every advantage. An equally exhausted commander stands and asks for one last act of courage. A coach acknowledges that no one picks them to win. The other team is bigger and stronger, but she reminds players of historic upsets. "No one comes into our house and pushes us around!" Players clap in unison as they head to the field.

As counterpublics we long to have such a moment. In the face of fierce opposition we take a stand and courageously present our convictions. If juries and soldiers can be moved by dramatic speeches, surely our opposition will be moved as well. While such scenes make for good drama, they seldom happen. Experienced counterpublics know that influence is gained in increments and stages. Opportunities to directly address strong publics are rare and usually come with time restrictions, crowded agendas, poor sound systems, page limitations, hostile audiences, and other complications. It's how a counterpublic handles these complications that will determine success. When given an opportunity to get my message out, what persona should I adopt? How does my audience feel about my topic? How can I identify with them? Should I use humor? What type of evidence should I use? Most importantly, how should I start?

How we answer these questions is just as important as the words we say. The first step of delivering your message is determining how you and your group want to come across to the audience.

DEVELOPING A PERSONA

Before you speak it's crucial to adopt a persona. Do you want to be seen as a teacher, prophet, preacher, expert, or fellow citizen? Add to these broad descriptors of personality traits such as rigidness, openness, conviction, empathy, or civility. Do you want to be seen as a rigid activist who isn't interested in compromise, or a fellow community member who wants what's best for everyone and is open to discussion on how to solve issues? Unfortunately, many counterpublics choose the former.

Cultural critic Paul Loeb argues that a "wall now separates each of us" as we increasingly take up residence in unwavering ideologies.[1] According to political experts, what fuels this separation is not merely disagreements about policy issues but how we view each other. Alan Abramowitz, a political scientist at Emory University, notes that our disagreements have become personal. "Ordinary Americans increasingly view members of the opposite party with contempt and scorn. They see them as less intelligent and more selfish, according to pollsters and political scientists."[2] The hatred runs so deep that "parents are more likely to say they wouldn't even want someone in the other party to marry their children."[3] The result of such acrimony is that "we have all but forgotten that public participation is the very soul of democratic citizenship."[4] The prerequisite for responsible citizenship—as discussed in chapter four—is humility. Loeb advises up-and-coming activists that none of "us has the final answers to such questions. But as you listen to this wide-ranging conversation, keep in mind that we're talking about common problems of our society, and their potential common solutions."[5] How does humility play out as we present our convictions?

In his preface to *Mere Christianity*, C. S. Lewis offers a helpful metaphor that might provide a persona for modern counterpublics. Lewis imagines those trying to decide between competing beliefs as standing in a hall

---

[1]Paul Rogat Loeb, *Soul of a Citizen: Living with Conviction in a Cynical Time* (New York: St. Martin's Griffin, 1999), 2.

[2]Max Ehrenfreund, "These Political Scientists Are Discovering Even More Reasons U.S. Politics Are a Disaster," *Washington Post*, November 3, 2015, www.washingtonpost.com/news/wonk/wp/2015/11/03/these-political-scientists-are-discovering-even-more-reasons-u-s-politics-are-a-disaster.

[3]Ibid.

[4]Loeb, *Soul of a Citizen*, 2.

[5]Ibid.

facing many doors. While in the hall, it's wise to check out rooms and explore why one room is appealing while another is not. "Is my reluctance to knock at this door due to my pride, or my mere taste, or my personal dislike of this particular door-keeper?"[6] After selecting a particular room, how should a person act? "When you have reached your own room, be kind to those who have chosen different doors and to those who are still in the hall. If they are wrong they need your prayers all the more; and if they are enemies, then you are under orders to pray for them."[7] Lewis's metaphor reminds us that we are all in the process of checking out different beliefs and we settle on particular perspectives for a multitude of reasons. Our communication with others will be greatly strained if we arrogantly assert our door is the only option.

In commenting on his son's presidency, former president George H. W. Bush criticized George W. Bush for surrounding himself with advisors who eschewed humility and adopted antagonistic rhetoric. Concerning former defense secretary Donald Rumsfeld, Bush notes, "There's a lack of humility, a lack of seeing what the other guy thinks."[8] He concludes that Rumsfeld's approach of "kick-ass and take names" came at a great relational price with fellow leaders. Vice President Dick Cheney receives a similar critique for adopting an "iron-ass" persona where he wanted to fight about everything. The result? Bush Sr. concludes that arrogant speech and personas hinder people from pulling together to solve diplomatic problems—a skill sorely needed after the terrorist attacks of 9/11. The writers of the book of Proverbs reach a similar conclusion: "pride and arrogance" are tied to "perverse speech" (Prov 8:13).

The 2016 election was marred by similar problems. Donald Trump took on a very distinctive persona—in this case, a persona that was reminiscent of what was described by sociologist Robert Bellah in his book *Habits of the Heart*. Bellah portrays a characteristic American hero, the outsider cowboy or the detective who "can be valuable to society only because he is a completely autonomous individual who stands outside it. To serve society, one must be

---

[6]C. S. Lewis, *Mere Christianity* (New York: Macmillan, 1952), 12.

[7]Ibid.

[8]Nancy Benac, "Elder Bush Criticizes Cheney, Rumsfeld," *Orange County Register*, November 6, 2015, News 3.

able to stand alone, not needing others, not depending on their judgment, and not submitting to their wishes."[9] This is certainly an apt description of Trump's persona as an outsider to American politics who was going into Washington to "drain the swamp." Again, one cannot help but wonder how this sort of arrogant individualism will play out in the actual challenges of governance.

One way to cultivate humility that is seldom utilized by counterpublics in today's argument culture is humor. When counterpublics take themselves too seriously it can lead to adopting a persona that never reflects on potential weaknesses or limitations. Philosopher Stephen Okey notes that humor can be an asset in developing humility.

> With a sense of humor, I can laugh at myself. I can remember that I am not actually the center of the cosmos. Whenever I become puffed up with pride and consider myself to be greater than I really am, gentle teasing might knock me down an appropriate number of pegs. It might help me to remain grounded in reality, not floating in my delusions of grandeur.[10]

There are two important qualifiers to the use of humor. First, there is a significant difference, notes Okey, between self-deprecating and self-deriding humor. Self-deprecating humor pokes at one's pride, while self-deriding humor undermines one's dignity. In poking fun at ourselves, we need to be careful not to demean ourselves or our reputations. Christian apologist G. K. Chesterton was a large man—tipping the scales at three hundred pounds— who easily could alienate others with both his physical appearance and his towering intellect. To offset others' impression of him and show that he could laugh at himself, he often good-naturedly joked about his weight and hosted theater parties where he dressed up in elaborate costumes and performed for dinner guests. Instead of hiding his flaws he joked about them. Christian author Philip Yancey notes that Chesterton's lightheartedness disarmed enemies and won many friends. "I think Chesterton's approach, making himself the main butt of his jokes, is a good model for all of us."[11] Second, your humor

---

[9]Robert Neelly Bellah, *Habits of the Heart: Individualism and Commitment in American Life* (Berkeley: University of California Press, 1985), 146.

[10]Stephen Okey, "The Virtues of Humor and Humility," Institute for Islamic, Christian, and Jewish Studies, May 30, 2013, http://icjs.org/articles/2014/virtues-humor-and-humility.

[11]Philip Yancey, "G. K. Chesterton: Christian History Interview—Exactly the Opposite," *Christian History* 75 (2002), www.christianitytoday.com/history/issues/issue-75/gk-chesterton-christian-history-interview--exactly.html.

must be directed at you, not your opponent. "Obese" or "egotistical" were labels Chesterton reserved for himself, not others.

These qualifiers were carefully negotiated by 2016 presidential hopeful Hillary Clinton when, in an attempt to rebrand her persona, she appeared in a *Saturday Night Live* skit. *SNL* cast member Kate McKinnon impersonated Clinton sitting at a bar, while Clinton played a bartender named Val. The banter between the two allowed Clinton to acknowledge deficiencies and poke fun at herself. The skit addresses Clinton's unabashed desire to be president when Val asks Clinton for identification. In her best Hillary impersonation, McKinnon answers, "Identification? I have a one-year-old granddaughter. She calls me, 'Madam President!'" As they talk a couple comes up to thank Clinton for supporting gay rights. After they leave, a somber Clinton confesses to Val, "I could have supported gay marriage sooner." "Well, you eventually did," replies Val. "Could have been sooner," states Clinton. "Fair point," agrees Val. Through humor Clinton is able to simultaneously laugh at herself and address concerns about her political ambition and charges of flip-flopping on key issues. Did it work?

The answer is complicated, suggests a study from the University of Missouri–Columbia. Lead researcher Christopher Robert states that the fundamental issue isn't the quality of humor, but rather the quality of the existing relationship. "If a good relationship between leader and the subordinate exists, then humor—be it positive or negative in tone—will only help to maintain the good relationship."[12] However, if the relationship is negative, then humor—no matter how positive—will be interpreted only in unproductive ways. The researchers suggest that instead of using humor to build good relationships, a leader must first establish a positive climate through fair treatment and clear communication. Once a relationship is established, humor can serve to augment or repair it. If Hillary Clinton's target audience in the *SNL* skit was those who deeply opposed her, then it's fair to speculate the humor accomplished nothing. However, if her goal was to address those who were neutral or supporters who had become critical, then it may have helped reaffirm the relationship by showing signs of self-deprecating

---

[12]Christopher Robert, Timothy C. Dunne, and Joyce Iun, "The Impact of Leader Humor on Subordinate Job Satisfaction: The Crucial Role of Leader-Subordinate Relationship Quality," *Group & Organization Management*, October 2015, 24.

awareness of perceived faults. For counterpublics, humor can be effective in establishing a tone of humility with those who have positive associations with us that have, over time, become strained.[13] Whether humor—among other things—is appropriate will be determined by what rhetoricians call the fitting response.

THE FITTING RESPONSE

In one short essay, rhetorician Lloyd Bitzer changed how we think about ways to construct and deliver a message. He argues that a speaker must be fluid in delivery and adapt to a specific speaking situation. This situation in turn helps the speaker determine a *fitting response*. Bitzer notes, "If it makes sense to say that the situation invites a 'fitting' response, the situation must somehow prescribe the response which fits."[14] A fitting response emerges as a speaker considers diverse constraints in the situation. Simply put, a constraint is anything—allotted time to speak, quality of the sound system, available evidence, oratory skills of the speaker, biases of the audience, length of a blog, 140-character restriction of a tweet—that limits a communicator.

When explaining the concept of constraints to my students, I have them watch a clip from the *Oprah Winfrey Show* where the host focuses on spirituality by inviting a panel of New Age speakers to address near-death experiences, reincarnation, and the supposed divinity that exists in all of us. At one point Oprah turns to the audience for questions. A woman raises her hand and declares she is a Christian. She then sets out to voice her objections and present a Christian perspective. In doing so, what constraints might she face? First, as an audience member she's expected to ask questions, not give a sermon. Also, how long will Oprah allow her to speak before interrupting? Once Oprah interrupts, will the audience member get a chance to respond?

---

[13]There is also anecdotal evidence that humor may even influence those who strongly disagree with us. Consider outspoken Christian and former vice-presidential candidate Sarah Palin's reaction to being spoofed by Tina Fey in a *Saturday Night Live* skit in September 2008. Fey's impersonation was so spot-on that she received a primetime Emmy Award for Outstanding Guest Actress in a Comedy Series. How would Palin respond to being the focus of Fey's jokes? Rather than being defensive, in subsequent interviews when Palin made a mistake she would quip that she was merely providing job security to *SNL* cast members. She also decided to join Fey and stand side-by-side during the show's opening sketch on October 18, 2008. The audience applauded wildly, and Palin won grudging respect from her critics—including Fey.

[14]Lloyd Bitzer, "The Rhetorical Situation," *Philosophy and Rhetoric* 1 (December 1968): 10.

How complex can her articulation of the Christian perspective be in light of severe time limits? Finally, what possible credibility does she have with a nationally syndicated host? How she answers these questions will determine a fitting response.

These same questions about constraints apply to all counterpublics in communicative settings. What credibility or *ethos* do I have? How much time will I be given to present my views? If I write a letter to the editor, what is my word limit? If I join an online conversation, how much can I write before people tune me out? Twitter and its limit of 140 characters presents a unique challenge to crafting a fitting response. While the inherent limits of Twitter prohibit giving a robust description of an event or telling a detailed story, it does allow you to provide links to full reports that readers may not know exist.

Most importantly, crafting a fitting response requires us to ask: Of all the available evidence I have, which is most strategic? Though it is beyond the scope of this chapter to present all the forms of evidence available to a counterpublic, we'll consider two that work in most situations—statistics and stories. In order to explore the strengths and limitations of these forms, we'll consider how a counterpublic seeking to advocate for Syrian refugees might use both.[15]

Syria's civil war, which began in 2011, has produced the worst humanitarian crisis of our time. Tragically, more than 11 million people—over half of Syria's population—have been either killed or forced to flee from their communities. Exhausted, separated from loved ones, dehydrated, sick, and dying, these homeless bands are being turned away as they seek refuge in other countries. Why? In part, the 2015 terrorist attacks in Paris that killed 130 people have produced fears that accepting Syrian refugees would inadvertently allow terrorists to infiltrate as well. In light of such concerns, polls show that a majority of Americans oppose resettling Syrian refugees within our boarders. In addition, over half of US governors oppose allowing these refugees to relocate in our cities.[16] Yet what if your group

---

[15]While these suggestions are applicable to both live speaking situations and social media, we envision you applying our advice while speaking in front of a local city council meeting.

[16]Margaret Talev, "Poll: Most Americans Oppose Letting in Syrian Refugees," *Orange County Register*, November 19, 2015, News 5.

wants to persuade civic leaders that the plight of these refugees far out-weighs concerns about allowing terrorist cells entrance? At the next town hall forum, you are given ten minutes to present your case. How might statistics and stories help your argument?

Statistics. A statistic is a numerical or quantitative measure of scope or frequency of occurrence. To help the audience and civic leaders at the town hall meeting understand the seriousness of the Syrian crisis, statistics might be useful. Consider the following:

- Fifty percent of Syria's population—more than 11 million Syrians—have been displaced.

- Over 400,000 people have been killed.

- More than 50 percent of Syrian refugees are children.

- The majority of refugees are frantically seeking entrance into five countries—Turkey, Lebanon, Jordan, Iraq, and Egypt. Each of these countries is significantly overburdened and thus turning away refugees.[17]

The strength of statistics is that they alert your audience to how widespread the tragedy has become. Statistics can also help alleviate fears of terrorists hiding in the midst of refugees. According to the US State Department, only 2 percent of Syrian refugees who have been admitted to the United States fit the demographics of terrorists—military age men with no families. The vast majority of refugees seeking access are women, children under eighteen, and the elderly.[18]

However, statistics also come with limitations. In our cynical world of political spin, audiences have become suspicious of statistics. American humorist Mark Twain once quipped that there are three types of falsehoods: lies, damned lies, and statistics. If you use statistics to buttress your case, you'll need to be prepared to cite the source and vouch for their validity.[19]

---

[17]"Quick Facts: What You Need to Know About the Syria Crisis," MercyCorps, October 13, 2016, www.mercycorps.org/articles/iraq-jordan-lebanon-syria-turkey/quick-facts-what-you-need-know-about-syria-crisis.

[18]Jonathan Merritt, "Three Facts About the Syrian Refugee Crisis Many Christians Overlook," Religion News Service, November 17, 2015, http://jonathanmerritt.religionnews.com /2015/11/17/3-facts-about-syrian-refugee-situation-that-some-christians-overlook/#sthash. fvewp0KX.dpuf.

[19]For an excellent discussion of how to assess the validity of statistics, see Jennifer Y. Abbot, Todd F. McDorman, David M. Timmerman, and L. Jill Lamberton, *Public Speaking and Democratic*

Also, while statistics give us scope they can also leave us emotionally un-moved. After all, it can be difficult to relate to a statistic. On the other hand, stories can put a face on statistics.

Stories. In the past few years there has been a major shift in communi-cation toward narrative and stories. The shift gained momentum when com-munication scholar Walter Fisher asserted that humans are *homo narrans*—natural storytellers.[20] Other scholars agree and argue that narrative isn't merely our preferred way to communicate, it "represents a universal medium of human consciousness."[21] In other words, we think in stories. While your statistics concerning the Syrian problem have introduced those at the town hall meeting to the massive size of the crisis, how might an individual story of suffering add to your argument?

A face was put on the Syrian refugee crisis when photos surfaced of the body of a three-year-old boy, Aylan Kurdi, washed up on the shores of Bodrum, Turkey. Aylan's parents had made the desperate decision to take their two sons and flee Syria, embarking on the treacherous journey across Turkey to Europe in hope of joining a relative in Canada. Spending all they had, they hired a Turkish smuggler and set off with nine other refuges in a five-meter-long dinghy. At the first sign of rough waters the smuggler jumped ship. Soon the boat capsized and all went into the water. The father frantically tried to hold on to his wife and two boys. Slowly, each one slipped through his arms and drowned. The father treaded water for three hours, searching for his family, before he was rescued. The next morning the world was shocked to see a picture of Aylan's lifeless body facedown in water.[22] The power of a story is that it helps the audience imagine how the Syrian crisis affects specific individuals and families. The weakness of a story is that

---

Participation: Speech, Deliberations, and Analysis in the Civic Realm (New York: Oxford University Press, 2016), 267-87.

[20]Fisher defines narration as "symbolic actions—words and/or deeds—that have sequence and meaning for those who live, create, and interpret them." Walter Fisher, *Human Communication as Narration: Toward a Philosophy of Reason, Value, and Action* (Columbia: University of South Carolina Press, 1987), 63.

[21]John Lucaites and Celeste Condit, "Reconstructing Narrative Theory: A Functional Perspec-tive," *Journal of Communication* 35 (1985): 90.

[22]Adam Withnall, "Aylan Kurdi's Story: How a Small Syrian Child Came to Be Washed Up on a Beach in Turkey," *The Independent*, September 3, 2015, www.independent.co.uk/news/world/europe/aylan-kurdi-s-story-how-a-small-syrian-child-came-to-be-washed-up-on-a-beach-in-turkey-10484588.html.

it is limited in how much it can portray. While the story of Aylan and his family is tragic, the death of three Syrians does not constitute a global crisis. When put together, statistics and narratives can show *both* scope and specific examples of injustice.

CONSTRAINTS AND SOCIAL MEDIA

Two constraints that counterpublics regularly face are how to mobilize fellow activists and how to engage an often-insulated rhetorical audience. Social media is well suited to help overcome these constraints in several ways.

Mobilizing counterpublics. First, social media allows you to get the word out quickly. Every day over 1.18 billion people log in to Facebook and roughly 500 million tweets are sent around the world.[23] Social media helps groups raise awareness of issues, spread critical information, and call for immediate response. Requests for donations or volunteers can be sent in real time in response to the particular needs of your community. Also, social media offers people an opportunity to slowly become more engaged and invested in your counterpublic group. Even if a person merely retweets or shares a Facebook post, it can cultivate an emotional commitment to your cause and potentially open the door for further action, thus converting social media enthusiasts into social media activists. Psychologist Pamela Rutledge argues that social media also brings people together in that a message from someone in your network gives the information a personal touch. Receiving a message through Facebook, Twitter, or Instagram has the validity and intimacy of hearing it by word of mouth.[24]

Engaging the rhetorical audience. Gaining access to individuals who have the power to evoke change is difficult and fraught with obstacles. Social media allows counterpublics the opportunity to bypass these constraints and make immediate contact. Consider the following example. Ed Royce is a congressman in California's Thirty-Ninth District and chair of the influential House Foreign Affairs Committee. In addition to an office in Washington, DC, he has an office in our hometown of Brea, California.

---

[23]"The Top 20 Valuable Facebook Statistics—Updated December 2016," Zephoria, https://zephoria .com/top-15-valuable-facebook-statistics; David Sayce, "10 Billions Tweets . . . Number of Tweets per Day?," David Sayce blog, March 2016, www.dsayce.com/social-media/10-billions-tweets.

[24]Pamela B. Rutledge, "Four Ways Social Media Is Redefining Activism," *Positively Media* (blog), October 6, 2010, www.psychologytoday.com/blog/positively-media/201010/four-ways-social-media-is-redefining-activism.

At his Brea office, appointments with him are made through a district scheduler and have to be booked months in advance. Royce's availability is limited and slots are in demand. However, like most members of Congress today, he has a Facebook page and Twitter account and is accessible through email. A staffer catalogues each and every email, post to Facebook, and tweet from constituents. If a consistent theme arises, Royce receives a personal briefing. My son, Jason Muehlhoff, served as an intern in Royce's Brea office, and his job was to daily monitor, catalogue, and chart trends from social media and pass them up the command chain if warranted. How should counterpublics strategically use social media to foster a positive communication climate with civic leaders such as Royce?

Willard Richan, professor emeritus at Temple University, has taught social welfare policy and lobbying for thirty years. He makes a key observation about members of the rhetorical audience: "There are two things nobody wants to be: evil and stupid."[25] The goal of organizing a social media blitz aimed at civic leaders is to assure them that you don't think they are either. We suggest the following. First, make sure to note and thank the official for decisions, bills proposed, or actions you find commendable. One aspect of a healthy communication climate is acknowledgment. Even with decisions that don't go your way, make sure to acknowledge how much time and consideration went into them: "I'm sure this wasn't an easy decision, and we thank you for seriously considering our views." Second, when organizing social media blasts remember that the first person reading the messages will be an intern. Numbers will have to be high for the topic to trend. However, only local constituents are important to a civic leader. It won't matter how many emails or tweets are sent if they are predominantly from outsiders. Jason Muehlhoff was told that every tweet or email from a local constituent would be seen as representing ten people. Third, remember that these officials are human beings who have birthdays, wedding anniversaries, and other meaningful events. So make sure to send cards and notes that recognize they have a life outside of politics.

Regardless of what type of evidence you offer or what medium you use, the most important aspect of your message is to foster identification with your audience that will allow them to consider your evidence.

---

[25]Willard C. Richan, *Lobbying for Social Change*, 2nd ed. (New York: Haworth Press, 1996), 119.

IDENTIFICATION

The most salient issue a speaker faces, asserts rhetorical scholar Kenneth Burke, is the perceived alienation or separation between the audience and the speaker. Thus, one of the main goals of a speaker is to proclaim some sense of unity. "If men were not apart from one another, there would be no need for the rhetorician to proclaim unity."[26] How can you help the rhetorical audience you are addressing see that although you may disagree about some issues, you can still identify with them? The answer to this question is at the heart of effective rhetoric. Burke forcefully states, "You can *persuade a man only insofar as* you can talk his language by speech, gesture, tonality, order, image, attitude, idea, identifying your ways with his."[27] Burke reminds us that every audience we encounter is both similar to and different from us. As a speaker, will you choose to focus on commonalities or divisions? Identification is achieved when a speaker doesn't ignore differences between her and the audience, but rather chooses to highlight how she is similar in either attitude or image. In our discussion of loose connections (chapter seven) we'll consider how similar ideas or causes can unify us, so our comments here will focus on the power of image. Simply put, when others view us do they see glimpses of themselves?

Most people in public office readily acknowledge that they hold a different status—by wealth or power—than their constituents. If you are a representative or senator, how do you show you still can relate to the public? Now, imagine you are married to the president of the United States. How can you possibly show you identify with average Americans? Target shoppers in Alexandria, Virginia, were shocked to learn that they had been shopping with an incognito Michelle Obama, dressed in a ball cap and sunglasses. While secret service members were scattered throughout the store, apparently no one noticed them or the first lady. When they were told what had happened, the response from unsuspecting shoppers was overwhelmingly positive and showed the power of image to foster identification. "Just shows she's regular people," noted one surprised shopper. One registered Republican wanted to make sure

---

[26]Kenneth Burke, *A Rhetoric of Motives* (Berkeley: University of California Press, 1969), 22.
[27]Ibid., 38 (emphasis added).

the reporter understood that he disagreed with Obama's policies, but thought her shopping at a store he regularly frequents was "terrific."[28]

Yet what is so terrific about it? Showing how two seemingly unlike things (a Republican voter and the spouse of the most powerful Democrat in the nation) can be brought together (shopping at Target) is what Burke calls *consubstantiality*. This odd-sounding religious term reminds us that despite all the causes of division—differing ideologies, convictions, styles of dress, backgrounds—there is a substance that brings us together—such as a desire for community, caring for families, love of the arts, common humanity, or pursuit of love. In what ways can we be brought together, even momentarily, with those who disagree with us?

The difficulty is that our coming together is often short-circuited when we Christians choose to separate from non-Christians in terms of education (home school or private Christian schools rather than public), sports (participating in church leagues), music (excluding secular music in favor of explicitly Christian), holidays (organizing a harvest fest rather than participating in Halloween), fashion (viewing tattoos or body piercing as worldly), and so on. For many Christian counterpublics the highest value seems to be to communicate how different we are from others. However, the goal of rhetoric is to show how similar the speaker is to the audience.

While identification can be rhetorically powerful, it also entails the same risks as the use of humor discussed earlier. Michelle Obama encountered criticism when during the same shopping trip to Target she also wanted to claim identification with those who experience racism. According to her, a woman came up to her in an aisle and asked if she could reach something on the top shelf for her. Though oblivious to her political status, the woman wasn't oblivious to Michelle's race and felt comfortable imposing on her. When later discussing the issue of race, the first lady used this encounter as an example of impositions that happen regularly to people of color—including herself. Did she go too far in attempting to identify? Is asking a person of color to reach for the top shelf comparable to examples of racism repeatedly shown on local and national news? Did her attempt to identify help or hurt her image? Public opinion in this case was split.

---

[28]Shomari Stone, reporter, "First Lady Michelle Obama Shops at Target," NBC Washington, September 30, 2011, www.youtube.com/watch?v=4WfrmWwE8UY.

In contrast, civil rights activist Rachel Dolezal's attempt to cultivate identification was roundly denounced. As a black woman Dolezal was proud to
be a graduate of the historically black Howard University and to lead the
Spokane, Washington, chapter of the National Association for the Advancement of Colored People (NAACP). However, when it surfaced that
Dolezal was born to white parents and only *identified* as being black, she
faced a storm of criticism and questions. Pictures surfaced of a white teenage
Dolezal, contradicting her current look of a woman with dark skin. When
asked whether she was black her answers ranged from "I'm black" to "I'm
definitely not white" to "I identify as black." She explains: "Nothing about
being white describes who I am . . . I'm more black than I am white. So on
a level of values, lived experience—currently, I mean, in this moment, that's
. . . that's the answer. That's the accurate answer from my truth."[29] One
NAACP organizer felt "duped," while another angrily tweeted, "BEING
BLACK is not a pair of earrings that you can just throw on to match your
outfit when you feel like it!"[30] In the face of such criticism Dolezal was
forced to resign, her reputation irrevocably compromised.

While identification is central to persuasion, Christian counterpublics
will need to carefully navigate being seen as "one of us" without being
disingenuous or unethical. Burke forces us to wrestle with probing questions: What causes can we legitimately adopt as being central to God advancing his kingdom? Are there causes that we should adopt simply to
support and identify with others? How can we commune with others—in
terms of styles of dress, participation in community life, forms of entertainment—to show we identify with fellow community members without
compromising biblical standards?

HOW TO BEGIN?

After adjusting to meet whatever constraints you are facing and negoti-
ating the fitting response, how do you actually start? While each situation
and subsequent fitting response will be different, we suggest a communication strategy that not only presents a persona of humility but also

---

[29]Dylan Stableford, "Rachel Dolezal: 'I Identify as Black,'" Yahoo News, June 16, 2015, http://news
    .yahoo.com/rachel-dolezal-naacp-black-white-misrepresenting-interview-today-110003467.html.
    [30]Ibid.

shows an audience that you understand and can identify with the merits of their position. Professional mediators Douglas Stone, Bruce Patton, and Shelia Heen suggest that most speakers make a pivotal—and sometimes unrecoverable—mistake in how they open lines of communication. "Often, we start from inside our own story. We describe the problem from our own perspective and, in doing so, trigger just the reactions we hope to avoid. We begin from precisely the place the other person thinks is causing the problem."[31]

These experts remind us that within every disagreement there are at least three stories or perspectives. Every disagreement includes each group's story and an invisible third story. The third story is "one a keen observer would tell, someone with no stake in your particular problem."[32] One key in presenting your message is to begin with a version that fairly represents both sides of the issue.

Going back to the divisive issue of allowing Syrian refugees sanctuary in our country, how would an outsider describe differing perspectives? The answer to that question in turn lays a foundation to your opening statement. Consider the following possible introduction:

> All of us are aware of the plight of Syrian refugees—especially the threat to children—and want to find a compassionate solution. We also recognize the potential risks of allowing refugees entrance in light of recent terrorist attacks. One side argues that we can secure our borders and still offer assistance to refugees through sending money and medical supplies to those in need. Others think the way to help refugees—with minimal risk—is to open our borders. Each side wants to find a solution that is both compassionate and prudent.

It is absolutely vital that a third story objectively state the best version of each position. It's also imperative to be generous to the intentions and actions of both sides. As Christians we seem to struggle with acknowledging the positive aspects of another group's actions—particularly if, in our estimation, they don't match up with biblical standards. For example, when movies tackling biblical themes—such as *Noah* and *Exodus: Gods and Kings*—went mainstream, Christians were quick to attack. "How dare Hollywood alter

---

[31]Douglas Stone, Bruce Patton, and Shelia Heen, *Difficult Conversations: How to Discuss What Matters Most* (New York: Penguin, 1999), 148.
[32]Ibid., 150.

biblical stories!" A film critic from *Christianity Today* offered an alternative perspective that may be useful to Christian counterpublics.

> Rather than bashing another not-perfectly-biblical Bible movie, what if we praised its beauty? What if we celebrated the fact that, as *Noah* did back in April, *Exodus: Gods and Kings* will likely increase online searches for relevant Bible passages by 300 percent or more? What if instead of issuing nitpicky complaints as the theological police, Christians extended compassion and thanks as the people of God, grateful to see parts of the Bible's story told on screen?[33]

The same could be said about those who are opposing your solution to the Syrian refugee crisis. Instead of starting with a negative assessment of your opposition, why not start with a third story that praises the other's attempt to balance protection from terrorists and acts of compassion? The alternative to starting with a third story rooted in goodwill was evidenced by former President Obama in his attempt to goad Republican leaders into allowing sanctuary to Syrians: "Apparently they are scared of widows and orphans coming into the United States . . . they are scared of 3-year-old orphans. That doesn't seem so tough to me."[34]

The benefit of starting with a third story that depicts the good intentions of others is that it begins a positive communication spiral where generosity, common ground, and goodwill garner generosity, common ground, and goodwill.

CONCLUSION

"Plans fail for lack of counsel, but with many advisers they succeed" (Prov 15:22). In this chapter you've received counsel on the many steps—choosing a persona, identifying with your audience, providing evidence, starting with a third story—to delivering an effective message. While it may seem like a lot to keep in perspective as you address your audience, remember this simple rule from ancient advisers: "A person finds joy in giving an apt reply— and how good is a timely word" (Prov 15:23). This applies not only to those

---

[33]Brett McCracken, "Exodus: Gods and Kings," *Christianity Today*, December 10, 2014, www.christianitytoday.com/ct/2014/december-web-only/exodus.html.

[34]Carl M. Cannon, "Unsettling Words on Resettling Refugees," *Orange County Register*, November 22, 2015, Opinion 5.

imparting wisdom but to counterpublics seeking to cultivate a *timely word* that fits diverse communication situations. Rather than forcing your topic on others, it's wise to allow the situation to shape your message.

Perhaps the best occasion to deliver your message isn't when you're standing behind a podium watching the clock as your time allotment dwindles, or increasing the word count in your blog. How might your message be more effective if given on the streets as you form partnerships with those who disagree with you? How might loose connections with opposing counterpublics and strong publics help you advance your message?

HARRIET BEECHER STOWE AND *UNCLE TOM'S CABIN*

WHEN ABRAHAM LINCOLN MET Harriet Beecher Stowe, the author of *Uncle Tom's Cabin*, he is reported to have said, "So you're the little woman who wrote the book that made this great war!"[1] On the face of it, this seems an outrageous statement. So many enormous political forces converged in the Civil War that it would be stunning if a single work of fiction even made the list of contributing factors. But though there is an element of hyperbole in Lincoln's statement, even in the more subdued language of Will Kaufmann, a twenty-first-century Civil War scholar, Stowe's work is acknowledged as helping to "lay the groundwork for the Civil War."[2] Stowe is noteworthy not as the creator of a counterpublic—abolitionism long preceded her—but as a person who completely transformed the discourse of a counterpublic by the way she crafted and delivered her message. Therefore she is a particularly apt example of several principles mentioned in the last two chapters: adopting an appropriate persona, appealing to shared starting points, moving people to hate what you hate and love what you love, and effectively operating within constraints.

ADOPTING AN APPROPRIATE PERSONA

When *Uncle Tom's Cabin* was published in 1852, America was in the midst of a culture war not unlike the one we are experiencing today. By the 1850s the core of the abolition movement had abandoned the hope of civil discourse and embraced outrage and direct confrontation. One of the most famous voices of outrage belonged to the abolitionist journalist William Lloyd Garrison:

---

[1]Mark Galli, "Christianity and the Civil War: A Gallery of Firebrands and Visionaries," *Christian History* 33 (1992), https://www.christianhistoryinstitute.org:443/magazine/article/civil-war-a-gallery-of-firebrands-and-visionaries.

[2]Will Kaufman, *The Civil War in American Culture* (Edinburgh: Edinburgh University Press, 2006), 18.

On [slavery] I do not wish to think, or to speak, or write, with moderation. No! No! Tell a man whose house is on fire to give a moderate alarm; tell him to moderately rescue his wife from the hands of the ravisher; tell the mother to gradually extricate her babe from the fire into which it has fallen;—but urge me not to use moderation in a cause like the present. I am in earnest—I will not equivocate—I will not excuse—I will not retreat a single inch—AND I WILL BE HEARD.[3]

Garrison advocated that abolitionists "secede from the government." He refused to vote. He condemned the Constitution as a "covenant with death and an agreement with hell" because it protected slavery, so he celebrated the Fourth of July by burning a copy of it.[4] In all cases, he took the tactic of abandoning shared starting points and embracing the persona of a culture warrior. There was no humility in his persona, no humor, no appeal to common ground—all of which had a predictable effect. Garrison and other abolitionists were like tourists shouting to make themselves understood without learning the language of their audience. Their stridency squandered the moral high ground through belligerence, impatience, outrage, and schism.

A similar ethos had spread aboard. An American academic traveling in Great Britain wrote home about his experiences with the British abolition movement. He commented that "ultra Abolitionism here has the same *nasty Radicalism*, the same dogmatic narrowness, that it has in America."[5] Though he personally disdained slavery, he noted that his experience at home and abroad left him moving further way from the abolitionist movement. Interestingly enough, that traveler was none other than Calvin Stowe, Harriet Beecher Stowe's husband.

Harriet Beecher Stowe's response to these rather dismal rhetorical conditions was to adopt the persona of a storyteller. It seems Stowe share Fisher's conviction mentioned in chapter six that humans are *homo narrans*. Rather than fight a battle, she told a story—or painted a picture, as she put it in a letter to her editor, Gamaliel Bailey:

---

[3]Nancy Koester, *Harriet Beecher Stowe: A Spiritual Life* (Grand Rapids: Eerdmans, 2014), 184.
[4]Ibid., 185.
[5]Joan D. Hedrick, *Harriet Beecher Stowe: A Life* (New York: Oxford University Press, 1994), 100 (emphasis original).

My vocation is simply that of a painter, and my object will be to hold up in the most lifelike and graphic manner possible Slavery, its reverses, changes, and the negro character, which I have had ample opportunities for studying. . . . There is no arguing with *pictures*, and everybody is impressed by them whether they mean to be or not.[6]

Writing a novel rather than an abolitionist pamphlet allowed her to steal past the "watchful dragons" of the heart. This is a phrase C. S. Lewis used to describe the ability of fiction to get behind our normal defenses.[7] Appeals to both reason and sentiment seem to gain a different access when put into a fictional account, a fact that Stowe masterfully employed a full century before Lewis. Among the most powerful pictures she painted were the characters caught up in the moral issues surrounding slavery. Stowe had a genius for using these fictional characters to get past "the watchful dragons." She cast slaves as leading characters instead of bit parts or literary stage props. Stowe wanted her readers to see slaves as human beings in their own right, thereby forcing her readers to feel the fundamental contradiction of slavery: that a human being, by definition, cannot be owned.[8]

Interestingly enough, Stowe serves as an example of not only the effective use of story but also the effective use of statistics. The year after *Uncle Tom's Cabin* was published, Stowe wrote a treatise titled *A Key to Uncle Tom's Cabin*. Its descriptive subtitle explains the work well: "Presenting the Original Facts and Documents upon Which the Story Is Founded, Together with Corroborative Statements Verifying the Truth of the Work." Her fiction was compelling, but it was fiction. To convince minds and not just move hearts, she had to respond to her critics who claimed that her novel exaggerated the evils of slavery. Stowe collected and summarized mountains of statistics and carefully recorded personal testimonies of numerous slaves. The resulting *Key to Uncle Tom's Cabin*, a bestseller in its own right, never had the impact of the novel but was no less vital to the cause of abolition since it so effectively complemented and supplemented her work of fiction.

---

[6]Ibid., 129.
[7]C. S. Lewis, *On Stories: And Other Essays on Literature* (New York: Harvest Books, 2002), 47.
[8]Koester, *Harriet Beecher Stowe*, 129.

APPEALING TO SHARED STARTING POINTS

Though Stowe wrote at a time when discussions of slavery on both sides were vicious, violent, and vitriolic, there was actually common ground hidden just beneath the surface. To put it in the language of chapter five, Stowe recognized that there were shared starting points and universal values that could be used to make an argument that would be persuasive to the other side—or at the very least comprehensible. In the early 1800s many leaders in the antislavery movement came from the South. In 1818 Presbyterians *unanimously* declared at their General Assembly that "the voluntary enslaving of one part of the human race by another" is "utterly inconsistent with the law of God."[9] Many of the members of this assembly were from the South. On the other hand, Northerners were not nearly as distant from the slave trade as they appeared to be. Much of the foreign slave trade in the United States came through New York's harbors. It is unrealistic to paint the moral intuitions and values of the North and South as being completely opposite on the matter of slavery. There was certainly some common ground to which abolitionists could appeal if they were simply willing to avoid moral outrage and direct confrontation.

Stowe's strategy for exploiting this common ground was brilliant. She refused to demonize the South or deify the North. Not only did she avoid making Northern whites morally superior to Southern whites in her book, she shunned almost all the traditional stereotypes. Simon Legree, the quintessential evil slaveholder, was a Northerner by birth. Miss Ophelia is a good Christian Northerner, but is confronted with her own deep-seated prejudice. Augustin St. Clare is a slaveholder, but surprisingly enlightened and opposed to the institution as a whole. One might expect him to be a devout Christian, but again Stowe surprised her readers by making him deeply cynical of religion. She skillfully skirted her reader's defense mechanisms by not pointing the finger of moral outrage at conveniently evil individuals. Instead, she portrayed slavery as an institution that corrupted all it touched: black or white, male or female, old or young, religious or irreligious. She invited her readers to stand on common ground, avoid ad hominem arguments and stereotypes, and simply consider the institution of slavery on its own (de)merits.

---

[9]Galli, "Christianity and the Civil War."

MAKING THE MESSAGE COMPELLING

Chapter five states that a profound challenge for counterpublics is motivating people to "hate the things you hate, love what you cherish, and feel sorrow over issues you find disheartening." Few people have done this more effectively than Harriet Beecher Stowe. Once she slipped past the watchful dragons and obtained access to the heart, she knew exactly how to move that heart. Her novel was published as a serial, and is therefore filled with tear-jerking and cliffhanger moments. The transparent appeal to emotion has led critics such as Ann Douglas to claim that *Uncle Tom's Cabin* is "a great book not because it is a great novel, but because it is a great revival sermon, aimed directly at the conversion of its hearers."[10] But this book reached far more than unsophisticated readers prone to cheap sentimentalism. Henry James noted that Stowe's novel was, "for an immense number of people, much less a book than a state of vision, of feeling and of consciousness in which they didn't sit and read and appraise, . . . but walked and talked and laughed and cried."[11] Leo Tolstoy includes *Uncle Tom's Cabin* on his short list of "examples of the highest art flowing from love of God and man."[12] Vincent van Gogh was also an outspoken admirer of the book. Stowe's writing did not merely leave marks on a page, it left marks on the hearts and souls of all who read it.

Stowe also moved people through humor. She obviously did not read the University of Missouri study discussed in chapter six, but her intuitions on the use of humor were flawless. Her readers laughed at the bumbling of those appointed to prepare horses to pursue a runaway slave, the light-hearted caricatures of otherwise loathsome figures, the antics of Topsy, and the comic irony of a senator who condemns sentimentality even as he finds himself spellbound beneath its sway. Thomas Gossett notes that "humor was a way of establishing the reality of the characters of the novel, especially that of the blacks," making the reader's sympathy with the black characters "less abstract and more personal."[13]

---

[10]Ann Douglas, *The Feminization of American Culture* (New York: Knopf, 1977), 245.

[11]David S. Reynolds, *Mightier Than the Sword: "Uncle Tom's Cabin" and the Battle for America* (New York: W. W. Norton, 2011), xi.

[12]Andrew Delbanco, "The Impact of 'Uncle Tom's Cabin,'" *New York Times*, June 24, 2011, www.nytimes.com/2011/06/26/books/review/book-review-mightier-than-the-sword-by-david-s-reynolds.html.

[13]Cited in Koester, *Harriet Beecher Stowe*, 130.

A FITTING RESPONSE GIVEN CONSTRAINTS

As stated in chapter six, there are constraints in every communication situation, and Stowe did not merely adapt to her constraints—she exploited them. She worked in volatile times; even in Northern cities like Philadelphia, abolitionists often risked angry mobs. If they went farther south, they would certainly be lynched. An obvious alternative was to send literature. Huge numbers of newspapers, tracts, and pamphlets had been sent South. But few reached their intended destination because the flood of abolitionist pamphlets had led to the establishment of postal censors in most of the South.[14] Stowe responded differently to these constraints when she wrote *Uncle Tom's Cabin*. Since it was first distributed by serialized release in a magazine, it gained a huge following before the last pages had even been written. Upon release as a completed novel, it was an instant bestseller. Then its distribution relied on people actively seeking the book rather than passively receiving unsolicited mail.

Stowe is a striking contrast to William Lloyd Garrison, who shouted "I will be heard!" Ultimately it was Stowe who was heard, not Garrison. Hedrick notes,

> In just one week the entire print run of five thousand copies sold out. The next week, another five thousand sold out. After three months, the *New York Daily Times* reported Stowe's earnings to exceed $10,000—more than any author had ever received from a book in that length of time. Within one year *Uncle Tom's Cabin* had sold 300,000 copies in the U.S. and 1.5 million in Great Britain.[15]

The novel was translated into at least twenty-three languages, and stage adaptations played to capacity crowds.[16] In the United States, one million copies were sold before the Civil War.

Perhaps even more impressive is the testimony of critics. One Southern critic described *Uncle Tom's Cabin* as "perhaps the most influential novel ever published, a verbal earthquake, an ink-and-paper tidal wave."[17] When a Confederate diplomat in London failed to win formal British support for the South, he explained to Jefferson Davis that too many Britons had read

---

[14]Galli, "Christianity and the Civil War."

[15]Hedrick, *Harriet Beecher Stowe*, 138.

[16]Mark Galli and Ted Olsen, *131 Christians Everyone Should Know* (Nashville: B&H Publishing Group, 2000), 120.

[17]Ibid., 118.

Uncle Tom's Cabin.[18] Susan Bradford stated, upon the secession of the state of Florida, "If Mrs. Harriet Beecher Stowe had died before she wrote *Uncle Tom's Cabin*, this would never have happened. . . . Isn't it strange how much harm a pack of lies can do?"[19] If imitation is the sincerest form of flattery, Stowe was well flattered. *Uncle Tom's Cabin* spawned nearly thirty proslavery knock-offs with titles such as *Aunt Phillis's Cabin*, *Southern Life as It Is*, *Frank Freeman's Barber Shop: A Tale*, and *Uncle Robin in His Cabin in Virginia, and Tom Without One in Boston*.[20]

Though thousands of gallons of ink had been spilled in decades of abolitionist articles and pamphlets, all of them combined had less impact than Stowe's *Uncle Tom's Cabin*. Truly Stowe stands as an exemplar of one who transformed the discourse of a counterpublic. Her wisdom, creativity, sensitivity, and ability to understand her times and audience make her a particularly salutary model for Christian counterpublics today. In all likelihood, applying Stowe's wisdom and example now would involve making movies rather than writing serialized novels. However, her studied avoidance of predictable stereotypes, skillful practice of her genre, and refusal to descend into sermonic interjections to get her point across are every bit as apropos to twenty-first-century movie making as they were to nineteenth-century novel writing.

---

[18]Koester, *Harriet Beecher Stowe*, 245.

[19]Galli and Olsen, *131 Christians Everyone Should Know*, 118.

[20]"Anti Uncle Tom Novels," Uncle Tom's Cabin and American Culture, http://utc.iath.virginia .edu/proslav/antitoms.html (accessed July 24, 2015).

7

LOOSE CONNECTIONS

Forging Unlikely Partnerships

FIVE HUNDRED STUDENTS MEET TO PRAY that the Christian perspective will make inroads on campus. In small groups they ask for open doors to further God's kingdom by helping others and showing Christ's compassion in tangible ways. They don't realize that less than half a mile away their prayers are being answered.

In the center of campus, one hundred students are gathered in a bold show of solidarity: a "Take Back the Night" march. The event, sponsored by feminist student groups, is designed to reclaim dangerous sections of campus by marching through them and shouting into the night, "We will not be afraid!" While the event attracts a diverse spectrum of students, not one of the twenty Christian organizations on campus is represented.

Imagine a different scenario.

Five hundred students march arm-in-arm for the safety of women. Their roar is heard across campus: "This is our campus. We will not be afraid!" "What brought you out tonight?" a member of a feminist group asks the person next to her. She replies, "I'm part of a Christian group on campus that is concerned for the safety of women. It's a neglected issue and we want to lend our voice."

What other conversations might ensue in the days ahead as fellow marchers see each other in the cafeteria or classroom? What tasks might be accomplished and doors opened as we strategically link arms with non-Christians to act as co-counterpublics for community concerns? In *Soul of a Citizen*, social critic Paul Loeb observes that the idea of a private sanctuary is an illusion. In contrast, social activism gives fragmented communities and individuals a sense of camaraderie and helps them build significant friend-ships and partnerships.[1] The problem is that Christians and non-Christians often respond independently as they seek to meet needs, fortifying their sanctuaries. Only if we dismantle these sanctuaries through key partner-ships will our message be heard. The challenges our communities face provide an opportunity for counterpublics to overcome barriers and develop influential relationships.

The question for Christian counterpublics is not *if* we should respond to the physical and spiritual needs surrounding us. If we aim to imitate Christ, we must act. The question we must ask is, *How* will we meet the needs of our community—by ourselves or by linking arms with counterpublics outside our churches? In this chapter we will address this question as we consider the early church's willingness to partner with others to meet community needs, the benefits of linking arms with non-Christian counterpublics, and what attitudinal and communication changes need to occur to make short-term partnerships successful.

THE HISTORY OF LINKING ARMS

While modern Christians are tempted to retreat from culture and form for-tified sanctuaries, our history is filled with followers of Christ who felt an ownership and obligation to the cities in which they lived.

Helping Greco-Roman cities flourish was not easy and required Chris-tians and non-Christians to work together to rise above the often inhumane conditions. For example, though the city of Antioch was only two miles long and one mile wide, by the end of the first century it had a population of about 150,000. Its population density would be roughly 75,000 inhab-itants per square mile or 117 per acre.[2] To put this in perspective, in Chicago there are twenty-one inhabitants per acre, while New York City has thirty-seven per acre. Only the wealthy in Antioch could afford private houses, while most families were forced to live in cramped rooms within decaying

---

[1]Paul Rogat Loeb, *Soul of a Citizen: Living with Conviction in a Cynical Time* (New York: St. Martin's Griffin, 1999), 7.

[2]Rodney Stark, *The Rise of Christianity: How the Obscure, Marginal Jesus Movement Became the Dominant Religious Force in the Western World in a Few Centuries* (San Francisco: HarperCollins, 1996), 149.

multistoried tenements. Historian Jerome Carcopino estimates that in ancient Rome there was only one private house for every twenty-six blocks of apartments.[3] Due to such small dwellings, most of Antioch's citizens spent much time outside interacting with others. The massive crowding caused many challenges when it came to basic sanitation issues such as obtaining clean water, disposing of human waste, and removing garbage. Most cities did a poor job of managing these challenges, resulting in filth and disease that contributed to a life expectancy of less than thirty years.[4] To make city life work, all citizens had to pull together. In such dire situations Christian converts had a decision to make: Do we merely care for our own, or do we link arms with fellow citizens?

Two ancient letters give us a clue as to the response of these early Christian counterpublics. In a letter to the high priest of Galatia in AD 362, the emperor Julian expresses disappointment that religious leaders fail to equal the compassion shown by Christians, whom he refers to as Galileans. He writes: "I think that when the poor happened to be neglected and overlooked by the priests, the impious Galileans observed this and devoted themselves to benevolence."[5] In another letter, his exasperation grows: "The impious Galileans support not only their poor, but ours as well."[6]

The compassion of these early Christian counterpublics was not limited to merely helping fellow citizens, but included giving their lives for them. In an Easter letter, Bishop Dionysius commends believers for sacrificing for neighbors during a devastating plague that ravaged the Roman Empire around AD 260. "Heedless of danger, they took charge of the sick, attending to their every need and ministering to them in Christ, and with them departed this life serenely happy; for they were infected by others with disease, drawing on themselves the sickness of their neighbors and cheerfully accepting their pains."[7]

However, Christians sharing a common concern for the cities in which they lived was not limited to dire situations. Church historian Bruce Winter

---

[3]Jerome Carcopino, *Daily Life in Ancient Rome* (New Haven, CT: Yale University Press, 1940), 23.

[4]Keith Hopkins, "On the Probable Age Structure of the Roman Population," *Population Studies* 20 (1966): 245-64.

[5]Quoted in Paul Johnson, *A History of Christianity* (New York: Atheneum, 1976), 75.

[6]Ibid.

[7]Quoted in Stark, *Rise of Christianity*, 82.

points out that Christians often served as benefactors to help better city life. They "paid for public works from their private resources in order to enhance the environs of their cities."[8] Government officials made sure to take notice of such benefactors—both religious and nonreligious—and publicly acknowledge them. Winter argues that this type of public praise is what the apostle Paul is referring to when, in discussing the power local officials have to punish bad behavior and reward good, he writes, "Do what is right and you will be commended" (Rom 13:3). The apostle Peter adds to this theme when he suggests that God has specifically established authorities to publicly commend and draw attention to those who do civic good (1 Pet 2:14). Winter sums up his argument: "The picture emerges of a positive role being taken by rich Christians for the well-being of the community at large and the appropriateness and importance of due recognition by ruling authorities for their contribution."[9]

Early Christians thought it their duty to assist fellow citizens in caring for cities they both desired to flourish. John Stott notes that Christ "had himself come into the world, in order to share in the life of the human community, and he sent his followers into the world to do the same."[10] The followers of Jesus so mimicked his life and concerns in Antioch that there they first earned the name Christians, or "little Christs" (Acts 11:26).[11]

Many Christians today also feel the desire to meet the needs of their communities, but remain isolated when projects are accomplished internally with church funds and volunteers. Unlike Christian benefactors in the New Testament, believers today often give only to explicitly Christian projects. While we may minister to a community, are we perceived as being an integral part of it? Sociologists refer to the resources a community has at its disposal as social capital. Much like a hiker takes stock of supplies—three matches, one flashlight, a single canteen of water—a community takes stock of its resources when facing a tragedy. For instance, they may know that the

---

[8]Bruce Winter, *Seek the Welfare of the City: Christians as Benefactors and Citizens* (Grand Rapids: Eerdmans, 1994), 26.

[9]Ibid., 39.

[10]John Stott, *Decisive Issues Facing Christians Today* (Old Tappan, NJ: Revell, 1990), 11.

[11]Stott suggests that citizens of Antioch were known for their wit and that the term "little Christs" most likely originated not as a term of derision but merely one of familiarity or even jocularity. John Stott, *The Spirit, the Church, and the World: The Message of Acts* (Downers Grove, IL: InterVarsity Press, 1990), 205.

Rotary Club can answer an appeal for money, the local high school can be used for an emergency shelter, and so on. A local church must ask whether it is perceived as vital to the community's social capital or just a group of people who merely take care of their own.

In his provocative study of how a marginalized group of religious followers became a dominate power in the Western world, sociologist Rodney Stark argues that early Christians in cities like Antioch were clearly seen as a vibrant part of social capital. "Since Antioch suffered acutely from all of these urban problems, it was in acute need of solutions. No wonder the early Christian missionaries were so warmly received in this city. For what they brought was not simply an urban movement, but a *new culture* capable of making life in Greco-Roman cities more tolerable."[12] Far from being isolated, these Christian counterpublics were welcome comrades in the fight to make daily life workable.

In any society Christians will be to some extent out of place. Yet if we are to follow the tradition of these first followers, or little Christs, we must give ourselves to strategic partnerships in order to meet civic needs. How would these partnerships work on a practical level?

LOOSE CONNECTIONS

What we advocate is described by sociologist Robert Wuthnow as *loose connections*. Through his research, Wuthnow has found that many Americans sense a fragmentation of their communities and are open to making connections with others to meet complex communal challenges. However, these connections are often informal, temporary, and topic specific. "Instead of cultivating lifelong ties with their neighbors, or joining organizations that reward faithful long-term service, people come together around specific needs and to work on projects that have definite objectives."[13] What characterizes a loose connection is the understanding that communities or organizations can have divergent, even contradicting beliefs but still partner in addressing a common concern.

For any association to work, participants will need to navigate what sociologists call the definition of the situation. The effectiveness of our

---

[12]Stark, *Rise of Christianity*, 162.
[13]Robert Wuthnow, *Loose Connections: Joining Together in America's Fragmented Communities* (Cambridge, MA: Harvard University Press, 1998), 8.

interaction will be determined by answers to three questions. First, what are the beliefs I value for my group and myself? Second, what beliefs do I perceive that you and your group value? Third, what are we trying to do together? For example, consider the Take Back the Night march described earlier in this chapter. As a feminist organizer interacts with Christians joining the march, how would she answer these questions? While she believes her motives center on making the campus more safe for female students (question 1), what does she believe about the motives of unexpected Christian participants (question 2)? If she believes they are equally concerned about campus safety (question 3), then the loose connection can flourish. However, if she believes joining the march is merely a cover for trying to convert her to Christianity, then the partnership is doomed to failure. Equally important is how Christian marchers define the situation. Do I care about the safety of women, or do I merely want to evangelize? While it is reasonable for Christians to hope participating in civic activism will allow discussions about faith, is that the primary reason for partnering? If the only reason we participate in the march is to convert, then we risk being disingenuous at the start.

Loose connections sound inviting, but what would it look like for a Christian counterpublic to partner with a distinctively non-Christian counterpublic? Is it possible for two vastly different organizations to come together for a common good? There are two distinct voices that seek to garner the attention of citizens in Colorado Springs, Colorado. The *Independent* is a fiercely liberal newspaper, while Focus on the Family is a staunchly conservative voice in today's culture wars. Their views on gay marriage, abortion, politics, and religion could not be more opposed. For years the *Independent* had unrelentingly attacked the founder of Focus on the Family, James Dobson. However, when Dobson retired and turned the leadership of his organization over to Jim Daly, an unexpected opportunity for a loose connection arose. Daly became aware of the *Independent*'s desire to address Colorado's ineffective foster care system. He too was concerned, and he set up a meeting with the paper's editors. While differing worldviews were obvious during the meeting, these two organizations were able to agree on a common project. The editor of the *Independent* explained, "There was at least one issue on which Focus and the *Indy* can agree: We want all kids to grow up in a loving home."[14] Foster care was the issue that allowed them to link arms for a common good.

While supporters of both the *Independent* and Focus on the Family were leery of the partnership, Daly stated, "Of course, we're going to have our differences philosophically; we understand that. But we're all big boys and girls, and so we can do the good things that we can do for the community without giving up our principles on either side of the aisle."[15] Together they sponsored an event called "Fostering Celebration," which focused on the needs of Colorado's foster care system.[16] This partnership led to Daly being on the cover of the *Independent* and giving an amazingly candid interview discussing significant issues facing Americans. Working on a common project and adopting a loose connection allowed two different organizations to address a common civic need. But why even form a partnership? Each organization had the resources to address this issue independently. Why risk cooperation? Specifically, what benefits does a conservative counterpublic organization like Focus on the Family gain by forming a loose connection with self-described liberal counterpublics? Are the benefits worth the cost?

BENEFITS OF LOOSE CONNECTIONS

Christian counterpublics gain five key benefits from merging resources and forming loose connections with non-Christian activists. First, stereotypes can be counteracted. Stereotyping consists of "exaggerated beliefs associated with a categorizing system."[17] People stereotype by ascribing a certain perceived characteristic to most or all members of a group, and by applying a particular generalization or characteristic of a group to a specific individual. In *Media, Culture, and the Religious Right*, two social critics select one word to describe conservative Christians: *mean*. These scholars assert

---

[14]J. Adrian Stanley, "Change of Focus: As the 'River of Culture' Rages On, Jim Daley Will Stay Rooted—but Respectful," *The Independent*, June 9-15, 2011, 17.

[15]Ibid.

[16]Distinguishing between macro- and micro-goals can protect this tenuous loose connection between Focus and the Indy. The macro-goal for both groups is strengthening a faulty foster care system, while the micro-goal is to define "family" in a way that matches each group's ideology. Daly's decision to first focus on macro goals allowed him time to garner trust and create a communication climate that eventually opened a door for communicating his organization's vision of what constitutes a family.

[17]Ronald Adler, Lawrence Rosenfeld, and Russell Proctor II, *Interplay: The Process of Interpersonal Communication* (New York: Oxford University Press, 2013), 125.

that Christians often rhetorically attack those who have little defense, such as welfare recipients or distraught women seeking abortions. They conclude that the form of social justice pursued by religious conservatives "is defined by compassion toward 'people like us,' with little regard for the effects on everybody else."[18] After surveying nonreligious Mosaics (those born between 1984 and 2002) and Busters (those born between 1965 and 1979), David Kinnaman and Gabe Lyons from the Barna Research Group report that Christians are described as hypocritical, convert obsessed, hostile to homosexuals, isolated, politically conservative, and judgmental.[19] Once immersed in a community that stereotypes others, adults tend to engage in stereotyping effortlessly and often unconsciously. "Once we create and hold stereotypes, we seek out isolated behaviors that support our inaccurate beliefs."[20]

By linking with other counterpublics to address concerns, Christians have a chance to counteract stereotypes held by other groups that keep them from hearing our message. However, counteracting stereotypes is a two-way proposition. For example, when we have students at our conservative Christian university write down the first word they think of associated with "feminists," common responses include *angry, man-haters, bra-burners, anti-family, lesbian, aggressive,* and *radical.*[21] Many of these students are merely reflecting the negative stereotypes held by religious authors and leaders. For example, regarding the fiftieth anniversary of Betty Freidan's landmark book *The Feminine Mystique*, conservative religious leader Pat Robertson commented, "Feminism is a socialist, anti-family, political movement that encourages women to leave their husbands, kill their children, practice witchcraft, destroy capitalism and become lesbians."[22]

---

[18]Linda Kintz and Julia Lesage, *Media, Culture, and the Religious Right* (Minneapolis: University of Minnesota Press, 1998), 18.

[19]David Kinnaman and Gabe Lyons, *UnChristian: What a New Generations Really Thinks About Christianity and Why It Matters* (Grand Rapids: Baker Books, 2007), 84-85.

[20]Adler, Rosenfeld, and Proctor, *Interplay*, 125.

[21]Some of these stereotypes are based on widespread misperceptions and have been debunked. For instance, gender scholars have long noted that the infamous "bra burning" protest of the 1968 Miss America pageant never happened and was the creation of a misinformed news reporter eager for a sensational scoop. For more, see Julia T. Wood, *Gendered Lives: Communication, Gender, and Culture,* 11th ed. (Stamford, CT: Cengage Learning, 2013), 80-89.

[22]"What Is Feminism? Some Famous Voices Give Their Opinion on What 'Feminism' Means," *Orange County Register*, February 26, 2013, Life 1.

When Christian and non-Christian counterpublics work together, both have the opportunity to decategorize each other by consciously setting aside assumptions or stereotypes and allowing individuals to define themselves based on present interactions.

A second benefit of partnering with other counterpublics is that we can explore radical solutions for complex issues. Today, *radical* is synonymous with extremism. Yet the word can be traced to the Latin *radix*, meaning "root." Christian counterpublics are not satisfied with addressing the symptoms of social problems; we desire to get to root causes. We are not alone in our desire. A few years ago, Germany's leaders struggled to make sense of a tragedy that has become all too common in our country. A teenage boy, recently expelled, returned to his school armed with a shotgun and five hundred rounds of ammunition. In ten horrifying minutes he murdered thirteen teachers, two students, and a police officer. "We now must ask ourselves the deeper questions," suggested the German minister of education, "of what is actually going on in our society when a young person causes such a disaster in such a way."[23] As Christian counterpublics we agree. While it would be foolish not to acknowledge the role violent video games, availability of hand guns, gun laws, and the absence of parental supervision play in school violence, it would be equally foolish to ignore the spiritual antecedents as expressed in the Scriptures. Though the Scriptures state that government and laws were instituted by God to curb evil (Rom 13:1), ultimately the human heart is desperately twisted and needs spiritual transformation (Jer 17:9). Partnering with others allows us to jointly explore the root reasons that undergird complex social issues, foster common ground, and explore possible solutions, including explicitly Christian ones.

Third, by linking arms we can develop trust. When two people start speaking, a communication climate is created. A climate is determined by factors such as, Does the other person acknowledge my perspective as valid? Are my expectations for the relationships being met? How committed is this person to me? Can I trust this person to be there when I need him or her? Communication scholars note that trust is foundational to a healthy relational climate. Without trust being firmly established, nothing else can

---

[23]Associated Press, "Expelled Student Kills 16, Self at School in Germany," *USA Today*, April 27, 2002, http://usatoday30.usatoday.com/news/world/2002/04/26/germany-shooting.htm.

proceed. Sadly, trust among Americans is at an all-time low. In 1972, when the General Social Survey first asked questions about trust, half of the respondents indicated they had trust in fellow Americans. Forty years later only one-third said they trust fellow citizens. Even more concerning, sociologists fear that it's too late for many Americans to become more trusting since the basis for a person's lifetime trust levels is established by the mid-twenties and is resistant to change.[24] If trust can be rebuilt, what factors cultivate it? Central to rebuilding trust is creating community and civic life, particularly in response to a catastrophic event or perceived threat. At the heart of being a counterpublic is the idea that key social issues, if not addressed, will cause harm to those around us. Responding to perceived threats provides time necessary to cultivate trust with others as we address common concerns. Simply put, you cannot rush trust. Communication scholar Julia Wood notes that we "learn to trust people over time as we interact with them and discover they do what they say they will and they don't betray us."[25]

Fourth, we can learn from others. A few years ago our university made it a point to address diversity and potential hidden racism. While it was beneficial to consult fellow faculty and leading Christian scholars and theologians, it would have been shortsighted not to consult those outside the Christian community. Postmodern authors such as Michael Eric Dyson, Anna Deavere Smith, Trin Minhah, and bell hooks have all embraced race as the key issue of our day. They each have deeply felt the sting of racism and have chosen to bring these issues under the microscope of postmodern thought. As believers called to address these same issues, we would benefit by learning from their observations. While some of our answers may differ, we most certainly care about the same questions. After spending years researching and writing about social activism, Paul Loeb advises, "The lesson I learned—and it helped to discover this early on—was the importance of remaining open to other points of view and letting new arguments, information, and perspectives change my mind. . . . A mind that admits no new light eventually withers."[26]

---

[24]Connie Cass, "Americans Have Trust Issues with One Another," *Orange County Register*, December 15, 2013, News 8.

[25]Julia Wood, *Interpersonal Communication: Everyday Encounters*, 6th ed. (Boston: Wadsworth, 2007), 257.

[26]Loeb, *Soul of a Citizen*, 52.

Finally, as we join others we allow the possibility of uncovering common values. Describing friendship, C. S. Lewis wrote that companions "look in the same direction."[27] What might surprise Christian counterpublics is how much we look in the same direction as non-Christian counterpublics. In their issue on mending a torn culture, the liberal magazine *Utne Reader* asked readers to identify issues that they sought to address through giving and volunteering. Their top fifteen included peace, women's rights, hunger, civil liberties, income inequity, and the poor suffering disproportionately. One of the oldest descriptions of what God considers to be "true religion" features a spokesperson for the marginalized in society who have no advocate or rhetorical voice (Jas 1:27). Many of the marginalized groups represented in the *Utne Reader*'s list should also be present on ours. Most importantly, these counterpublics are actively looking for others to join in their fight. "More generally, *UR* [*Utne Reader*] readers are almost by definition community organizers. They talk to their neighbors, both online and in person, meet in each other's living rooms, and knock on doors across town and around their block on behalf of their preferred candidates and issues."[28] Linking arms with others may be as easy as listening to the concerns of those who knock on our doors looking for help.

If these benefits were even partially accomplished, they would create a climate in which exploration and understanding could be cultivated between differing counterpublics. Communication scholar Norman Denzin uses the term *epiphanies* to describe "those interactional moments that leave positive and negative marks on people's lives."[29] We mistakenly think that epiphanies are only dramatic moments of understanding that touch every part of a person's life. Denzin notes that minor or cumulative epiphanies slowly, over time, change how we view ourselves or others.

As mentioned earlier, after partnering with the *Independent* to address Colorado's foster care system, Focus on the Family president Jim Daly agreed to be interviewed by the paper. Daly offered perspectives that not only muted the impressions left by his predecessor, James Dobson, but

---

[27]C. S. Lewis, *The Four Loves* (New York: Harcourt, Brace and Javanovich, 1960), 96.

[28]Eric Utne, Jay Ogilvy, and Brad Edmondson, "Have You Given Up?," *Utne Reader*, March–April 2014, 41.

[29]Norman K. Denzin, *Interpretive Interactionism*, 2nd ed. (Thousand Oaks, CA: Sage Publications, 2001), 143.

allowed him the possibility to cultivate minor epiphanies. After the interview, *Independent* staff writer J. Adrian Stanley compared quotes from Dobson and Daly concerning potentially volatile issues. On the topic of same-sex marriage, Dobson described homosexuals as individuals who "want to destroy the institution of marriage," resulting in the eventual destruction of our planet.[30] In contrast, Daly opened the door for discussion by asking, "How can [a civil union] be done in such a way that it recognizes where the culture's at and the needs that are between same-sex couples?" He concludes: "And I think if those laws can be written in such a way to strengthen their legal rights, but still protect marriage as a special union between a man and a woman, for the sake of the culture, the sake of rearing children, procreation, all those things, I think that is something that is being talked about."[31] In discussing abortion, Dobson argued that Christian activists are merely assuming a "holding action" while culture is "awash in evil and the battle is still to be waged."[32] Daly acknowledged the passion of Christian activists, but placed the focus on women wrestling with the decision to abort. "We know there's desperate situations for women when they have an unplanned pregnancy. [But] we would love to see abortion radically reduced."[33] Such admissions by Daly perhaps create minor epiphanies for staff and readers of the *Independent* that could motivate them to explore these issues further.

OBJECTIONS TO LOOSE CONNECTIONS

Not everyone supports adopting loose connections with non-Christian groups. For example, if we partner with a feminist group in a Take Back the Night March to make our campus safer, are we not in danger of endorsing any aspects of their agenda that run counter to biblical convictions? Is helping the campus become safer (a good intention) worth the risk of inadvertently supporting unbiblical goals (a bad result)?

Philosophers have long wrestled with such concerns and have created guidelines for ethical thinking called the principle of double effect. First

---

[30]J. Adrian Stanley, "Cooling the Rhetoric," *The Independent*, June 9-15, 2011, 23.
[31]Ibid.
[32]Ibid.
[33]Ibid.

conceptualized by Thomas Aquinas, the principle comprises four factors summarized by philosopher Alison McIntyre:

1. The act a person is doing must itself be morally good.

2. The bad effect must not be the means by which a person achieves the good outcome.

3. A person must intend only the good effect with the bad outcome being an unintended side effect.

4. The good outcome must compensate for the unintended negative outcome.[34]

With these guidelines in place let's apply them to Christians participating in the march. *Principle 1*: Participating in a march to make a campus safer for students is a good thing that furthers God's kingdom. *Principle 2*: The primary goal of Christians participating in the march is not to give credence to the feminist group so they can more effectively recruit and achieve unilateral goals—including ones that run counter to a biblical agenda. *Principle 3*: The Christians participating in the march intended only to address safety concerns with fellow students. Bringing notoriety to the feminist group and perhaps helping them achieve unethical goals would be unintended and undesirable. *Principle 4*: Does the good achieved during the march outweigh the potential bad side effect?

Principle 4 is perhaps the most helpful to the question we are addressing. What actual goods are accomplished by forming a loose connection with a feminist group to address campus threats toward women? In this chapter we mentioned several benefits of Christians forming temporary alliances with non-Christians: counteracting stereotypes, exploring radical solutions, cultivating trust between groups, learning from each other, and discovering common values. In addition, when we tackle common projects a door is open to presenting the Christian worldview.[35] Yet does this compensate for the possibility of students being recruited into an organization

---

[34]Alison McIntyre, "Doctrine of Double Effect," *The Stanford Encyclopedia of Philosophy*, ed. Edward N. Zalta, Winter 2014 ed., http://plato.stanford.edu/archives/win2014/entries/double-effect.

[35]Could Christians simply address campus safety concerns by organizing their own march? Yes, but then none of the benefits of forming a loose connection would be accomplished. In fact, negative effects could result, fostering a deeper separation between communities.

that promotes abortions? Are the benefits worth the risk of even one abortion? In this case we are deciding between actual goods we will achieve (e.g., safer campus, gospel proclaimed, trust developed) versus possible negative effects (e.g., increased abortions). Helping to make a campus safer by partnering with non-Christians is within our power; how non-Christians respond to our help is out of our control. Neighbor love should not be withheld for fear of how that love could be misused.

CONCLUSION

After many inhabitants of Judah had been deported to Babylon, the prophet Jeremiah received a surprising message from God for the exiles. Instead of remaining isolated or becoming embittered toward the Babylonians, they are to "seek the peace and prosperity of the city" to which they have been taken, because "if it prospers, you too will prosper" (Jer 29:7). As Christian counterpublics and resident aliens, we seek the good of our cities so that all inhabitants can flourish. It may surprise us that non-Christian counterpublics desire many of the same things we do and might be open to linking arms. If these temporary partnerships give voice to the oppressed and marginalized, not only will our communities flourish, but private sanctuaries—once thought impregnable—may be dismantled.

WILLIAM WILBERFORCE
AND PARLIAMENT

WILLIAM WILBERFORCE IS ONE OF THE GREATEST social reformers who has ever lived. He is justly acclaimed for abolishing slavery in Great Britain. He is among the greatest political orators of all time. He was charming, witty, outgoing, generous, and hospitable to friend and foe alike. He was gracious yet persistent, idealistic but also pragmatic; he had a strong moral compass but also a vibrant love of life. Though he lived among the mighty, he always seemed to find time for children, the poor, and the forgotten. He has rightly been called a hero for humanity. A contemporary reflecting on his death stated that he was "great among the good and good among the great . . . ages yet to come will glory in his memory."[1]

Wilberforce also cultivated the gifts and abilities of others. As John Pollock notes, "he was proof that a man may change his times, though he cannot do it alone."[2] Indeed, Wilberforce did not work alone. He led the Clapham Sect, a group of social reformers who attended a church on Clapham Common in southwest London. Their work reshaped English social life in the late eighteenth and early nineteenth centuries. They were a classic counterpublic, working within mainstream culture to challenge the dominant beliefs and ultimately reweave the moral fabric of their day. Though often mocked and derisively called "Clapham Saints" by their contemporaries, they proved to be one of the most elite and effective bands of social reformers in all of Christian history.[3]

WILBERFORCE'S LOOSE CONNECTIONS

But Wilberforce's personal gifts and dedicated supporters do not tell the whole story. His success was due in no small part to his ability to cultivate

---

[1]Kevin Charles Belmonte, *Hero for Humanity: A Biography of William Wilberforce* (Colorado Springs, CO: NavPress, 2002), 327.
[2]John Pollock, *Wilberforce* (New York: St. Martin's Press, 1978), 307.
[3]Ibid., 89.

loose connections, often with very unlikely individuals. For example, Charles Fox was a political enemy of William Pitt, Wilberforce's closest friend and political ally. Consequently, on most political issues of the day—the revolution in France, the war with France, the Regency Crisis, the Test and Corporation Acts, or the Sedition and Treason Acts—Wilberforce and Fox were fiercely opposed to one another. Fox was an eloquent orator in his own right and more than capable of saying hurtful things if they contributed to political victories. In personal moral conduct Fox was famously dissolute, while Wilberforce modeled and promoted the "reformation of manners"—a movement that could be neatly summarized as opposing the morality of nearly everything that Fox did in his private life. Two more unlikely political bedfellows could hardly be imagined. Yet despite their profound differences, they agreed on one thing: the necessity of the abolition of slavery. They became firm collaborators on abolition throughout the long parliamentary struggle. They cultivated a deep mutual respect that transcended their personal, moral, religious, and political differences. It is unlikely that Wilberforce would have succeeded without the support of Fox.

And Fox was only one of many people with whom Wilberforce maintained loose connections. He and the Clapham Sect were pragmatic regarding means, and quite happy to use whatever instruments God made available to them. Richard Sheridan, one of the greatest public speakers of the day, was also known as an alcoholic. Nonetheless, he proved a useful ally; as a member of the Clapham Sect wryly noted, we are "happy to work with the celebrated orator Richard Sheridan whether drunk or sober."[4]

Perhaps the most easily overlooked of his loose connections are those Wilberforce formed with the British Parliament itself. From the outset, he understood that slavery would have to be abolished by law. That meant that Wilberforce would not just need to speak *to* Parliament, but before he was done he would have to speak *for* Parliament. Success required that his clarion call for abolition be answered by a majority of the members of Parliament. Given the state of the legislature upon Wilberforce's entry into the House of Commons, such a possibility was exceedingly difficult to imagine.

---

[4]Bruce Hindmarsh, "Aristocratic Activists," *Christian History* 16, no. 1 (1997): 27.

CONNECTING WITH PARLIAMENT

The body that confronted Wilberforce was not predisposed to favor abolition. They were not moral reformers or philanthropists. As Pollock notes, this was "a body of men elected to maintain and strengthen British interests and . . . the interests of their class, the men of land and property."[5] England was emerging as a great global empire, and this sort of power inclines people to paper over inconvenient moral issues—especially when the victims are politically weak and live on a distant continent.

Taken as a whole, the Parliament was morally tepid. They did not disdain morality, but neither was it their most central concern. They were lukewarm to principle. In this sense they were the absolute opposite of Wilberforce. For Wilberforce, abolition was the clearest of moral issues, and once this dawned on his consciousness all other concerns fled before it. As he noted in his diary, "So enormous, so dreadful, so irredeemable did the trade's wickedness appear that my own mind was completely made up for abolition. Let the consequences be what they would; I from this time determined that I would never rest until I had effected its abolition."[6] However, most members of Parliament lacked Wilberforce's moral clarity. They "vaguely shared the Enlightenment's rejection of slavery as inhuman . . . yet they [were] uneasy lest tampering with the Trade should damage British commerce."[7]

Furthermore, slavery was not seen with anything like the unambiguous moral disdain it evokes today. Some slavers seriously argued that theirs was a moral trade because they were trying to help people who'd been captured in African wars, who were otherwise going to be executed, and they were taking them to a safe place and a new life. Others were convinced that it was essential to the economic well-being of the colonies and therefore the British nation. If in places like the West Indies slavery was required to make things work, so be it.

Also working against Wilberforce were external political realities. The British nation had real enemies and constant threats. Abandoning the slave trade would mean letting Spain, or worse yet France, take over the trade and reap an economic windfall. In effect, this meant funding the treasury of one's

---

[5]Pollock, *Wilberforce*, 89.
[6]Christopher Hancock, "The Shrimp Who Stopped Slavery," *Christian History* 16, no. 1 (1997): 16.
[7]Pollock, *Wilberforce*, 88.

enemies. England and France were either at war or on the verge of war for most of the time Wilberforce was campaigning for abolition. Though he hoped to foster abolition in France as well, and eventually in Spain, there were certainly no guarantees of this. The prospect of abandoning the slave trade to the French in the midst of wartime was perceived to be foolhardy at best and treasonous at worst. This was not merely a smokescreen or over-stated fear. Liverpool historian Ramsey Muir records that in 1807 alone some 17 million pounds changed hands in the slave trade in Liverpool. In present-day terms this would be approximately the equivalent of the housing market or the IT sector of the British economy.[8]

So on the night of May 11, 1789, when Wilberforce rose to address Parliament and advocate for abolition, the deck was stacked against his success. Connections, loose or otherwise, were going to be hard to find.

THE GREAT SPEECH

The story of this famous speech is well worth the telling. In early 1789 the Privy Council's report on the slave trade had been completed and Wilberforce read it with interest. Though the final report contained no recommendations, it did include 850 pages of damning evidence of the evils of the slave trade. Wilberforce realized that this was his opportunity to bring the question before the House of Commons. Twelve resolutions were drawn up in response to the Privy Council report, and after lengthy consultation with friends and advisors Wilberforce presented these resolutions to the House. His speech was an oratorical masterpiece, but also a skillfully laid foundation for a long and fruitful loose connection. Several lessons can be drawn from his approach.

1. Wilberforce left his opponents room to join him without humiliation. Despite abundant evidence of the evils of the slave trade, Wilberforce did not employ the rhetoric of moral outrage. He was calm, rational, and moderate. He did not distance himself from the morality of his peers but chose to paint himself with the same brush: "I mean not to accuse anyone, but to take the shame upon myself, in common indeed with the whole Parliament of Great Britain, for having suffered this horrid trade to be carried on under

---

[8]"William Wilberforce," BBC Religions site, May 7, 2011, www.bbc.co.uk/religion/religions/chris
tianity/people/williamwilberforce_1.shtml.

their authority."[9] He kept the focus on the morality of slavery itself instead of the morality of his peers and colleagues.

Wilberforce's moderation allowed his colleagues a place to stand. He was with them, not above them. He shared with them complicity in a policy that was deeply corrupt. It was a national policy, benefiting (so it was perceived) the nation as a whole. Its practitioners served the nation as a whole, and the nation as a whole was guilty of neglect in allowing the trade to flourish. Though Wilberforce had a better excuse than most to exculpate himself, he refused to do so. He understood that his peers were people he had to work *with*, not *against*. He was courting a loose connection with a group that owed him nothing. If he painted them as moral enemies in his first speech, then every bit of future cooperation would require his collaborators to admit their failure and acknowledge Wilberforce's rectitude. Such conditions would simply impede progress and make support harder to cultivate.

2. Wilberforce refused to make the battle personal. Wilberforce also avoided naming the names of his hardened opponents. This included people who were telling lies, offering false testimony, practicing deceit and obfuscation, and deliberately trying to derail the investigation. He refuted their arguments but allowed them to remain anonymous—at least within his own statements. As Metaxas notes, "Wilberforce did not humiliate the wicked men who had given [false] descriptions as he might have, and if ever anyone had been given the gifts with which to verbally smash his opponents like eggs, Wilberforce had. Instead, he coolly countered each of these false accounts."[10]

3. Wilberforce let the facts, not his rhetoric, be the fuel of moral outrage. Instead of angry shouting, finger pointing, and inflammatory language, Wilberforce used facts. Facts upon facts upon facts. Facts were his rebuttal, his outrage, and his ally against all opposition. Facts drawn from personal testimonies—from slaves, from slave traders, from disinterested third parties, from doctors and lawyers employed by the slave plantations. These facts were meticulously researched and carefully documented. This became a hallmark of Wilberforce's work and that of his colleagues. At one point fellow abolitionist Thomas Clarkson searched systematically through every

---

[9]Eric Metaxas, *Amazing Grace: William Wilberforce and the Heroic Campaign to End Slavery* (New York: HarperSanFrancisco, 2007), 133.

[10]Ibid., 134.

ship in England to find a sailor who he thought could provide evidence against slavery. Clarkson finally found him on the fifty-seventh ship.[11]

One of the most compelling pieces of evidence was also one of the most understated. Wilberforce had found a chart that meticulously represented the way to stack and load the maximum possible number of slaves aboard a ship for the Middle Passage. The figures look like sardines in a can; it is hard to tell they are human beings. However, every aspect of the image is orderly. It faithfully records the placement of 292 slaves on the lower deck and 130 additional slaves "on the wings and sides of the lower deck by means of platforms or shelves." Other smaller compartments were also diagramed, as was the cross-section of the ship, showing how the slaves could be stacked with two feet and seven inches of clearance between layers, clarifying where this allowed for four levels and where it only allowed for two. All the drawings are devoid of flourishes or augmentation designed to evoke horror. No chains, manacles, or whips are shown. The chart intentionally avoids the horrific, and in so doing it maximizes the power of the mere facts. Most disturbing of all is that the number of slaves depicted in this ship is exactly the new legal limit of the "improved" slaving regulations. Before these changes, the ship could have carried up to 740 slaves instead of the 482 shown in the drawing.

4. Wilberforce refused to fall into the all-or-nothing trap. Finally, the resolutions that Wilberforce put forward were moderate, especially given the magnitude of the evidence. Though he longed for complete abolition and emancipation, he knew it was not a political possibility. He also accepted the general view that it would produce anarchy and great distress. Therefore, his immediate aim was to stop the slave trade. This would secure two ends. First, eliminating the devastating cruelty of the Middle Passage would end an untold amount of human suffering. Second, limiting the supply of slaves would force slaveholders to treat their existing slaves better since they could no longer be easily replaced. But his willingness to take incremental steps never deflected Wilberforce from the ultimate goal. As he later explained to a young Quaker:

> It is most true, that . . . the real and the declared object of all the friends of the
> African race, to see the West Indies slaves GRADUALLY *transmuted* into a

---

[11]Hindmarsh, "Aristocratic Activists," 26.

free Peasantry; but this, the ultimate object, was to be produced progressively
... and to appear at last to have been the almost insensible result of the various
improvements ... like the progress of vegetation which appears to have gradually changed barrenness and desolation into virtue and beauty.[12]

THE SURPRISING RESULT

With these observations in mind, it is shocking that the result of this remarkable three-and-a-half-hour speech was almost complete failure. There
can be no doubt about Wilberforce's oratory. Perhaps the most telling testimony to his eloquence comes from Edmund Burke, himself one of the
great orators of the day. He was present for the speech and commented that
"principles so admirable, laid down with so much order and force, were equal
to anything he had ever heard in modern oratory; and perhaps not to be
excelled by anything to be met with in Demonsthenes."[13] And Burke's affirmation was joined by that of other notables, including Fox and Pitt.

However, when confronted with the actual prospect of abolition, most
of the House feared it would precipitate an economic and political disaster.
Therefore, when the debate resumed a few days later they eagerly supported a motion from Alderman Sawbridge to further research the matter
because "the House could not proceed to so rash and impolitic a measure
as unqualified Abolition without hearing evidence at their own bar."[14] Despite pleas from Fox and Burke, Wilberforce's resolutions were not discussed and never came to a vote. Ironically, after all the facts of the evils
of the slave trade had been presented, the House pleaded ignorance and
called for more research.

So is all of this just a study in failure? I believe not. Wilberforce did not
achieve his stated objective, but he did lay the foundations of a long-
enduring loose connection with Parliament itself. He had not passed a bill,
but he had passed a test. He had proven himself to be a person with whom
others could work. His demeanor and eloquence did not carry the day, but
they did prepare the way. He had been heard, and he would be heard again.
And again. He brought forward legislation that was defeated in 1791, 1792,

---

[12]Pollock, *Wilberforce*, 71.
[13]Ibid., 89.
[14]Ibid., 91.

and 1793. After a brief gap caused by war with France, legislation was again introduced and defeated in 1797. Thereafter, Wilberforce's bills for abolition became an annual event, gaining ever-increasing support until finally, on February 23, 1807, at four o'clock in the morning, the House of Commons voted 283 to 16 to abolish the slave trade.

It was a wonderful victory, but his work was not yet done. He had pledged himself not to rest until slavery was completely abolished, and this meant not only the end of the slave trade but also the emancipation of every slave in English territory. To accomplish this feat, he had to cultivate his loose connections for another twenty-six years, until on July 26, 1833, the House finally passed a resolution that secured the emancipation of every British slave. With his life work complete, Wilberforce passed away three days later. As a final testimony to the effectiveness of his loose connections, within hours of his death almost every member of Parliament had signed a letter requesting the family to allow Wilberforce to be buried in Westminster Abbey, an honor reserved for only the greatest of their nation's citizens.

Part III

PRESSING QUESTIONS FOR CHRISTIAN COUNTERPUBLICS

When the US Supreme Court ruled in June of 2015 that a state ban on same-sex marriages is unconstitutional, the cultural sand shifted under Christian counterpublics. A chorus of conservative and religious voices asserted that it was perhaps the darkest period in our nation's history. Accordingly, some advocate that we take a page from Martin Luther King Jr. and—through nonviolent resistance—make same-sex marriage as difficult as possible to enact. Is this the correct course of action? Surely our communities, churches, and religious institutions will feel the reach of the court's decision. How should we respond at the local level? More specifically, what should be the first step in our response? In the next two chapters each of the coauthors independently answers this question and then responds to the other's suggestions, acknowledging areas of common ground and pushing each other's thinking. We hope it will spur your thinking about how Christian counterpublics should address this complex issue.

8

HOW SHOULD WE RESPOND TO THE SUPREME COURT DECISION ON SAME-SEX MARRIAGE?

Tim Muehlhoff

To FRAME MY CHAPTER, I'LL ADDRESS ONE QUESTION: *As we ask those who disagree to consider our argument for traditional marriage, how should we respond if they suffer relational crisis?* As with any communication there are (at least) two distinct aspects: the content and the relational level. The content is our message, while the relational level is the amount of acknowledgment, respect, compassion, and concern that exists between communicators. Since in my estimation our content—biblical support for traditional marriage—is unwavering, I will focus on the relational level—how we treat those with whom we disagree.[1] My goal in this chapter is to raise key questions of how we should relationally respond to those outside the Christian community with whom we find ourselves embroiled in passionate debate.[2] As counterpublics our support of traditional marriage (i.e., the content of our message) will *not be heard* unless we firmly establish the relational level.

---

[1]For a summary of the argument for traditional marriage, consult Kevin DeYoung, *What Does the Bible Really Teach About Homosexuality?* (Wheaton, IL: Crossway, 2015).

[2]I understand that there are many perspectives within the Christian community concerning this topic. For example, some maintain that same-sex marriage is unbiblical, yet still argue for the legalization of gay marriage; others are not convinced the Bible condemns modern notions of same-sex marriage. How to structure those in-house conversations is beyond the purview of this chapter. For suggestions on how to have productive conversations, see my book *I Beg to Differ: Navigating Difficult Conversations in Truth and Love* (Downers Grove, IL: InterVarsity Press, 2014).

TO HELP OR NOT TO HELP

Let me begin with a scenario that seems not to be controversial and then move to one that could be. For the first scenario, imagine that three houses down in your neighborhood is an unchurched lesbian couple raising two kids. Over the years you've casually interacted with them enough to know that they are aware of the stance of your church toward same-sex marriage. Through word of mouth you learn that one of the women is having significant health problems requiring frequent trips to the hospital. Do you— along with other neighbors—offer to bring them meals? Do you watch the kids as they go for treatment? Do you drive the woman who's ill to an appointment if her spouse can't do it? Few of my Christian friends balk at this point. "Of course I'd help. I'd do so gladly," is a common response. Why? First, caring for this couple and their family in a time of need is a powerful expression of neighbor love. Second, from a communication standpoint spending time with this couple allows you to look for opportunities to explain your church's position, which to them must seem harsh and unloving and may cause them to harbor strong negative feelings toward us.

Our decision to help in the midst of debating the nature of marriage is merely following the advice of Paul and Jesus. To the counterpublics in Rome, Paul writes, "If the one who hates you is hungry, feed him. If he is thirsty, give him water" (Rom 12:20 NLV). Paul does not assume that the opposition is asking for assistance. Rather, it's the follower of Christ who after becoming aware of another's need graciously responds. In commenting on the proverb Paul is quoting, Old Testament scholar David Hubbard notes, "No one who fears the Lord dare stand by and let another person suffer if he has the means to meet the need."[3] Paul here is clearly echoing Jesus' command to love, pray for, and do good toward our adversaries (Mt 5:44-47). Paul's hope is that when we establish the relational level—showing concern and compassion—those who have strong negative feelings toward Christians will not only authentically experience Christ's love but may also soften their view. With this softening, could it also be possible that hate and negative emotions will be replaced with civility and renewed dialogue?

---

[3]David A. Hubbard, *Proverbs*, The Communicator's Commentary (Dallas: Word Books, 1989), 402.

Now imagine a different scenario. Through word of mouth you learn that this same neighbor couple is having marital problems, evidenced by loud shouting matches in front of their kids. Raising two kids is proving difficult and costly, resulting in increasingly angry outbursts. What is your response? Do you inquire to see how they as a family are fairing? If they confide that they need help, do you offer marital advice? Instead of offering material goods—meals, babysitting, shuttling to office visits— you now offer relational goods. At this point some of my Christian friends become increasingly uncomfortable. "I can't offer marital advice for fear of condoning a sinful relationship. I'm not going to help a couple sin more effectively. So no, I don't offer relational help." Such legitimate concerns require careful consideration. These concerns can be expressed in two questions.

In providing relational counsel to same-sex couples, am I helping them sin? No. Helping to diffuse toxic anger, emotional or verbal abuse, and incivility within a relationship results in creating relational goods that God affirms; it doesn't mean we are affirming the entire relationship. Jesus makes this distinction when he acknowledges that the crowd in front of him is composed of sinful parents, but they still "give good gifts" to their children (Mt 7:11). Acknowledging the good gifts does not mean Jesus is condoning the person's overall lifestyle. Whenever we encourage individuals to be more humane to each other, we are introducing relational goods that God acknowledges as good. To be clear, we are not helping a couple engaged in a relationship we deem unbiblical simply move on to the next level of intimacy. Rather, we are helping a couple remove toxic elements—abuse, rage, damaging words— from their relationship.

Those who disagree with my application of Paul's call to help our opposition counter, "But when those who oppose me consume the food and water I provide, that is not, in and of itself, sin." Yes, but neither is an individual beginning to treat others more humanely a sin. When a gay couple adopts your advice regarding how to diffuse toxic communication that is ripping the family apart, you are not aiding them in sin. Rather, you are helping two people made in the image of God treat each other in a way advocated by the Scriptures (e.g., avoiding speaking death to each other as suggested by Prov 18:21).

Won't others see my helping same-sex couples relationally as condoning an unbiblical relationship and thus sending contradictory messages about Christian convictions? As Christians we should be wary of sending mixed signals by seemingly supporting perspectives or lifestyles that run counter to a biblical worldview. No doubt this is a delicate dance. However, should that be our greatest concern? It seems that neighbor love—the second greatest commandment (Mt 22:39)—should be a higher value. In a story that has come to be known as the parable of the good Samaritan, Jesus informs us what constitutes being a good neighbor: showing mercy (Lk 10:37).

I find it interesting that Jesus, in his participating in table fellowship with known sinners, shows a remarkable *lack* of concern for being seen as condoning sin. New Testament scholar Craig Blomberg describes Jesus' decision to break bread with sinners as an act that "goes beyond a casual association with the ritually impure to a scandalous intimacy with the profoundly immoral."[4] Blomberg notes that religious leaders who witnessed his fellowship with notorious sinners described Jesus as a glutton and drunkard. To them, his decision to have table fellowship with the unsavory was synonymous to sharing in their sin. How does Jesus respond to such charges? "Jesus discloses not one instance of fearing contamination, whether moral or ritual, by associating with the wicked or impure."[5] Will some view our decision to give relational help to a gay couple as affirming their relationship? Perhaps. But Jesus' example compels us to place love and mercy above the fear of being seen as condoning sin.

Let's make this last scenario even murkier. What if this couple isn't in relational crisis, but through interacting with them you see signs that they are heading toward crisis? You witness occasional bursts of anger or a critical spirit that demeans another. If these patterns continue unchecked, you know they'll lead to a full breakdown of the relationship, which will deeply affect the kids. Do you wait until they are in crisis, or do you step in and attempt to prevent one? My assertion is that if we are willing to help couples *in* crisis, we should also help them address patterns that will *lead* to relational crisis. What virtue is there in watching couples and families be torn apart?

---

[4]Craig Blomberg, *Contagious Holiness: Jesus' Meals with Sinners* (Downers Grove, IL: InterVarsity Press, 2005), 133.
[5]Ibid., 167.

To summarize, my answer to the question that began this chapter is that when those who are considering our argument for traditional marriage show signs of moving into relational crisis or are in crisis, we should respond with both material and relational help. However, the focus of this book is how communities or groups interact with each other, not merely how individuals interact. Thus, what would the group version be of a Christian couple responding to the needs of a gay couple three doors down? This is what I suggest your local church should consider. What might this look like conceptually and practically?

CONCEPTUAL CONSIDERATIONS

What if, several years into this unprecedented social experiment of same-sex marriage, we start to see signs that same-sex couples are experiencing significant relational problems? Like many heterosexual couples, what if same-sex couples start exhibiting toxic traits that harm and rip apart marriages? Evidence of a struggle may already be surfacing. Julie and Hillary Goodridge, lead plaintiffs in the case that led to same-sex marriage being recognized in Massachusetts, quickly married only to separate two years later. Three years after the separation, they divorced. Rosie O'Donnell, TV host and outspoken gay marriage activist, is on her second divorce and currently is in a bitter custody battle with her estranged wife. How should our churches and Christian organizations respond if same-sex couples move into relational crisis evidenced by harmful communication practices that damage adults and children? And what if they come to us for help?

In the surrounding community where I live and go to church there are over twenty-five organizations that support same-sex couples and families. How should my church respond if we receive a call for help? Simply put, it depends. If one of those organizations calls and suggests we cosponsor a marriage workshop that helps couples doing well move to the next level of relational intimacy, I would respectfully decline. The invitation feels like a celebration of marriage with a few communication principles thrown in. I would explain that our differing convictions concerning marriage make it an uncomfortable fit. However, if another organization calls and explains that many couples they are working with are in varying degrees of distress, ranging from anger issues to perhaps signs of abuse, would we respond differently? Invoking Paul's command to aid those in need, we shouldn't hesitate to respond.[6]

Conceptually, what would our response entail? Rather than cosponsoring a public one-day marriage conference for both heterosexual and homosexual couples, I envision something subtler. Couldn't a church send its top marriage and family counselors to this organization to conduct an in-house workshop designed to provide strategies to diffuse harmful communication? Our response to this group is not something we publicly advertise. Not because we should be embarrassed to do it; rather, we should be careful not to make this kindness serve as some form of self-promoting public relations gesture in order to demonstrate that we are not homophobic. Our motive for sending help is to exhibit neighbor love in time of need.

The weakness of what I'm advocating is that—based on today's negative communication climate—it is highly unlikely we'll ever get a call for help from organizations supporting same-sex couples. "You guys hate gays," is the response I once received from a community organizer. It is unreasonable for us to wait by the phone for an invitation that will never come. Paul didn't wait to help those who opposed him. "If the one who hates you is hungry, feed him" (Rom 12:20 NLV). His command presupposes that we are aware of the needs around us. Are we? Do we know the needs of our surrounding community, including LGBTQ members?

Two essential steps are needed. First, we should be proactive in assessing the needs of all in our community.[7] How would we attain such information? I suggest reaching out to organizations to ask where the greatest needs are—especially those addressing same-sex couples. Not only will our initiation open lines of communication, but it will help us engage in perspective taking on behalf of those with whom we disagree. If an organization designed to support same-sex couples tells us they are fine or is closed to

---

[6]Why help in the one case and not the other? My organizing principle is that whenever Christians become aware of individuals treating each other *inhumanely* or showing patterns of harmful communication, we are compelled to act. As a starting point, I assert that any form of abuse (emotional, physical, or verbal) or the signs of abuse warrant our assisting groups or organizations.

[7]This also entails our seeking to understand and respond to the needs of those with same-sex attraction within our churches. As people seek to navigate their struggles with sexual identities, will we come alongside them?

our help, we respectfully move on. If an organization is transparent about couples showing signs of material or relational crisis, we discuss how we might respond in Christlike fashion. Second, we should act on what we *already* know.

Without making one phone call, we already know of an element within the LGBTQ community who are in crisis—the transgender. The National Gay and Lesbian Task Force and the National Center for Transgender Equality surveyed 6,450 transgender and gender nonconforming individuals. They discovered that respondents were four times as likely as the general population to be living in extreme poverty (less than $10,000 yearly income). While in kindergarten through twelfth grade respondents reported harassment (78%), physical assault (35%), and sexual assault (12%), resulting in one out of six being forced to leave school. Most alarming, 41 percent of the transgender community has reported attempting suicide in order to make the pain, public shame, and bulling stop.[8]

How should we respond to such heartbreaking information?[9] We need to begin by rhetorically cleaning house. In our churches how do we talk about transgender people? Do we mock people like Caitlyn Jenner, or do we acknowledge their courage or pain? Do the transgender or those struggling with same-sex attraction within our churches feel welcomed and loved? If people had access to our hidden transcripts, what would they reveal about our level of concern for a contingent within our community in crisis? We need help in understanding how our biblical view is coming across to others. Is our message inadvertently adding to bullying, harassment, and even

---

[8]Jaime M. Grant, Lisa A. Mottet, and Justin Tanis, *Injustice at Every Turn: A Report of the National Transgender Discrimination Survey, Executive Summary* (National Center for Transgender Equality and National Gay and Lesbian Task Force, 2011), www.thetaskforce.org/static_html/down loads/reports/reports/ntds_summary.pdf.

[9]Some have responded by noting that what transgender people experience, while tragic, isn't necessarily greater than what heterosexual students encounter in school. For example, in the 2001 study *Hostile Hallways*, 83 percent of girls and 60 percent of boys surveyed in grades eight through eleven reported being sexually harassed (*Hostile Hallways: Bullying, Teasing, and Sexual Harassment in Schools* [Washington, DC: American Association of University Women Educational Foundation, 2001], www.aauw.org/files/2013/02/hostile-hallways-bullying-teasing-and-sexual-harassment-in-school.pdf). Even if one grants these findings, what separates the two studies is the students' ability to cope. In *Hostile Hallways* nearly half (47%) of students reported feeling very or somewhat upset. Thoughts of suicide did not make the list of student responses. In the transgendered study 41 percent of respondents (including but not limited to high school students) contemplate or attempt suicide. Surely transgender people urgently need our support.

thoughts of suicide for the very individuals we seek to minister to? In an effort to engage in perception checking we should meet with organizations that support transgender people to hear how our rhetoric is coming across.

A few years ago three graduates who self-identify as gay or transgender were invited to speak to faculty and administrators about what it was like to be an undergraduate at Biola University. With powerful emotions surfacing, these graduates described the pain and isolation that came from balancing being a Christian with same-sex attraction or gender confusion. It was gratifying to hear that most faculty were sympathetic when presented with their struggles. However, it was disturbing to hear stories of crude jokes, harsh characterizations of gay and transgender people, and uncompassionate pronouncement of biblical positions by other students unaware of the struggles of these students. That day, presenters and audience alike shed many tears. Along with the tears came a realization that truth (content level) must always be accompanied by love (relational level) as prescribed by the Scriptures (Eph 4:15).

PRACTICAL CONSIDERATIONS

I was encouraged recently to learn of a church program in my community that practically reflects the values and strategies offered in this chapter. Their goal is to be a resource to fellow community members who are in relational crisis. Through advertising on Craig's List and other media they let it be known that there is help for those dealing with destructive anger. Hundreds of couples of all types have responded, including ones from the gay community. Each week in this program during the first hour couples are placed in support groups, where they describe—free of judgment—struggles they are experiencing. Carefully selected Christian couples serve as facilitators and also share personal struggles. During the second hour communication principles are presented and discussed in the group. Each session ends with "back from the brink" couples sharing how anger and toxic communication almost destroyed their marriages and families. Each of these couples consists of Christians who share how their faith helps them remove damaging patterns of interaction. Anyone interested in hearing more about God is invited to attend church or to meet privately with facilitator couples, who discuss what constitutes a relationship with God. Time and again, organizers of this program confirm the central claim of this chapter: the relational level of communication opens the door to the content level. One attendee commented that she was terrified, as a gay woman, at how she might not be accepted. She thanked organizers for treating her and her partner with what was offered to all who attended—respect.[10]

CONCLUSION

As our communities and laws are shaped by the implications of the Supreme Court decision, Christian counterpublics must wrestle with how to balance affirming Christian convictions while addressing the needs of *all* community members. The strategy I advocate in this chapter at times may seem to place a priority on ministering to those outside the Christian community above the concerns of those within. It's a perception I can accept. I concur with the leadership at Hillsong Church in New York as they seek to find a balance in ministering to the LGBTQ community. "[Hillsong's] heart on this matter is to reach all people, even communities that present extreme complexities," states pastor Carl Lentz. "We would rather be misunderstood and look 'messy' to some in the Christian community that do not agree with us and help some, than appease people that think differently and reach none."[11]

---

[10]I sometimes wonder whether when people ask us to "accept" their views they may be merely asking that we respect their perspective. Clearly as Christians we can give people the respect that is warranted by their bearing the image of God, and we can do this without anyone thinking that we are agreeing with everything they stand for.

[11]Jonathan Merritt, "Carl Lentz on How Hillsong Church Is Becoming 'Gay Welcoming' Without Compromising Their Convictions," Religion News Service, August 10, 2015, jonathanmerritt .religionnews.com/2015/08/10/carl-lentz-on-how-hillsong-church-is-becoming-gay-welcoming -without-compromising-their-convictions.

9

HOW SHOULD WE RESPOND TO THE SUPREME COURT DECISION ON SAME-SEX MARRIAGE?

Rick Langer

ON JUNE 26, 2015, THE SUPREME COURT decided *Obergefell v. Hodges* in such a manner as to require all states to issue marriage licenses to same-sex couples and to recognize same-sex marriages performed in other jurisdictions. This decision made same-sex marriage the law throughout the United States. Some celebrated, including some Christians. Others, including many Christians, responded with sadness, feeling that our culture had lost its way. Suggested reactions to *Obergefell* have varied widely.[1] Some call for Christians to withdraw from secular society and form alternative communities that support a coherent moral vision in the midst of an increasingly amoral society. Others urge ramping up protest in the public square and overturning *Obergefell*. Others have advocated for a strategic civil disobedience to the decision. And finally, many Christians feel it is time to just get over it and get on with life, viewing the controversy over same-sex marriage as a distraction from more central issues facing the church.

---

[1]For the responses cited here and more besides, see "After Obergefell: A First Things Symposium," June 27, 2015, www.firstthings.com/web-exclusives/2015/06/after-obergefell-a-first-things-symposium.

PROPHETIC CIVILITY

Dissatisfied with each of these options, I suggest we practice what I will call *prophetic civility*. The biblical grounding is found in 1 Peter 3:15-16:

> But in your hearts honor Christ the Lord as holy, always being prepared to make a defense to anyone who asks you for a reason for the hope that is in you; yet do it with gentleness and respect, having a good conscience, so that, when you are slandered, those who revile your good behavior in Christ may be put to shame. (ESV)

Peter exhorts us to give a defense and to do it with gentleness and respect. In other words, we are to declare the truth (be prophetic) and we are to show gentleness and respect (be civil). Prophetic civility. I find this compelling because I frequently see Christians being so prophetic that they are uncivil, or so civil that they are unprophetic. If prophetic civility sounds oxymoronic, consider the life of Jesus. He was "a friend of sinners"—a moniker his enemies gave him because it was descriptively accurate. He actually was a friend of sinners. And though he befriended tax collectors and prostitutes, he never denied their sins. Indeed, in his presence the tax collectors and prostitutes often called *themselves* sinners. Here is my argument: Jesus modeled prophetic civility, Peter commands it, so we should practice it.

But how? Peter talks about giving a defense or a reason—words that convey not just speaking truth, but speaking truth to a particular audience, one that disagrees with or doubts our truth claim. So we must know both the truth and our audience. Knowing our audience means perspective taking, crafting and delivering a message, and a host of other skills we have discussed in previous chapters. To put this in counterpublic language, we must know the public we are countering and counter it wisely.

KNOWING THE PUBLIC WE ARE COUNTERING

Identifying the public we are to counter is not as easy as it sounds. Some Christians want to counter the gays and lesbians who will actually seek to be married under the new laws. Some Christians want to counter the self-congratulatory elites who celebrate this change as a major moral advancement. Some Christians want to counter the "judicial activism" of the Supreme Court. And yet others want to counter the ascending LGBTQ activism in contemporary American culture. To which of these publics should we speak?

I choose none of the above.

Indeed, this is my most important claim. In my view, Christian counterpublics should not focus on the *Obergefell* decision at all. *Our focus should be not on same-sex marriage but on straight marriage.* Simply put, our culture has a faulty understanding of marriage, largely characteristic of Christians and non-Christians alike. The fault in this understanding of marriage has little or nothing to do with the gender of the marriage partners, and everything to do with a host of practices, technologies, and social policies related to straight marriage. Let me explain.

The last century was one of relentless change for marriage practices: arranged marriages have been replaced by marriage for romantic love, reliable birth control has become cheap and widely available, in vitro fertilization has become commonplace and reproductive technologies greatly expanded, no-fault divorce has become the legal norm, and the sexual revolution of the '60s has morphed into the hook-up culture of the twenty-first century. Many of these changes were well-intended by their advocates, were often uncontested by Christians, and had nothing to do with homosexuality. But over the decades the intended and unintended consequences of these changes transformed heterosexual marriage in America. Marriage has become almost completely grounded in romantic love and personal satisfaction. Childbearing is no longer an essential good of marriage, and is not even mentioned in many marriage ceremonies. No longer is marriage a precondition for having children. Indeed, having a partner is not a precondition—a sperm bank can do as well. Cohabiting before marriage is not only permissible but viewed as normative and prudent. Divorce is seen as a legitimate unilateral decision when a partner no longer finds the relationship satisfying; it does not require the violation of a vow. And of course, with many couples writing their own vows using ambiguous wording, it is extremely difficult to argue that a vow has been violated at all. Brad Wilcox, a scholar at the University of Virginia, helpfully distinguishes the two models of marriage we have been discussing:

> Americans have moved away from . . . an "institutional" model of marriage, which seeks to integrate sex, parenthood, economic cooperation,

and emotional intimacy in a permanent union. This model has been over-written by the "soul mate" model, which sees marriage as primarily a couple-centered vehicle for personal growth, emotional intimacy, and shared consumption that depends for its survival on the happiness of both spouses.[2]

The shift from an "institutional" model to a "soul mate" model is a shift in our *straight* marriage practices. But the consequences of these changes for social policy concerning same-sex marriage are enormous. Adam Haslett, writing over a decade ago for *New Yorker* magazine, notes:

> The choice of whom to marry has become less about satisfying the demands of family and community than about satisfying oneself. When you add the contraceptive and reproductive technologies that have separated sex from procreation, what you have is a model of heterosexual marriage that is grounded in and almost entirely sustained on individual preference. This is a historically peculiar state of affairs, one that would be alien to our ancestors and to most traditional cultures today. And it makes the push for gay marriage inevitable.[3]

I agree. To return to Wilcox's terminology, the soul-mate model of marriage makes same-sex marriage practically inevitable. As long as such an understanding of marriage is in place, reversing *Obergefell* would be a fleeting and Pyrrhic victory. It would prove unsustainable and fruitless in the soil of contemporary America. Furthermore, demographically, gay marriage directly affects only a tiny portion of the population. That it is indicative of a pervasive deterioration of marriage is true, but my point is that gay marriage is the consequence of this deterioration, not the cause. And eliminating gay marriage would likely have little or no effect on the cultural deterioration of marriage since almost all of the deterioration was in place before same-sex marriage was even on the horizon of our political discussions.

Changing a culture's perception of marriage is an incredibly difficult task, but it is exactly the sort of task that counterpublics are suited for. Traditional political activism is insufficient because it focuses too narrowly on laws and social policies. A counterpublic is better suited to the long, hard work of

---

[2]W. Bradford Wilcox and Elizabeth Marquardt, "The State of Our Unions: Marriage in America 2010" (University of Virginia, The National Marriage Project, Institute for American Values, 2010), 38.

[3]Adam Haslett, "Love Supreme," *The New Yorker*, May 31, 2004, 76-80.

transforming the social imagination of a culture. Such a task is what Wilberforce faced, and I imagine his forty-six years of sustained campaigning is a good starting point for our thinking about the duration of this task. Or perhaps it would be better to compare this to a different part of Wilberforce's labor. He famously declared that God had called him to two tasks: the abolition of slavery and the reformation of manners. *Manners* here refers to a broad range of social ethical issues, including loose sexual practices, gambling, drunkenness, lewd entertainment, coarse language, and blasphemy. Wilberforce's success in this second task was probably less complete and certainly harder to measure than his success in abolishing slavery; however, he did make substantial inroads over the course of his life. It is his example, and the example of other historical counterpublics we have considered in this book, we must follow. All of these worked to accomplish pervasive change in the social imagination of their time, and this is exactly the sort of task that faces us as we look ahead.

COUNTERING WISELY

Here are four suggestions to keep in mind when building a counterpublic related to marriage.

1. Choose our ethos *wisely.* Chapter four stressed the importance of *ethos* for a counterpublic, so one might assume Christians should adopt an *ethos* of sympathy, compassion, and humility toward the gay and lesbian community. However, if we are a counterpublic against revisionist straight marriage practices, the public we address is not primarily gays and lesbians but practitioners of the received marriage wisdom of our day. Many of our opponents will be sitting beside us in the pew! Articulate opposition is fundamental to this project, and so I suggest adopting an ethos of prophetic civility. While I favor sympathy, compassion, and humility all around, I do not think this is very helpful guidance for the task at hand. If we focus on these virtues, I worry that we will end up being civil but not prophetic. As noted in chapter one, oppositionality is part of every counterpublic; to avoid it is to avoid being a counterpublic.

Perhaps an analogy would help. Since the earliest days of Christianity, certain Christians have seen pacifism—the complete rejection of coercive violence and war—as a direct entailment of the gospel. Peace-church

Christians (as they are sometimes called) have generally adopted an ethos of sympathy, compassion, and humility toward individuals who are soldiers, policemen, or politicians. Well and good. However, their mission is not sympathy, compassion, and humility. Their mission is opposing war. They oppose war through civil, nonviolent means, but they always oppose it. That is just who they are.

A necessary skill of prophetic civility is the ability to achieve disagreement. Achieving disagreement requires people to understand each other and clearly identify the issues about which they disagree. The great enemy of achieved disagreements is talking past one another—whether in disagreement or agreement. When a nonpacifist calls a pacifist war protestor a coward, they have not achieved disagreement, they are merely talking past each other. The pacifist protesting that he values courage does not solve this problem. A surface agreement on courage must also be set aside to achieve a respectful disagreement. It must be pointed out, for example, that for a nonpacifist the soldier might be the archetype of courage whereas for the pacifist the martyr would be the archetype. The two exemplars mark out very different ways of being courageous. They can be contrasted gently and respectfully, but the differences must be laid bare and owned as a disagreement.

Major differences also lie within disagreements about marriage. Fidelity is an important virtue to advocates of both traditional marriage and gay marriage. However, traditional marriage has understood fidelity to mean absolute sexual monogamy. Some (not all) gay marriage advocates are explicit about conceiving of fidelity not as absolute monogamy, but rather as never lying or being deceitful about one's sexual relations outside of marriage.[4] It is unhelpful and deceptive to say "We agree! We all favor fidelity" if fidelity meant such different things to different parties in the conversation.

---

[4]Torsten B. Neilands et al., "Development and Validation of the Sexual Agreement Investment Scale," *Journal of Sex Research* 47, no. 1 (January 2010): 24-37, found 49 percent of the sexual agreements of gay men included exclusive sexual monogamy. Katherine Gass et al., "Sexual Agreements in the Partnerships of Internet-Using Men Who Have Sex with Men," *AIDS Care* 24, no. 10 (2012): 1255-63, found approximately 56 percent included exclusive sexual monogamy. See also Scott James, "Many Successful Gay Marriages Share an Open Secret," *New York Times*, January 28, 2010, www.nytimes.com/2010/01/29/us/29sfmetro.html. Some well-known advocates of nonmonogamous fidelity include gay journalist and founder of the It Gets Better project, Dan Savage, conservative political commentator Andrew Sullivan, and founder of the Metropolitan Community Church, Troy Perry.

Such disagreements must be captured in language that is deeply respectful but also perfectly clear.

2. Form loose connections. The previous historical sketch noted the unlikely loose connections formed by William Wilberforce as part of his alliance for abolition. Our own opportunity for loose connections is near at hand. The revisionism of sexual and marital practices will not end with same-sex marriage. Chief Justice Roberts pointed out that the *Obergefell* decision may lead to the expansion of marriage rights to polygamy, and it took under a week for a Montana family to file suit to have their polygamous marriage recognized.[5] The legal reasoning in *Obergefell* may even more directly support a bisexual person who wants to have both a male and a female spouse. Other revisions loom as well. Elizabeth Brake advocates for "minimal marriage" in which "individuals can have legal marital relationships with more than one person, reciprocally or asymmetrically, themselves determining the sex and number of parties, the type of relationship involved, and which rights and responsibilities to exchange with each."[6] It is a bewildering terrain that defies one's moral compass, and the winds of change have only begun to blow.

As we stand in the gale, some unlikely partners could stand at our side. For example, Jonathan Rauch, a gay journalist, is a long-time advocate for traditional marriage and a more recent advocate for same-sex marriage. Listen as he tells his own story:

> So I'm 25, and I'm on the verge of finally acknowledging to myself and the world that I'm gay, after all those years of twisting and tormenting myself to deny it. . . . I'm thinking to myself, "I don't want to be gay, I don't want to be gay, I don't want to be gay." And the reason for that is not that I am homophobic or anti-gay. It's that it's 1985, and being gay means I'm condemned to a world, I think, of anonymous sex and late-night bars and poppers and AIDS and early death. And that's not what I wanted.[7]

[5] "Montana Polygamist Family Applies for Marriage License," KRTV.com, July 1, 2015, www.krtv.com/story/29450937/montana-polygamist-family-applies-for-marriage-license.

[6] Sherif Girgis, Ryan T. Anderson, and Robert P. George, *What Is Marriage? Man and Woman: A Defense*, Kindle ed. (New York: Encounter Books, 2012), loc. 360-63.

[7] "Transcript for David Blankenhorn and Jonathan Rauch—The Future of Marriage," *On Being*, hosted by Krista Tippett, April 16, 2015, www.onbeing.org/program/david-blankenhorn-and-jonathan-rauch-the-future-of-marriage/transcript/7483.

Rauch looked at the prevailing sexual practices of gay men in the 1980s and found them deeply disordered. For him the disorder did not attach to same-sex orientation, but what might be called the sexual culture of the gay community. He was repelled by both the practices and the consequences of anonymous sex, promiscuous sex, and drugs mixed with sex. He longed for a committed, life-long relationship with a single partner.

At the time, in his vocation as a journalist Rauch was writing about a variety of social ills that emerged from broken family structures. He began to advocate for traditional marriage. Gay marriage was not even on the horizon as a legal institution. He simply wanted to help fix American marriage practices:

> But in order for you to fix it, you're going to have to realize that this is not just
> a private contract between two individuals. When I talk to young people on
> college campuses, they all think marriage is—it's a thing two people do . . . a
> piece of paper from the state, that's just a convenience. I tell them, no, no, no,
> no. . . . This is a commitment that two people make, not just with each other,
> but with their community. And that commitment is to have and to hold from
> this day forward, for better or for worse, for richer or for poorer, in sickness
> and health, till death do us part. That's a promise you as a couple are giving
> to care for each other and your children forever to your whole community,
> and the community has a stake in it.[8]

Even though Rauch is gay, he understands many aspects of marriage more clearly than large portions of the straight population. I certainly disagree with him about the gendered aspect of marriage since I see it as essential to the definition of marriage itself, but that should not keep me from seeing many points of agreement. Depending on what future storms may blow out of the seas of sexual revolution, Rauch may stand beside me and other advocates of traditional marriage as a co-belligerent on issues such as plural marriage, group marriage, minimalist marriage, and open marriage.

3. Protect religious freedom. Rather than focusing legislative efforts on overturning the *Obergefell* decision, we should focus on protecting religious liberty. The authors of the decision acknowledge the need to protect religious liberties, and it is urgent that we capture this sentiment in specific

---

[8]Ibid.

legislation. Many others have already advocated along these lines and I applaud and support their efforts.[9]

We must also become sensitive to the problems of conscience facing people who are outside of the religious mainstream, whether sectarian Christians or non-Christians. Returning to the example of pacifist Christians, imagine how they feel about summer blockbuster movies that are spectacles of violence and destruction. Heroes do not turn the other cheek or love their enemies; they destroy them. Many holidays celebrate war either directly (Memorial Day and Veterans Day) or indirectly (Independence Day celebrations climaxed by a flyover of bombers from a local Air Force base). Our national anthem is a sustained lyric image of war. Our so-called peace officers have been weaponized and militarized. On almost every level, American society seems to disdainfully disregard or actively insult pacifist convictions, and most of us are completely blind to this fact. But this is not just a matter of insensitivity. Consider the possible legal issues. Is an Anabaptist wedding photographer required by law to provide services for the wedding of an Air Force pilot and a Navy SEAL who are planning to pass beneath swords for their recessional while a phalanx of fighter planes flies overhead? Is there room in our society for a pacifist to respectfully decline to participate? For decades, evangelicals have been close enough to mainstream American convictions that they could afford to have little regard for day-to-day challenges of a "sectarian" religious conscience. With *Obergefell*, those days have gone.

Defending religious liberty and freedom of conscience is a particularly important place to make good use of loose connections. Again, the words of Jonathan Rauch are helpful. He notes the temptation for gay people to pick up the momentum of the *Obergefell* decision and use it to crush religions that oppose homosexuality:

> It is very tempting for us to say, "Let's drive this out of society altogether. All forms of discrimination, whether religious or not, should be illegal." And I'm saying to gay people, no, we've got to share the country. . . . We want to be in a live-and-let-live society where no one gets treated as a prisoner of conscience

[9]John Huleatt, "After Obergefell: Liberating Christian Witness," *Plough Quarterly* 6 (Autumn 2015), www.plough.com/en/topics/life/marriage/after-obergefell. Note especially the account of the Laycock Amicus Brief.

and feels the need to stay in the closet, frightened because of what they believe. That's what we fought against all those years. . . . We need to be champions of all reasonable protections for religious people who may not agree with us. . . . We need to let them share this country with us.[10]

These words are an invitation to form a loose connection and advocate for the legal protection of religious conscience. We should eagerly accept the invitation.

4. Form alternative communities of faithful practice. The church must understand that practicing traditional marriage will make it a misunderstood minority. This is problematic because marriage practices are communitarian and must be sustained in social contexts larger than the nuclear family. Since civil marriage has now diverged substantially from traditional marriage, we can no longer count on civil society as a support structure. The church, not society at large, must sustain traditional marriage. Peter Leithart expresses this well:

> Churches must take responsibility for marriages and families. . . . The best argument for traditional marriage is a thriving traditional marriage. Creating an alternative public sounds like a plan to intensify the culture war, but it's the opposite. Culture war continues because . . . we've tried to politick our values back on top. We failed, but for the church this is a skirmish in a spiritual war crossing millennia. We have the luxury of patience. Attending to our own house is now our best strategy for evangelization and prophetic witness. It's also the way of peace, perhaps the only way of peace remaining.[11]

For a marriage counterpublic, the lesson to learn is simply that we must accept the feeling of being an outcast as a companion and consequence of our moral convictions. There is little point in being angry or resentful, but it is equally untenable to try to blend in to the prevailing marriage landscape. We must decide whether we are hoping to fit in or to be faithful. If we decide to be faithful, our first concern must be the integrity of our own marriage practices, and our second concern any changes that we might make in the culture at large.

---

[10]"Transcript for David Blankenhorn and Jonathan Rauch—The Future of Marriage."
[11]Peter Leithart in "After Obergefell: A First Things Symposium."

ENGAGING EACH OTHER

A Guided Conversation

I T   I S   C L E A R   T O   A N Y   C A R E F U L   R E A D E R of the last two chapters that the coauthors of this book do not completely agree on how to respond to the 2015 Supreme Court decision regarding same-sex marriage. Rather than trying to brush our disagreements under the carpet of our many agreements, we would instead like to identify them more clearly and examine them more closely. We feel this is important and instructive since modern counterpublics must learn to explore potential disagreements in a way that is productive. One of the problems that Christian counterpublics have faced is the assumption that we must all agree on every important social issue because we are all Christians. We do not believe this is true. In fact, since well-meaning Christians disagree on important theological issues, it is hard to imagine that we would automatically agree on sociological and political issues. We need to be able to have gracious disagreements within Christian circles—indeed, this is good training for having gracious disagreements in the public square. So we have condensed many long hours of our own conversations into a single dialogue. We invite our readers to join with us and our friend, Todd, to explore both common ground and areas of disagreement over the first steps in addressing this cultural shift in how we view marriage.

DIALOGUE

TODD: Along with your readers, I've read both of your chapters. I really appreciate your willingness to step into areas where there are no clear answers.

TIM: (Laughing) We excel at making things murkier.

RICK: It's our specialty.

TODD: (Smiling) While there are many areas of agreement, I want to explore differences between your perspectives. Tim, let's start with you.

TIM: Sure.

TODD: Rick, how do you feel about Tim's desire to reach out to elements of the gay community that may be facing relational crisis? He's advocating offering relational advice to help people communicate in more humane ways.

RICK: I'm particularly struck by how well Tim captures the personal and relational side of the issue of same-sex marriage, and I commend him for it. When we think of counterpublics, we are thinking of communities; we must remember that we are not dealing with a set of principles but a set of people. Good job!

TIM: Thanks. Well, I think our dialogue is over!

TODD: (Laughing) Not so fast. I want to clarify what you're advocating. You suggest that we should step in when couples of any kind are exhibiting inhumane or toxic communication. However, doesn't that put us on a type of moral slippery slope? For example, you say we need to help not only same-sex couples in relational crisis but also those moving toward crisis. I fear the slope is getting progressively slippery, and at some point you will cross over a moral boundary that shouldn't be crossed. Can you mark out this terrain for us?

Developing Criteria for Helping Others

TIM: Sure. Remember, the question my chapter addresses is: *As we ask those who disagree to consider our argument for traditional marriage, how should we respond if they suffer relational crisis?* So it's assumed that people are aware of our stance toward same-sex marriage. Yet how do we respond if we learn those we are debating fall into relational crisis? Paul gives our answer when he advocates that we give food and drink to those who harbor ill feelings toward us (Rom 12:20).

TODD: Granted. But what constitutes a crisis? What happens when you realize a gay couple is failing to communicate effectively, but they are headed for quiet despair, not a crisis? They are not getting violent; they are getting passive and withdrawn. Do you offer counseling?

TIM: Good questions. If we view this as type of continuum, then I think we can agree on what's on opposite ends. On one end is celebrating or condoning a relationship we deem unbiblical and on the other end is fulfilling Paul's command to love and meet the needs of those who oppose us. In between these two extremes, we need wisdom to discern how to love our neighbors without giving tacit approval to behaviors we believe are unbiblical.

TODD: I still want specifics. When do you help and when do you not?

TIM: Before I answer, it's interesting to note that Paul himself doesn't offer specifics. When he sees that the opposition is in need he responds. He doesn't raise your question.

TODD: Okay. I'm not talking to Paul. I'm asking you. When do you help, when do you not?

TIM: To go back to the continuum, if I'm asked to offer advice to a same-sex couple of how to spice up their dating life or enhance sexual intimacy, then I pass. To give that type of advice moves me toward the end of the continuum that seems to celebrate a lifestyle I deem immoral. However, if I have the opportunity to offer advice on promoting humane communication, I gladly accept the offer. That is just a good way to love my neighbor.

TODD: Is it realistic to think we'll have opportunities to offer that kind of advice?

TIM: Yes! It's already happening. In my chapter I mention a group of Christians in my city who offer seminars to the public on how to deal with anger. They advertise through social media, and couples of all kinds—gay and straight—come out to hear advice. In addition to providing ways to cope with anger, facilitators carefully weave in the Christian perspective and offer every couple the opportunity to hear more. Over the last few years hundreds of couples of all kinds have gone through these seminars. Over time, that can have an impact on how a community views Christian counterpublics.

TODD: Let me play devil's advocate. Why not offer a seminar to the public on how to improve your sex life?

TIM: I wouldn't. If same-sex couples—or for that matter unmarried couples living together—attend, then I'm in danger of moving toward the end of the continuum that celebrates what is unbiblical. The Bible specifically prohibits *any* sex outside the bounds of traditional marriage.

TODD: But it's not wrong to help those same couples learn to cope with out-of-control anger?

TIM: That's right. While it's a sin to have sex outside of traditional marriage, it's not sin to remove toxic anger. In fact, it's something the Scriptures applaud. What I'm advocating will entail what is commonly called *agenda setting*. We offer to the public advice on how to handle issues on the end of the continuum that we affirm.

Agenda Setting

TODD: Does your agenda also entail helping couples that are moving toward crisis?

TIM: Yes. If we are willing to address toxic anger, then we would do well to offer relevant advice on how to avoid the antecedents of anger. The key is offering relevant advice that is related to the topic.

TODD: Hate to push back . . .

TIM: Go for it.

TODD: Couldn't you argue that an active dating life would help prevent anger from building up? Why not offer advice to same-sex couples for having romantic nights out?

TIM: First, while my lack of romantic nights together with my wife may cause her to be upset at times, it's far removed from the topic at hand—toxic anger. Again, we want to avoid moving toward that end of the continuum that celebrates a lifestyle outside the bounds of Scripture. So I would set the agenda for my community seminar on issues most everyone—communication scholars and psychologists—agree foster toxic anger, such as latent conflict, verbal aggression, bitterness, and so on. We control the agenda.

TODD: Rick, what do you think of Tim's idea of a continuum and offering community seminars that address relational crisis issues?

RICK: Tim, I like your idea of a continuum, but it still gets a little murky when we get to the middle, and I can imagine all kinds of difficulty when you try to put this into practice.

TIM: Agreed, but do you have an alternative that is free of difficulties? When Paul commands us to respond to the needs of those who hate us by giving food and drink, he appeals to a proverb rooted in wisdom literature, which means we'll have to use discernment when moving along the continuum. I don't think Paul or the book of Proverbs gives us a moral formula for dealing with the opposition. *If you offer this advice you're fine, but one step further and you are condoning sin.* Where a church or community of Christian counterpublics draws the line will be up to them and the leading of the Spirit.

Loose Connections

TODD: Rick, what about Tim's idea of offering community workshops or seminars dealing with removing inhumane communication?

RICK: I'm curious. Would these seminars be sponsored solely by a church, or cosponsored with advocacy groups for same-sex marriage? I ask this question because one's institutional affiliations make statements.

TODD: Before Tim answers, could you elaborate?

RICK: Sure. To me it's analogous to a nonprofit not wanting to accept a donation from a gambling casino because it might be understood as a tacit approval of gambling. I am aware of a situation like this where the nonprofit stated it would be willing to accept donations from the individuals, listing them as they would other individual donors, but they would not accept the money from the corporation and they would not list the casino as a sponsor. The casino refused to make the donation on these conditions. In general, I think most organizations carefully guard their associations with other groups, and I think this is as it should be. When it comes to loose connections, sometimes they are best made anonymously, sometimes publicly, and sometimes not at all.

TODD: Tim, want to respond?

TIM: I agree that Christian counterpublics need to be careful in what loose connections we form with non-Christian groups. However, if the *ethos* or credibility of the Christian group is strong enough, then a loose connection formed to provide a social good is warranted. For example, in our chapter on loose connections we use as a case study Jim Daly—president of Focus on the Family—and his decision to form a loose association with a liberal newspaper to bring attention to Colorado's broken foster care system. The *ethos* of Focus on the Family was strong enough that he didn't think they would send the wrong message by partnering with a liberal organization.

TODD: So, to be clear, you would partner with an organization that affirms same-sex marriage to offer a marriage seminar to the public?

TIM: Depends. Let's go back to the continuum. If the topic of the seminar was just marriage in general, then I wouldn't form a loose connection. However, if the topic was addressing out-of-control anger or the dark side of communication, I would consider it.

RICK: I agree that the example Tim offers about Focus on the Family and *The Independent* is a great partnership and a good example of healthy loose connections. But because both Focus on the Family and *The Independent* have wide-ranging social agendas, there is not an immediate and obvious confusion that arises when they work together. But imagine that Mothers Against Drunk Driving is asked to partner with Jack Daniels Distillery for a telethon to raise money for children who have lost parents to drunk drivers. Of course, Jack Daniels wants to help orphaned children as much as anyone, but the product they make is part of the problem. It sends a very confusing message to the public, and I imagine Mothers Against Drunk Driving would be reluctant to have their telethon endorsed by a distillery—even if the distillery was very sincere about wanting to help the kids.

TODD: Tim, you look lost in thought.

TIM: Stay with me as I try to verbalize what I'm thinking. I'm hesitant to say MADD could never partner with Jack Daniels.

RICK: This should be good. Go on.

TIM: First, MADD isn't a teetotaler group opposed to drinking on any level. Rather, they are opposed to drinking and driving—a stance Jack Daniels would firmly support. Second, truly changing how we view responsible drinking will only come when the major players—Budweiser, Anheuser-Busch, Jack Daniels—use their massive platform and resources to evoke change. Third, from a rhetorical standpoint the last thing MADD wants to do is to shun the very groups that have power to evoke the change MADD wants. Again, offering goodwill to Jack Daniels we can assume they are also utterly opposed to drunk driving and that common ground needs to be explored. If MADD wants to change cultural perceptions about drunk driving, they'd better reach out to major players in this cultural discussion and start a dialogue of how to evoke that change. Would such a partnership be incredibly messy and perhaps impossible? Undoubtedly. Should it be explored? I say yes.

The same attitude should be adopted by Christian counterpublics with seemingly polar opposite groups who share the same social concerns.

TODD: Good conversation and a lot to think about. Let's move on to Rick.

RICK: No, I'm fine. Let's continue to focus on my coauthor.

TIM: (Laughing) I bet you would.

Starting with Traditional Marriage

TODD: Rick, in your chapter you offer two different action steps Christian counterpublics need to take in light of the Supreme Court's decision. You suggest that we carefully select the public we should counter and that we adopt what you call prophetic civility.

RICK: Yes.

TODD: However, you write that we should respond to the Supreme Court decision by advocating that we *not primarily* focus on the decision. Actually, you suggest that we should start by strengthening traditional marriage. Isn't that just dodging the issue?

RICK: I think the problem with focusing on the *Obergefell* decision is that it puts the focus in the wrong place. It makes the problem the fact that gays and lesbians want in on the institution of marriage. I think the real problem is that we so eroded our marriage practices, both within the church and in broader society, that contemporary American marriage is practically unrecognizable as an expression of traditional marriage.

TODD: Tim, it looks like you want to jump in.

TIM: First, I couldn't agree more!

RICK: Thanks (smiling).

TIM: Paul himself states that Christians should avoid anything that would discredit the ministry (2 Cor 6:3). Our mistreatment of marriage no doubt caused others to disvalue it and seek alternatives. In the end our credibility was compromised, so I understand why Rick might think our counterpublic needs to withdraw and address in-house concerns. However, along with these times of regrouping come dangers.

TODD: Like what?

TIM: The biggest concern I have is that as necessary as times of withdrawal are to put our house in order, it does not absolve our responsibility to respond to groups *currently* in crisis. It took years to devalue and weaken traditional marriage and will no doubt take years to strengthen it. We have to be careful not to create a false dichotomy that pits withdrawal and engagement against each other, or suggest you cannot do both at the same time. How will the gay or transgender community interpret our decision to utilize our resources to strengthen traditional marriage? We can't put up a sign: "Sorry, church is closed for in-house cleaning. Come back in ten years!" What separates us as counterpublics is our goodwill—addressing the crisis of other communities *simultaneously* or even *before* we address our own crisis. We simply cannot put neighbor love on hold as we attend to our own relational needs and get our house in order.

RICK: But let me be clear that focusing on our straight marriage practices is *not* an example of what we have called "withdrawal." It is *not* about restoring our credibility. It is *not* the precondition for getting on with the really important business of responding to the gay community, or the public as a whole, regarding same-sex marriage. Getting traditional marriage straight (pun intended) really is the point in and of itself! Traditional marriage practices are foundational to a healthy society. Traditional marriage is the way the next generation of human society is produced, nurtured, sustained, guided, and launched into adulthood. There is no replacement for heterosexual sex when it comes to the demographics of human societies. Focusing on traditional marriage is not an attempt to close the church for in-house cleaning. It is a corrective to a society that is so infatuated with individualistic marriage practices and romantic love that it has no idea why a particular form of sex or a particular way of organizing male-female relationships might be conducive to the common good.

TIM: I agree that establishing traditional marriage is what our communities most need, but activists on the other side could say the very same thing about advocating for sexual diversity and tolerance for same-sex marriage. Differing ideological stances on what is the *real* common good are at the heart of our disagreements. So of course strengthening traditional marriage is in-house cleaning and much needed. However, we also need to be ready to respond to the needs of our opponents as they arise. We even should be ready to temporarily set aside our agenda if the need is dire.

TODD: Rick, to be clear. Are you saying same-sex marriage is really not an important issue?

RICK: I think it is important, but it is not of primary importance. To put it another way, we could overturn the *Obergefell* decision and still have almost no positive impact on American marriage practices. As I mentioned in my chapter, almost all of the deterioration of traditional marriage practices in America took place long before same-sex marriage even emerged as a social issue, and they would remain even if same-sex marriage were to be revoked.

Prophetic Civility

TODD: You also suggest that we adopt prophetic civility toward those we are countering. Could you elaborate?

RICK: Prophetic civility is about speaking the truth in love. I am truly worried that the church is in the midst of a pendulum swing from the evangelicals of 1980s, who were known for speaking truth without much love, to an emerging generation of evangelicals who are so concerned with loving and being loved that they have little room for inconvenient truths. Prophetic civility simply reminds us that we cannot choose either of these alternatives. Rather, the church is called to speak the full truth, but to do it with gentleness and respect.

TODD: Tim, how does prophetic civility strike you as a communication professor?

TIM: Your idea of prophetic civility mirrors my concern that we always balance our content (view of traditional marriage) with the relational level of communication (amount of compassion and acknowledgment shown to another).

RICK: Sounds like I hear a "but I have concerns" coming. True?

TIM: (Smiling) Yes.

TODD: How did you know?

RICK: We wrote a book together (laughing).

TIM: In today's argument culture, will adopting prophetic civility markedly set us apart from others? There are many secular activists who passionately and prophetically argue for their particular ideology. In addition, there are individuals such as Georgetown linguist Deborah Tannen who are gaining momentum in recruiting others to reject the incivility of the argument culture.

RICK: I really don't think that is a problem. I welcome any and all who would like to join us in advocating for civility. If our political discourse as a nation becomes so civil that our civility does not stand out, I will be the first to celebrate. But that said, in today's heated rhetorical climate, I think being civil will get us noticed for a good time to come.

TIM: No doubt. But will it move the needle as much as we want in changing how the opposition views us? Let me suggest that what separates us is sacrificial and compassionate neighbor love. Specifically, what distinguishes us from others is precisely how we react when others do *not* exhibit prophetic civility toward us. What will be our response when others not only disagree with us but harbor hatred, incivility, and ill will? Will being merely civil to those hostile to us change the communication climate? I have my doubts. Most importantly, what happens when those very people show evidence of material or relational suffering and move into crisis? I argue that we set aside the debate and sacrificially respond as neighbors providing material and relational goods. Not only will such a compassionate response minister to those who are in need, it will also establish the relational level of our communication (amount of respect, sympathy, commitment, and compassion between groups).

RICK: I agree completely that when we are treated with hostility and respond in love we are doing something quite distinctive and uniquely Christian. So yes, by all means, let us be people who turn away wrath with soft answers and kind deeds. Let us return blessing for cursing. My worry is that we will end up being so similar to the rest of our society that no one would think of treating us with hostility. This is what I mean by my fear of being so civil we fail to be prophetic. I think if we would do what you advocate, the net effect might be improved relationships with the gay and lesbian community, but only to the extent that we silence our voice about our areas of disagreement regarding morality of homosexual practices and same-sex marriage. I would like to do what you are advocating, Tim, but also become more skillful and articulate in conveying our prophetic message.

TIM: But we'll never get a chance to voice our differences if we don't first establish the relational foundation. Based on communication research, it is the relational level that opens the door to our prophetic content. In a communication climate dominated by angry prophetic communicators, it is at the relational level—compassion in the face of hostility, *not mere civility*—that will distinguish us and perhaps open dialogue. When insulted, advises Peter, give a blessing (1 Pet 3:9).

TODD: How can we lead with the practical? Are there practical ways we can show the relational level?

TIM: Yes. One practical area where we can start is being open and compassionate toward the idea of transgender bathrooms. A communication scholar once stated that *how you start a conversation is how you'll end it*. Sadly, Christians often start the conversation by stating in no uncertain terms, "Over my dead body will we consent to public transgender bathrooms! We will not open the door for pedophiles!" Instead of starting the conversation with compassion and openness to address the needs of transgender people in our community, we adopted a culture war stance!

RICK: I very much agree with Tim concerning the recent debates over transgender bathrooms. We are very much at risk of squandering all of our social capital on an issue that makes very little sense to most of the population, and over which even many Christians disagree. Would I rather have an individual who is genetically female but to all appearances looks male using a male or a female bathroom? I'm not sure. I'm far less likely to have awkward conversations with my young children or grandchildren if people use bathrooms that correlate with their apparent gender rather than their birth certificate.

To give a specific example, an article in the *LA Times* recently told the story of August Branch, a resident of Greeneville, North Carolina. He sports a full beard, but as a transgender man he is legally supposed to use the women's bathroom. It creates awkward situations: "It makes everybody uncomfortable," Branch said. "For me in general, it's safer to use the men's room. . . . I'm, like, a 200-pound bearded guy. That's the bathroom I should be using."[1] I realize that some would feel differently than I, but it is not at all clear to me that my Christian convictions would point to one way to solve the bathroom problem as opposed to another. Christians may not favor gender reassignment, but we cannot deny that this is done in our society. Surely our desire is not to refuse access to public bathrooms for transgender people. In short, I feel like we are burning an enormous amount of political capital for little or no social gain.

---

[1]Matt Pearce, "What It's Like to Live Under North Carolina's Bathroom Law if You're Transgender," *Los Angeles Times*, June 12, 2016, www.latimes.com/nation/la-na-north-carolina-bathrooms-20160601-snap-story.html.

TODD: I think I agree. However, what would you say about the pedophile concern?

TIM: When our first response is to bring up the pedophile issue, we equate transgender people with pedophiles. The transgender community is just as concerned about protecting young children from predators as we are! Any consideration of a public transgender bathroom must address this concern and I think both sides would want to address it. Last, even if we can't fully embrace all the needs or demands of the transgender, at least we've compassionately considered them.

TODD: At this point some readers may be thinking, *What do public transgender bathrooms have to do with protesting the Supreme Court decision?* How would you respond?

TIM: It has everything to do with it! We'll never make significant strides in our conversation with the LGBTQ community about the nature of marriage *until* they know we care about them and the issues they face. By lovingly addressing an element of their community we develop an *ethos* to speak into other areas.

RICK: I would also point out that these issues are also related in public perception. Our attitudes and actions toward the usage of bathrooms by transgender individuals are likely to be read as strong indicators of our attitudes toward gays and lesbians. There are so many issues that will be coming up that we need to carefully choose winnable battles that don't needlessly squander our political capital.

TODD: So is coming to the aid of the LGBTQ community a rhetorical strategy meant to improve public relations or open the door to the gospel?

TIM: No. We do neighbor love because we want to be good neighbors and love people. Period. While open doors to the gospel or improved *ethos* may be a side benefit, it is not the goal.

TODD: One last question: What issues *would* you engage in legal battles over?

RICK: A good example is a bill that is currently before the California Assembly that restricts Title IX exemptions for universities in such a way that they can only be granted for religious instruction for preparing religious ministers. The effect of this bill would be that Christian universities could not require chapel, or have classroom prayers, or require that all their faculty or all their students be professing Christians. And of course the same would be true for any other religion with similar higher-educational institutions.

TODD: Tim, do you agree?

TIM: Yes. I think this bill is legally problematic at several levels, and unfairly constrains the free exercise of religion. It also affects the practices of a large number of religious universities, including not just evangelicals but members of every world religion. I think a wise counterpublic could marshal broad opposition against this bill. It is a potentially winnable battle, it attaches to central issues related to religious freedom, and it is an issue that can be effectively addressed by legislation. All of these facts make it a great example of a legal battle that is worth fighting.

TODD: So you feel there is a place for legal and political action, not just for civil conversations?

RICK AND TIM: (together) Absolutely!

TODD: (laughing) It sounds like we have found some agreements after all! Well, even if all of our questions are not answered, perhaps this is a good place to end the conversation.

CONCLUSION

"Aren't we trying to go over there?"

If you've ever learned how to sail or sat on a sailboat seemingly going in the wrong direction, you've experienced the principle of tacking. When a boat is heading into the wind, you simply can't go directly from point A to point B—the wind and currents won't allow it. If you sailed straight into the wind, you would soon find yourself increasingly off course. In order to get to your destination you must tack or zigzag in slow, planned increments. The detours are frustrating until you realize that each tack brings you closer to your goal. In today's ever-changing cultural landscape Christian counter-publics must become proficient at rhetorical tacking. The more our culture finds the Christian worldview offensive, the more we'll need to resist the urge to push too quickly or stridently for our convictions.

What makes us impatient is a belief that we have absolute truth on our side. "Why can't I simply present what the Bible says?" is a common refrain. The real question is, What function should our absolutes—rooted in the Scriptures—perform? We argue that absolutes should guide our choice of ends, but they do not in and of themselves determine the best means or methods to achieve these ends. The moral truth that slavery is wrong led Wilberforce to seek to abolish it. But the method he employed was not to immediately and directly demand the abolition of slavery. Rather, he strategically tacked by first trying to eliminate the slave trade. This goal seems to be a compromise because it left all existing slaves in bondage. However, even that lesser goal required twenty years of effort and was achieved by a bill that did not so much abolish the slave trade as make it financial impractical. It took over twenty *more* years to actually emancipate slaves and achieve the final goal of abolition. Again, the means used were problematic because they involved "buying" the slaves from their current owners. Such purchasing actually implied the legitimacy of buying and selling human beings, but it was the best means available to accomplish the end. Eventually, after forty years of zigzagging Wilberforce arrived at his final destination and slavery was abolished.

Laws based on faulty moral premises need to be changed. However, the best means to effect a change might not be a law that fully embodies a given absolute. Changing embedded cultural practices often requires slow and gradual pressure. It is analogous to straightening teeth. Orthodontists apply slightly increasing pressure over a long period of time to turn teeth gradually. Using pliers to align a tooth instantly might be possible, but it is not desirable; it would be extremely painful and ultimately fail to achieve the goal since the tooth would most likely be lost. We believe all-or-nothing demands to change social policy or public opinion are often analogous to instantly straightening teeth—it is likely to be both painful and unsuccessful.

"Better a patient person than a warrior," suggest ancient Jewish writers (Prov 16:32). Applying the principles of this book—cultivating *ethos*, reading the rhetorical situation, adjusting to constraints, speaking in humility, crafting a third story, forming loose connections with outsiders—may seem like unnecessary diversions to those who want to be warriors in the culture war. Yet through patience, perseverance, and strategic tacking, we believe entire communities can be introduced to a Christian perspective that has as its goal returning us all back to God's shalom.

NAME AND SUBJECT INDEX